IT IS NO DREAM

Israel: Prophecy and History—The Whole Story

COMPLETELY UPDATED AND REVISED

ELWOOD MCQUAID

The Friends of Israel Gospel Ministry, Inc.

In memory of those victims we must never forget.

CONTENTS

FOREWORD

My intention in approaching this work was not simply to produce one more volume on Bible prophecy. There are many works available that deal effectively with prophetic and dispensational themes. Furthermore, I shrink from the thought of contributing a sensationalized work that makes extravagant claims but in actuality delivers little substance.

What I feel can be helpful is a book that scans the entire biblical and prophetic program for Israel while integrating documented, historical insights into the outworking of God's program for the Jewish people. Essential to this aim is an understanding of the Chosen People, what they have experienced, why they have been thus dealt with, and where their journey through history will finally bring them. I have, therefore, restricted research to predominantly Jewish sources. I spent many weeks in Israel conducting research and interviewing individuals holding positions that allowed them to provide vivid perspectives.

Although specific acknowledgments are given elsewhere, I must immediately recognize the graciousness, availability, and patience of the Israelis who have unhesitatingly cooperated in this venture. Military officials, Zionist Agency personnel, government leaders, and religious representatives have sacrificed both their official and personal time to open offices, libraries, and homes to assist in the compilation and review of the content you're about to read. In the United States, staff members of the Embassy of Israel in Washington, DC, and the Jewish Consulate in New York responded graciously to my requests. My earnest and enduring gratitude is offered to these men and women, many of whom have become friends.

This book is written from an evangelical Christian point of view. Certainly, great differences exist between my religious views and the majority of the people mentioned above. Their official and personal cooperation does not imply an endorsement of the Christian content. However, it is everywhere obvious that the people of Israel wish all segments of our fragmented world to understand the Jewish people's inherent right and desire to live in peace in the land given to Abraham and his posterity.

My ultimate purpose is twofold:

The first is to help Christians understand the Jewish people and their problems, aspirations, and divinely destined place in history. I hope to show, through the unfolding of God's prophetic program, the unchallengeable miracle of Israel, her sons, and daughters; to give believers a fresh sense of kinship with the land and the Jewish people; and, consequently, to provide a renewed awareness of our responsibility to share what a sovereign Messiah has accomplished in the lives of true Christians.

The second is to help Jewish readers differentiate between Christendom in general—which has heaped scorn, ridicule, suffering, and persecution on them—and true Christians who emulate the genuine spirit of Christ toward the Chosen People of God. I pray this work will help Jewish people comprehend the enormous dimensions of their unique relationship to the God of the universe, as well as show Jehovah's faithfulness in delivering all the irrevocable promises to Abraham, Isaac, and Jacob and his seed.

It is my fervent hope this book will, in some measure, accomplish these purposes. Of course, my readers must judge the relative success of the effort. If I have failed, be assured the deficiency is due to a lack of literary skill, not to a lack of heartfelt concern for the Jewish people or God's Land.

Elwood McQuaid

SETTING THE STAGE

> When the LORD brought back the captivity of Zion, we were like those who dream. Then our mouth was filled with laughter, and our tongue with singing. Then they said among the nations, "The LORD has done great things for them." The LORD has done great things for us, and we are glad (Ps. 126:1–3).

For millennia, the Jewish people have held a hope in their hearts, a dream embodied in the Israeli national anthem, "Hatikvah." That dream is "to be a free nation in our land, the land of Zion and Jerusalem."

The unshakable belief that one day the Jewish people will "possess their possessions" (Obad. 1:17) in the ancient land of their fathers is perfectly consistent with what the Scriptures have taught for thousands of years.

During the years of dispersion and wandering in inhospitable Gentile environments, the vision never waned. It was never far from the Jewish mind and heart. Equally true is the fact that buffeted and beleaguered Jewry has never been out of the heart of God.

The great wonder we have witnessed in this modern age is the merging of Jewish desire with divine design. The Jewish people are returning to their land. History is playing out before us; and prophecy, splashed across the pages of the biblical record—Old Testament and New—provide details yet to unfold.

But what has unfolded sent shockwaves through the nations, as they witnessed an event the vast majority thought impossible.

HISTORY'S GREATEST STORY

When Theodor Herzl coined the phrase, *If you will it, it is no dream,* he actually spoke of two worlds: the "will" God infused in Jewry, a quality that has persisted throughout the ages; and the "dream," which the Jewish people have tenaciously held on to and struggled to make reality. Thus we have before us a story told in the Holy Book and acknowledged by history; and it is history's greatest story. It could be said that the telling in itself—without theology or related disciplines—captivatingly reveals all to be cherished or loathed in humanity's march through the ages. Above all, this narrative anticipates a spectacular consummation, the much-sought-after "happy ending" to the greatest drama on this planet.

The drama revolves around the record of a people deemed insignificant, written off as dispensable by the secularist powers that be. The truth is that the Jewish people and their Holy Land are unparalleled gifts from God to humanity.

And yes, Jerusalem is the center of the earth and focus of the future. And lest we forget, Jesus the Christ—God's supreme gift—came to us in Bethlehem of Judea, born of a Jewish woman.

What can we then take away from history's greatest story?

Foremost, we can accept it for what it is: life on the ground, not the stuff of myth or fable. It shows us real life, with all its bumps, bruises, tests, and triumphs. It shows us the hand of God, preserving what He promised.

It has been well said that if the Lord breaks one promise He has made to Abraham's posterity, we have no shred of assurance He'll be faithful to us. But He has not breached or broken those promises, and He never will.

That's good news. So it follows that we have much to learn and appreciate when we look at Israel's history and the Jewish people. Of utmost importance is the transformative heart-and-soul desire for peace and commitment that we see within this nation chosen to provide a light in the storm that is darkening the world around us.

THE STATE OF ISRAEL HAS RISEN

After more than 2,500 years of Gentile domination, the nation of Israel was about to rise from the ashes. The event was planned in secrecy, but half the city of Tel Aviv waited in the streets as David Ben-Gurion's car pulled up to 16 Rothschild Boulevard at 4 p.m. Wearing a dark suit and dark tie and carrying a portfolio under his arm, Ben-Gurion exited the back seat and ascended the steps of the Tel Aviv Museum of Art where a different crowd waited inside.

Residents of Tel Aviv wait for the delegates to leave the Museum Building there after the signing of the Declaration of Independence.

For the eyes of the Lord run to & fro throughout the whole earth to show Himself strong in the behalf of them whose heart is perfect toward Him.

II Chron. 16:9

other Jewish ministers of the National
nder, Theodor Herzl, hanging directly
s feet. "On the strength of the resolution
bly," he told the crowd in Hebrew, "we
ewish state in Eretz-Israel, to be known

leering, and crying. The man who would
ster read the country's freshly minted
; our trust in the Almighty, we affix our
s session of the Provisional Council of
he city of Tel Aviv, on this Sabbath eve,
)48)."

It was appropriate that Herzl's portrait seemed to survey the historic scene, for it was Jewish journalist Theodor Herzl who assessed the ominous clouds gathering over European Jewry in the late 1800s and concluded it was time to go home. To dissenters who thought a modern Jewish state in Ottoman-Turkish Palestine impossible, he uttered the now immortal words, *If you will it, it is no dream.*

Few people thought that dream would come true. After 2,000 years of surviving among nations often hostile to their presence, the Jewish people could return home. What occurred on the evening of May 14, 1948, was astonishing, a unique event in the annals of history. A nation long dead was being resurrected and restored to its original land. Surely nothing of that magnitude could transpire without God. He had promised in His Word, "I will bring you back" (Jer. 15:19; 29:14; Zeph. 3:20). And He was doing just that.

In a sense, the event was an awakening to a new reality. The Jewish people were returning as a nation—a resounding affirmation to some, a bewildering prospect to others. Sorely disquieted by the phenomenon were theologians who held to Replacement Theology (RT), which sees no biblical future for Israel.

RT scoffs at the idea that God will fulfill all of His promises to Israel literally. Theological revisionists postulate that somehow Old Testament Israel has morphed into the church, and the church has become the "New Israel," replacing Jacob's physical children.

However, the State of Israel's existence today should send a stark warning that God is the same yesterday, today, and forever. He does not make promises He doesn't keep. Jehovah is not a "force." He is God Almighty. "He said, and will He not do?...Has He spoken, and will He not make it good?" (Num. 23:19).

God is no one to trifle with, and *replacement* is not a word encoded in any aspect of the divine program. In fact, the concept in any form flies in the face of biblically charted history and its culmination, as assured by our Maker.

WHEN DOES FOREVER NOT MEAN FOREVER?

If asked to define the word *forever*, we Christians have a ready answer—no quibbling or equivocation. *Forever* means "forever." End of story. If asked about eternal life, we quote John 3:16: "For God so loved the world that He gave His only begotten Son, that whoever believes in Him should not perish but have everlasting life."

How long is "everlasting"? The dictionary says *everlasting* means "enduring through all time: eternal." In other words, it means "forever," for a time without limit. Scripture says God is an "everlasting God" (Isa. 40:28) whose righteousness is "everlasting" (Ps. 119:142) and whose Kingdom is "an everlasting kingdom" (145:13). God, His righteousness, and His Kingdom will endure forever, for all time. They will never cease to exist.

Ironically, some people fail to apply the same standard of certainty to *forever* when the promises are given to Israel. God told Abraham,

> And I will establish My covenant between Me and you and your descendants after you in their generations, for an everlasting covenant, to be God to you and your descendants after you. Also I give to you and your descendants after you the land in which you are a stranger, all the land of Canaan, as an everlasting possession; and I will be their God (Gen. 17:7–8).

Replacement theologians contend this promise does not mean what it says and is not to be taken literally. This new interpretation sprung up when some of the early church Fathers opted to plot a theological course not formerly traveled in order to make the church supreme. Yet in doing so, they deprived it of the whole story of Israel and the Hebrew people.

My intent here is not to parse semantics or grapple with divergent theological positions. Rather, I hope to tell the story of Israel and show why understanding the entire biblical portrait can enrich our lives and instill in us a clear vision of Israel's future, as well as that of the church.

It is overwhelmingly important to come to grips with the knowledge that we do not worship a God who deals in half measures. What He promises He will deliver in full—always, and in His time. Nowhere is this biblical truth more compellingly executed than in His program for Israel. To cut off the story half told and unfulfilled is like teaching about Christ's death without ever mentioning His resurrection. What a huge mistake that would be. We need the entire story of Israel to understand God and His wondrous program for humankind.

The saga of Israel's journey to its ultimate destiny far surpasses any novel that could ever be written or any historical documentary that could ever be produced. It depicts the birth of a nation and contains romance, unrequited love, struggle, indescribable suffering, survival against all odds, national resurrection, fiery trials, a coming King, reconciliation, fulfillment, restoration of relationships, and delivery in full of every promise made by the God who never fails to keep His word.

Contrary to the often-dreary depictions of life in our time, usually accompanied by sullenly depressing endings, Israel's epochal journey has a glorious consummation—a happy ending. One reflecting rich personal incentives for 21st-century believers—and one that assures us God will never stop loving us.

CHAPTER ONE

The Prophetic Nation

> Who, contrary to hope, in hope believed, so that he [Abraham] became the father of many nations, according to what was spoken, "So shall your descendants be." He did not waver at the promise of God through unbelief, but was strengthened in faith, giving glory to God, and being fully convinced that what He had promised He was also able to perform (Rom. 4:18, 20–21).

A solitary figure watched the sun creep over the lush meadows of his new land. As the light emerged, his eyes swept the horizon. To the west, the azure Mediterranean sent rhythmic breakers to wash its coastal sands. Before him lay a breathtaking panorama of plunging descents, rolling plains, and great valleys. Away to the east, the Galilee sparkled against the basalt cliffs of the Golan. Clearly visible was the point where the Jordan River quit the southern tip of Kinneret to furrow a serpentine course through the land and eventually find its terminus beneath the vaporous haze marking the place where the Dead Sea patiently garnered its treasures.

On the flanks of the lower Jordan rested a semitropical garden where the fruits of creation were gathered without regard for the times and seasons restricting husbandmen in other climes. In the distant south rose the soft, brown mountains of Judea, where barren Moriah silently anticipated its bedecking as the eternal Jerusalem. Farther on, the Negev watched Bedouin and trader ply their way down to the land of the pharaohs, ancient Egypt.

It was a unique land for a unique man, a man whose life would begin not at the proverbial 40, but at a patriarchal 75. Abraham would be one of a kind, yet he would endure as the spiritual prototype of all believers in Jehovah who would follow after him. In this first Hebrew, the world would witness a fresh phenomenon. A branch was being grafted out of humanity through which the divine purposes would flow, around which all history would revolve, and in which all biblical prophecy would one day triumphantly culminate. God was creating a new thing: Jehovah was forming His Israel.

THE STORY WITHIN THE STORY

We must never overlook, minimize, or ignore the people—as much a slice of humanity as you or I—who were essential instruments in the divine scheme of things. From their personal stories, we can learn life-transforming lessons as we open the Scriptures. In a dramatic sense, Abraham is among those people.

Soul-arresting indeed is the legacy of this godly man. Abraham's altars dotted his trek across the land that was Israel's inheritance. Though he did not know it, he was humanity's new beginning: A new era of faith—with promise, both personal and enduring forever—had arrived.

In the space of a few chapters in Genesis, God defined the parameters in His program for the new nation that would alter the course of history on Earth. In fact, so dramatic were the consequences of His intervention through Abraham that Israel would essentially become the center of the planet.

Through this man we encounter the greatest mountain peaks of promise found in all of God's Word, promises that span the whole of history and place markers never to be erased. Abraham touches not only the sons and daughters born of his seed but, in one way or another, every nation and individual.

You may be asking yourself, *What is it about this first Hebrew that matters to me?* It is this: "*Abraham believed God,* and it was accounted to him for righteousness" (Rom. 4:3, emphasis added). Simple as it may appear, believing

Artist rendition of Abraham journeying into the land of Canaan

faith—unquestioning obedience to God—is the spiritual staff of life for true believers. And, as was true with Abraham, such enabling faith guides us confidentially into the yet unseen. "Now faith is the substance of things hoped for, the evidence *of things not seen*" (Heb. 11:1, emphasis added).

Therefore, the impact of Abraham's call cannot be taken lightly. It would become the fountainhead of all biblical prescience. Consequently, it would become an essential study for all who aspire to understand history and its most enigmatic elements, the Jewish people and their land.

No people on the face of this sphere have been as consistently conspicuous as the descendants of Abraham. Certainly, none have aroused emotions, attracted a greater measure of attention, or made more indelible contributions to humankind than have the Jewish people. Why? Why, after all, did God call them? Why did He so obviously set them apart? What did (and what does) He intend to show the world through this tiny nation? How is every child of Adam influenced by the Jewish presence and Jehovah's program for Israel? The answers to these questions, as we shall see, are intriguing, illuminating, and potentially soul-satisfying.

Why does little Israel figure so prominently in the news? Why does little Israel matter? A partial explanation appears in God's Word:

> For you are a holy people to the LORD your God; the LORD your God has chosen you to be a people for Himself, a special treasure above all the peoples on the face of the earth. The LORD did not set His love on you nor choose you because you were more in number than any other people, for you were the least of all peoples; but because the LORD loves you, and because He would keep the oath which He swore to your fathers, the LORD has brought you out with a mighty hand, and redeemed you from the house of bondage, from the hand of Pharaoh king of Egypt (Dt. 7:6–8).

Through these Chosen People, God will manifest His love, as well as His faithfulness, to His promises; and through them He will bring the prospect of light and life to all people.

His program contains four phases: dispersion, preservation, restoration, and reconciliation.

I WILL BLESS THEE

To properly appraise the full significance of Abraham's place in history, we must view events from his introduction to us in the biblical record:

> Now the LORD had said to Abram: "Get out of your country, from your family
> and from your father's house, to a land that I will show you. I will make you
> a great nation; I will bless you and make your name great; and you shall be
> a blessing. I will bless those who bless you, and I will curse him who curses
> you; and in you all the families of the earth shall be blessed" (Gen. 12:1–3).

Embodied in this initial unveiling of Jehovah's plan for the future is a fourfold
application of *I will:*

1. I will show you a land. This involves *divine direction.*

2. I will make you a great nation. This speaks of *divine determination.*

3. I will bless you and make your name great; and you shall be a blessing.
   This reveals *divine promotion.*

4. I will bless those who bless you, and I will curse him who curses you;
   and in you all the families of the earth shall be blessed. This shows
   the *divine program.*

These remarkable words were spoken to Abraham, the childless Shemite son
of an idolater from the ancient city of Ur in Mesopotamia. He accepted them
by faith and moved in the appointed direction without knowing his precise
destination. After arriving in the land God had identified to him, the declarations given earlier were amplified. Three passages illuminate the dimensions of
Jehovah's promises:

> And the LORD said to Abram, after Lot had separated from him: "Lift your
> eyes now and look from the place where you are—northward, southward,
> eastward, and westward; for all the land which you see I give to you and
> your descendants forever" (Gen. 13:14–15).

> On the same day the LORD made a covenant with Abram, saying: "To your
> descendants I have given this land, from the river of Egypt to the great river,
> the River Euphrates" (15:18).

> And I will establish My covenant between Me and you and your descendants
> after you in their generations, for an everlasting covenant, to be God to you
> and your descendants after you. Also I give to you and your descendants
> after you the land in which you are a stranger, all the land of Canaan, as an

everlasting possession; and I will be their God (17:7–8).

The magnificent sweep of these prophetic words was profound and permanently binding—but not immediately realized. A man, childless at 80 years old, is promised a son. This son, he is told, will become a great nation. The nation is given a land by God; it is to be theirs forever. Jehovah enters into a covenant with the Jewish nation, insuring the nation's longevity and national identity as long as history continues. Through Abraham's seed, a Messiah will come to bring blessing and benefit to the entire world.

God made these declarations some 4,000 years ago. If we accept the Bible as His instrument for communicating with us, we must also acknowledge that its trustworthiness and reliability will be evaluated based on whether His promises are faithfully fulfilled. Therefore, these declarations to Jacob and his progeny put the Bible to the ultimate test. Will all of them come to pass over the span of thousands of years? Furthermore, will the results establish beyond question that God's Word is to be taken literally?

If these predictions come true, it is folly to propose that the Bible is anything less than God's revealed Word to humanity. Fulfillment also will establish the fact that God is on the world scene, moving history toward an orderly culmination—one that He Himself has chosen.

THE UNBORN HEIR TO THE COVENANT

It is crucial to understand that the fulfillment of the divine Covenant program would come through Isaac and the Jewish people, not Ishmael, Abraham's firstborn son by Hagar, Sarah's Egyptian handmaid.

> Then God said: "No, Sarah your wife shall bear you a son, and you shall call his name Isaac; I will establish My covenant with him [not Ishmael] for an everlasting covenant, and with his descendants after him. And as for Ishmael, I have heard you. Behold, I have blessed him, and will make him fruitful, and will multiply him exceedingly. He shall beget twelve princes, and I will make him a great nation. But My covenant I will establish with Isaac, whom Sarah shall bear to you at this set time next year." Then He finished talking with him, and God went up from Abraham" (17:19–22).

THE WORLDS OF ISAAC AND ISHMAEL

Much of the political world these days is promoting the fiction that the vast majority of the world's problems are somehow related to Israel's existence and the fact that Israel insists on secure borders and adequate land to ensure its survival. Radical Islamists call for Israel's annihilation and the banishment or extermination of its people. They claim Ishmael was Abraham's favored son and, therefore, the legitimate heir to all rights to the land and sanctuaries.

Needless to say, Islam's claims concerning Ishmael and the Abrahamic Covenant are false and irrelevant. Islam did not exist until the 7th century AD, and God's promises in Scripture clearly go from Abraham to Isaac to Jacob to the Jewish people.

Respected scholars describe Ishmael's descendants as the Arab people who, for the most part, live in settlements and Bedouin-like camps in northern Arabia. In addition, the Muslim Arabs, following Muhammad's example, claim descent from Ishmael. Muslims further claim that Ishmael and his mother, Hagar, are buried in the Ka'aba at Mecca in Saudi Arabia. To Muslims, the Ka'aba, Muhammad's birthplace and home for half a century, is the most sacred place of worship; and Mecca is the most sacred city on Earth—not Jerusalem.

The fact that the Arab world engulfs 99.9 percent of the land across northern Africa and the Middle East, possesses enormous wealth, and wields major influence internationally testifies to the fulfillment of God's promise that Ishmael's descendants would receive a great heritage.

But as Jehovah specified to Abraham, "My covenant I will establish with Isaac."

In the course of time, Abraham received the promised son, Isaac. His son had a family, and the family moved to Egypt to escape a severe famine. Under Egyptian bondage, the family struggled through the birth pangs of delivering a nation. Some 500 years after those divine proclamations to a lone patriarch in a distant city, an estimated 2.5 million souls marched out of Egypt to again occupy the land promised to their forefathers.

THE NATION

Israel's exodus from Pharaoh's domain endures as one of the great sagas of all time. Moses contesting with Pharaoh, the successive plagues that rolled over the land, and Israel's miraculous deliverance through the Red Sea are all familiar events to Jews and Christians alike. Jewish people have celebrated the Exodus in annual Passover ceremonies worldwide for more than 3,000 years. Christians revere the memory of the Exodus as one of the great Old Testament previews of the sacrificial work of Christ. Hundreds of novels and historical works have been based on the Exodus, and filmmakers and songwriters have repeatedly used its theme. More recently, we think of it as we see Jewish people trek across the nations to return home since the birth of the State of Israel.

Sketch of the Tabernacle

Israel's deliverance from servitude in Egypt and its subsequent journey through the wilderness would be one of the most productive short periods in history. We are all beneficiaries of those momentous days. During that time God gave the Law to Moses, Moses wrote the first five books of the Bible (the Torah), and God established Moses as perhaps the greatest leader the world would know.

During the trip from Egypt to Canaan, the Israelites paused for nearly a year before Mount Sinai to receive unprecedented revelation from God. The priestly ministry was established; and the Tabernacle, the first national house of worship, was built. It was a time of great optimism. Israel had been favored by direct communication from God. Through the Law, He instructed them regarding their religious worship and service. The land of Abraham, Isaac, and Jacob lay before them. To Jewish people of the day, the future seemed aglow with glorious prospects.

But suddenly, God sent a prophetic shiver down the national spine. He introduced the Israelites to the principle by which they would occupy the land he had given them: They must obey Him. He had given Canaan to the Jewish people in perpetuity. They would own it forever. But if they failed to obey Jehovah, He would expel them from the land made sacred by His hallowed promises.

In the brief span of two chapters in the Bible (Leviticus 26 and Deuteronomy 28), the Jewish people's entire future is outlined. It is striking in its detail and precision. The facts of Jewish history recorded in the history books coincide so completely with these prophecies that even someone who doesn't believe in

God can't help but see the similarities.

This astounding revelation identifies four distinct movements in the divine program for the Jewish people: dispersion, preservation, restoration, and reconciliation. These periods mark the way of Jewry during its national pilgrimage. The sequence first appears in Leviticus and is restated in Deuteronomy.

Moses was the first prophet to touch on these points. Then the Old Testament writers who came after him reiterated them repeatedly. New Testament writers later took up the threads and wove additional patterns into the fabric. Around these four movements all international developments will revolve. From beginning to end, this little nation will be central to all of God's dealings with mankind. We can interpret history correctly only if we understand Israel's singular niche in the unfolding drama of global affairs.

As we look at Leviticus and Deuteronomy, we can easily see Israel's prewritten history as it came from the hand of God:

DISPERSION

And after all this, if you do not obey Me, but walk contrary to Me, then I also will walk contrary to you in fury; and I, even I, will chastise you seven times for your sins (Lev. 26:27–28).

I will scatter you among the nations and draw out a sword after you; your land shall be desolate and your cities waste (v. 33).

Then the LORD will scatter you among all peoples, from one end of the earth to the other, and there you shall serve other gods, which neither you nor your fathers have known—wood and stone. And among those nations you shall find no rest, nor shall the sole of your foot have a resting place; but there the LORD will give you a trembling heart, failing eyes, and anguish of soul. Your life shall hang in doubt before you; you shall fear day and night, and have no assurance of life (Dt. 28:64–66).

PRESERVATION

Yet for all that, when they are in the land of their enemies, I will not cast them away, nor shall I abhor them, to utterly destroy them and break My covenant with them (Lev. 26:44).

Now it shall come to pass, when all these things come upon you, the blessing and the curse which I have set before you, and you call them to mind among all the nations where the Lord your God drives you...(Dt. 30:1).

RESTORATION

My covenant with Jacob, and My covenant with Isaac and My covenant with Abraham I will remember (Lev. 26:42).

The Lord your God will bring you back from captivity, and have compassion on you, and gather you again from all the nations where the Lord your God has scattered you (Dt. 30:3).

RECONCILIATION

But for their sake I will remember the covenant of their ancestors, whom I brought out of the land of Egypt in the sight of the nations, that I might be their God: I am the Lord (Lev. 26:45).

Then the Lord your God will bring you to the land which your fathers possessed, and you shall possess it. He will prosper you and multiply you more than your fathers. And the Lord your God will circumcise your heart and the heart of your descendants, to love the Lord your God with all your heart and with all your soul, that you may live ((Dt. 30:5–6).

Behold, I will gather them out of all countries where I have driven them in My anger, in My fury, and in great wrath; I will bring them back to this place, and I will cause them to dwell safely. They shall be My people, and I will be their God; then I will give them one heart and one way, that they may fear Me forever, for the good of them and their children after them. And I will make an everlasting covenant with them, that I will not turn away from doing them good; but I will put My fear in their hearts so that they will not depart from Me. Yes, I will rejoice over them to do them good, and I will assuredly plant them in this land, with all My heart and with all My soul (Jer. 32:37–41).

Nothing approximating the scale of these restoration and reconciliation prophecies has yet occurred in the history of Israel. Some argue that the return spoken of in these passages took place when the Jewish people returned from captivity in Babylon under Zerubbabel, Nehemiah, and Ezra. However, there are obvious facts that refute that theory:

◆ Relatively few Jewish people went back to Israel during these returns.

The rest chose to remain in the more comfortable circumstances in Babylon. The number of Jews in the land from the time of the returns until the Romans destroyed the second Temple in AD 70 was always a remnant of the nation, not a full complement.

◆ The Jewish people's most extensive dispersion still lay ahead. Their scattering after the Romans scourged the land would take them farther from their ancient soil than ever before. For nearly 2,000 years, they would wander among the Gentile nations and suffer such severe persecution that it would defy parallel in the chronology of humanity.

◆ Israel as a nation has never been fully reconciled to Jehovah spiritually. There has never been a time when all the Jewish people have had "one heart and one way" in adherence to Jehovah's person and program. The final fulfillment of this promise awaits a future day. However, as we survey world events, we can recognize that the final realization of these aspirations is drawing near, and the quickening surge of prophetic movement should make us rejoice and give us confidence that God keeps His Word.

Many other prophecies in Scripture speak of Israel's divine regathering and promise the nation peaceful and blessed living conditions that will endure "forever"—something that clearly has not yet occurred. The fulfillment obviously is still future. One passage in particular is Ezekiel 37:25–26:

> Then they shall dwell in the land that I have given to Jacob My servant, where your fathers dwelt; and they shall dwell there, they, their children, and their children's children, forever; and My servant David shall be their prince forever. Moreover I will make a covenant of peace with them, and it shall be an everlasting covenant with them; I will establish them and multiply them, and I will set My sanctuary in their midst forevermore.

The detail and scope of these declarations are astonishing. God told us thousands of years ago the nation would be dispossessed and scattered. But it would also be preserved through centuries of dispersion, returned to its ancient soil, and be reestablished as a nation. What other ancient nation has accomplished the same feat? Given all the attempts to assimilate or exterminate the Jewish people, they should not even exist today. Yet here they are. Why? Because God ordained it. He made a promise, and He's a promising-keeping God.

The very existence of the Jewish people and the rebirth of the nation of Israel tell us we are living in the presence of a miracle—one as surely wrought by God as any from the days of the prophets and apostles. In the Bible, we possess a book unlike any other. We cannot casually lay it aside. Among other things, it reveals God's plan for the ages and accurately tells us the future—something only He can do. And He tells us so in Isaiah 46:9–11:

> Remember the former things of old, for I am God, and there is no other; I am God, and there is none like Me, declaring the end from the beginning, and from ancient times things that are not yet done, saying "My counsel shall stand, and I will do all My pleasure," calling a bird of prey from the east, the man who executes My counsel, from a far country. Indeed I have spoken it; I will also bring it to pass. I have purposed it; I will also do it.

Prominent scholar and historian Alfred Edersheim commented appropriately,

> Israel as a nation was born of God; redeemed by God; brought forth by God victorious on the other side the flood; taught of God; trained by God; and separated for the service of God. And this God was to be known to them as Jehovah, the living and the true God....God is the God of the present as well as of the future, and that even here on earth He reigneth, dispensing good and evil.[1]

DISPERSION

YET FOR ALL THAT, WHEN THEY ARE IN
THE LAND OF THEIR ENEMIES, I WILL NOT
CAST THEM AWAY, NOR SHALL I ABHOR
THEM, TO UTTERLY DESTROY THEM AND
BREAK MY COVENANT WITH THEM; FOR
I AM THE LORD THEIR GOD. BUT FOR
THEIR SAKE I WILL REMEMBER THE
COVENANT OF THEIR ANCESTORS, WHOM
I BROUGHT OUT OF THE LAND OF EGYPT
IN THE SIGHT OF THE NATIONS, THAT I
MIGHT BE THEIR GOD: I AM THE LORD.

LEVITICUS 26:44–45

BY THE RIVERS OF BABYLON, THERE
WE SAT DOWN, YEA, WE WEPT WHEN
WE REMEMBERED ZION. WE HUNG OUR
HARPS UPON THE WILLOWS IN THE
MIDST OF IT. FOR THERE THOSE WHO
CARRIED US AWAY CAPTIVE ASKED
OF US A SONG, AND THOSE WHO
PLUNDERED US REQUESTED MIRTH,
SAYING, "SING US ONE OF THE SONGS
OF ZION!" HOW SHALL WE SING THE
LORD'S SONG IN A FOREIGN LAND?

PSALM 137:1-4

CHAPTER TWO

Cast to the Four Winds

Mere human ingenuity could never begin to produce a work of fiction as absorbing, emotionally charged, or exhilarating as the actual drama being lived out in the story of the Jewish people. From the nation's birth in the call of Abraham and through the Exodus, conquest of Canaan, rule of the judges, and reign of its kings, Israel's early history runs the gamut from combat to tranquility to rebellion to captivity.

Stern voices of bold prophets ring across the Bible's pages as the nation is called to repent and give its allegiance to its God. Psalmists sing captivating melodies that will live throughout the ages as a source of strength and inspiration for men the world over. Kings, princes, and queens—good and bad—all add their deeds and voices to the chronicle.

But over it all, it seems that we hear the persistent footfalls of great empires and petty tyrants as they thrust and parry to possess the land God gave to the children of Jacob. This Gentile obsession over the millennia to take title to Israel and subjugate its inhabitants has led to periods of turbulence, captivity, and finally the Jewish people's worldwide dispersion.

As we view this segment of history, we should keep in mind two of its general features. We might characterize them as preliminary and primary, or captivities as opposed to dispersion.

CAPTIVITIES

The captivities were localized experiences during which major segments of the Jewish people were forced into exile in other countries for varying periods of time. Later they were allowed to return home and resume official national life once again. The major captivities involved two nations: Assyria and Babylonia.

Following the death of Israel's third king, Solomon, his son Rehoboam ascended the throne. Rehoboam initiated a series of repressive measures that alienated his subjects. He unwisely rejected the sound counsel of his elders, who warned him the Israelites were already overburdened and would serve him willingly only if he behaved leniently toward them. But Rehoboam was intransigent, and his extreme harshness resulted in the division of the kingdom.

In 922 BC, Jeroboam led a successful insurrection that severed the 10 northern tribes (thereafter identified as Israel) from the nation. That move left Rehoboam with the two southern tribes (Judah and Benjamin) referred to in Scripture as the southern kingdom of Judah.

ASSYRIA

Under the leadership of Tiglath-Pileser III, the Assyrians invaded Israel and forced the northern kingdom to pay tribute. Israel paid for a short time before joining with Damascus on a course of mutual resistance to this arrangement. The result was a new intrusion by Assyria. The engagement brought about the fall of Damascus and Israel's loss of territory.

In addition, Assyria took Jewish people into exile. A later Israelite king, Hoshea, joined his predecessor in resisting the payment of tribute, this time turning to Egypt for help. Consequently, Assyrian ruler Shalmaneser V besieged Samaria, Israel's capital city. Samaria withstood the siege for three years but finally fell in 722 BC. Shalmaneser's successor, Sargon, who had participated in the conflict, reported that 27,290 more Israelites were captured. The Assyrian conflict spelled the end of the northern kingdom. Israel ceased to exist; only the kingdom of Judah now remained.

The Assyrians recruited settlers from Babylonia and Syria to move into the region and dwell among the Israelites who remained in the land. Their assimilation with the Jews produced the Samaritan people who were so hated by the Judeans in the days of the New Testament.

WHERE ARE THE 10 LOST TRIBES?

For years cultists have constructed elaborate schemes and deluded many into believing the 10 northern tribes were "lost." Some have claimed these Israelites became either Anglo-Saxons, gypsies, or some other group that accommodates the cultists' personal whims or objectives. To substantiate their claims, they mutilate the Scriptures by trying to relate God's promises to these groups, rather than to Israel. In reality, the tribes were never lost at all.

They were taken by their captors to "Halah, Habor, Hara, and the river of Gozan" (1 Chr. 5:26). Authorities place this area near the Euphrates River in the region between southern Turkey and northern Syria, about 200 miles east of the northeast tip of the Mediterranean Sea. The obvious conclusion is that they remained there until the Babylonians overtook the Assyrian empire to become the dominant world power. Then the exiles either returned to their homes in Israel or stayed put, as they chose. Either way, they now fell under the jurisdiction of the Babylonian Empire.

We also have documentation that a great many Israelites remained in the land and never left at all. During the revival under Hezekiah, king of Judah, Scripture says the king sent invitations to the northern tribes "from Beersheba to Dan, that they should come to keep the Passover to the LORD God of Israel at Jerusalem" (2 Chr. 30:5). Hezekiah received favorable responses from members of five of the tribes of Israel: Asher, Manasseh, Zebulun, Ephraim, and Issachar. The passage indicates that many Israelites from the northern tribes joined the Judeans for the Passover celebration at Jerusalem.

We also must take into account the fact that many pious Jews would have migrated south after the Assyrians first introduced their ungodly influences and oppressive pagan practices. Furthermore, there was no Temple in the north. Solomon's Temple still stood in Jerusalem in the southern kingdom, and Jewish people from all branches of Jacob's posterity—men of faith, believers in the promises of Jehovah—would have moved there and/or traveled there to worship because they identified with Temple worship and the place of the Davidic throne.

We have sufficient evidence to rest assured that all of Israel is represented in present-day Jewry, and we need not search for the so-called 10 lost tribes.

BABYLONIA

Even though the Judeans escaped the Assyrian scourge, they eventually would share the same fate as their northern brothers. They would be dragged into exile by the Babylonians. Approximately 150 years earlier, God had warned Judah of its impending judgment:

> Be in pain, and labor to bring forth, O daughter of Zion, like a woman in birth pangs. For now you shall go forth from the city, you shall dwell in the field, and to Babylon you shall go. There you shall be delivered; there the LORD will redeem you from the hand of your enemies (Mic. 4:10).

The prophet Jeremiah even told the nation how long the captivity would last:

> And this whole land shall be a desolation and an astonishment, and these nations shall serve the king of Babylon seventy years (Jer. 25:11).

As the year 605 BC crested over the horizon, Egypt held control of Israel and Syria. Led by Nebuchadnezzar, the Babylonians dealt the Syrians and Egyptians a defeat that broke Egypt's power and left the way to Syria and Israel open to the victors. Nebuchadnezzar then advanced into Judah, resulting in Judean King Jehoiakim being forced to agree to make tribute payments to Babylon.

Later, however, Jehoiakim refused to honor his pledge and fell prey to Babylonian wrath. Although Nebuchadnezzar spared Jehoiakim's life, which in itself was a minor miracle, he raided the Temple and took a number of captives to Babylon. Among those making the long journey into exile were a young Daniel and his friends Hananiah (later renamed Shadrach), Mishael (Meshach), and Azariah (Abednego).

WHEN LOYALTY TRANSCENDS EVIL DEMANDS

Shadrach, Meshach, and Abednego epitomized the faith to which the captives clung during their enforced exile in Babylon. Celebrated in story and song, these three defied a mighty king and lived to tell the story. A remarkable aspect of the encounter was their age. As was true with their famous companion, Daniel, they were probably only in their late teens when taken captive.

The story is familiar to us: Nebuchadnezzar had an enormous image of gold made and issued a universal decree that everyone must bow down and worship it; refusal meant suffering horrendous execution by fire. To paraphrase the Jewish teenagers' unanimous answer to the king, "No need to ask us. We will not bend our knees to worship your image, nor will we perish in your furnace. Our God whom we serve is able to deliver us" (Dan. 3:17).

How deeply engrained in the heart and soul of Jehovah's faithful remnant was faith in Him whom, though not seen, was loved beyond even life itself. True faith does not craft cowards. It creates overcomers. In this case, we can learn from the young.

CONTINUING OBSESSION TO RULE OR RUIN

Later, in 597 BC, Nebuchadnezzar's emissaries placed Jerusalem under siege and took more Judeans captive. The prophet Ezekiel was among those taken to Babylon in this wave of deportation.

The city finally fell on August 1, 586 BC. In an attempt to instill an attitude of enduring subservience in the Jewish mind, the king ordered the magnificent Temple of Solomon sacked and its valuables removed. Then it was put to the torch, along with the city and the king's palace. Except for the extremely poor and nondescript, whom the king left behind, the Jewish people were taken into captivity.

The Judeans mounted one more futile uprising in 581 BC. The result was the same, and more Jews were carried off the Judean hills to the banks of the river Chebar. Some Israelites, contrary to Jeremiah's advice, fled to Egypt rather than become captives; and they hauled an unwilling Jeremiah with them. The prophet died in Egypt.

As Jeremiah had predicted, Babylon did indeed annex Judah. The first confirmed physical evidence of Judah's destruction was discovered by Israeli archaeologists during the 1975 digging season. Professor Nathan Avigad unearthed four bronze and iron arrowheads of Babylonian origin at the base of a defense tower in the Jewish quarter of the Old City.

And so the prophetic word came true once again. For 70 years the Hebrews labored in a strange land. They wept by the river of Babylon, raised their lament, and longed to see their beloved Jerusalem once more.

In 538 BC, the Persians swept aside the Babylonians and became entrenched as the power to reckon with. Their leader, Cyrus, granted the Jews permission to return to their land. Zerubbabel led the first return of about 49,000 people. By 516 BC, the returnees had reconstructed the Temple. Ezra the scribe led another band of about 6,000 people in 457 BC; and 13 years later, Nehemiah led yet another assembly of travelers on the rigorous trek back to the land God gave to the children of Jacob forever.

Compared to the number of Israelites taken into exile, relatively few returned. They had known a great measure of freedom and prosperity in the land of their conquerors. Consequently, many chose to remain there rather than face the dangers they would encounter en route and the uncertainties awaiting them when they got home.

Scholars estimate that the number of people who remained in Israel during the exile probably exceeded 120,000. These are the people who composed the remnant that shared the vigil through the long years of waiting for the return of the captives and the appearance of the promised Messiah.

With the Babylonian conquest of Judah and the destruction of the Temple began a period of Gentile domination known as "the times of the Gentiles" (Lk. 21:24). It continues today and will end when the Lord returns to Earth, and Israel receives the final fulfillment of all that God has promised.

THE MYSTERY OF THE MISSING ARK

With the Babylonian destruction of the Temple, the Ark of the Covenant dropped out of sight. It was the central piece of furniture in Solomon's Temple and had been at the heart of Jewish worship for approximately 800 years, since God introduced the Mosaic system at Mount Sinai.

Moses received instructions for its dimensions and construction directly from Jehovah. The Ark was a chest that measured 3.75 feet long by 2.25 feet wide and high. It was made of acacia wood and covered inside and outside with gold. Inside it held the two tablets of the Decalogue—the Ten Commandments.

It was from above this Ark, between the covering cherubim attached to the Mercy Seat that rested on the Ark, that Jehovah communed with Israel:

> And there I will meet with you, and I will speak with you from above the mercy seat, from between the two cherubim which are on the ark of the Testimony, about everything which I will give you in commandment to the children of Israel (Ex. 25:22).

Once a year the high priest entered the Holy of Holies in the Temple and stood before the Ark to make an offering on behalf of the people as a covering for their sins.

No one really knows what happened to the Ark. But there are some theories. Possibly, it was destroyed by the marauding Babylonians who would have been interested in salvaging its gold. Or it could have been taken to Babylon as a trophy of war. However, there is no mention of it as being among the valuables described in the list of confiscated items in 2 Kings 25.

A rabbinical tradition asserts that Jewish priests protected it from the Babylonians by burying it under the Temple Mount before the Babylonians captured the city. If this is true, it is still there, as we well know that no one has claimed to have unearthed it. A number of high-ranking rabbis today favor this view and contend that the ancient Ark is indeed buried beneath the Temple Mount and will yet be found.

Still another theory appears in the apocryphal book of 2 Maccabees. It attributes the Ark's removal from Jerusalem to Jeremiah:

> It was also contained in the same writing, that the prophet, being warned of God, commanded the tabernacle and the ark to go with him, as he went forth into the mountain, where Moses climbed up, and saw the heritage of God. And when Jeremy came thither, he found an hollow cave, wherein he laid the tabernacle, and the ark, and the altar of incense, and so stopped the door (2 Macc. 2:4–5).

This account says the cave's location was lost and awaits disclosure by the Lord at some later date.

Others believe the Ark was transported to heaven and rests there now. People who hold to this theory go to Revelation 11:19 for their proof text. Here the apostle John described his glimpse into the heavenly Temple: "Then the temple of God was opened in heaven, and the ark of His covenant was seen in His temple." The obvious question is whether John saw the manmade Ark known to Israel or a heavenly version that occupies the celestial Temple.

Dr. Benjamin Mazar, the revered archaeologist who was in charge of all excavations at the Temple Mount in Jerusalem in the mid 20th century, told me he did not believe the Ark to be in existence. He felt that if it were not destroyed, it would have long since decayed and disintegrated. This view, however, does not take into account the fact that the wood was encased in gold and contained stone articles or that it already had weathered 800 years of use before the Babylonians destroyed the Temple. He did concede, however, that were he and his associates to discover the Ark, it would dramatically affect the nation and, for that matter, the world.

It most assuredly would! Finding the Ark would rank with, if not surpass, the resurrection of the nation of Israel in 1948 and the reunification of Jerusalem in 1967 as a landmark in Jewish history. And to say the least, the prophetic implications of such a find would be monumental. Observant Jews around the world might immediately call for a proper place to house this unequaled national treasure. The only acceptable resting place, of course, would be a new Temple. This possibility illustrates the dramatic swiftness with which great events could unfold in these last days.

Artist rendition of the Ark of the Covenant (Exodus 37)

It is noteworthy that Jeremiah said the Ark will not be needed in Israel's ultimate future:

> "Then it shall come to pass, when you are multiplied and increased in the land in those days," says the LORD, "that they will say no more, 'The ark of the covenant of the LORD.' It shall not come to mind, nor shall they remember it, nor shall they visit it, nor shall it be made anymore" (Jer. 3:16).

Also, the description of the Millennial Temple in Ezekiel 40—44 makes no mention of the Ark, and for good reason. In that glorious day, our reigning Messiah-Savior, Jesus Christ, will be light, law, redemption, and righteousness. There will be no further need for a symbol when He appears on the scene.

THE GENERAL DISPERSION

Preparation for the final dispersion dawned with Roman domination of the Promised Land. Until the Roman period, a succession of foreign powers made themselves felt among the Jewish people. After the Babylonians came the Medes and Persians. In their wake entered the swift forces of Alexander the Great. Finally, the Romans arrived. This unwelcome, uneasy yoke of Roman domination prevailed at Christ's birth.

THE WORDS OF JESUS

The coming expulsion of the Jewish people from their land was spoken of by Jesus Christ in the Gospel records of the New Testament. A large number of Jewish people already were living in other countries. Famous Jewish communities had sprung up in Alexandria, Egypt, as well as in Babylon, and were vying with the Jews in Israel for theological supremacy. The great national feasts, held in Jerusalem, would swell with large numbers of Israelites arriving from far-off nations for a brief, spiritual respite within the environs of the sacred Temple Mount.

Jesus, however, predicted the destruction of the Temple and the siege and fall of the city of Jerusalem approximately 40 years prior to the event:

> These things which you see—the days will come in which not one stone shall be left upon another that shall not be thrown down (Lk. 21:6).

> But when you see Jerusalem surrounded by armies, then know that its desolation is near. Then let those who are in Judea flee to the mountains, let those who are in the midst of her depart, and let not those who are in the

country enter her. For these are the days of vengeance, that all things which are written may be fulfilled. But woe to those who are pregnant and to those who are nursing babies in those days! For there will be great distress in the land and wrath upon this people. And they will fall by the edge of the sword, and be led away captive into all nations. And Jerusalem will be trampled by Gentiles until the times of the Gentiles are fulfilled (vv. 20–24).

Christ's prophecy revealed four future events:

1. The Temple would be destroyed.

2. The nation would be dispersed.

3. The city of Jerusalem would come under Gentile domination until Israel returned to the land.

4. The time of Gentile world-supremacy eventually would end.

DESTRUCTION

The disciples were thunderstruck by Christ's statement that not one stone of the Temple would be left upon another. This magnificent edifice graced the crown of Mount Moriah in Jerusalem, and all of Jewish life—inside and outside Israel—revolved around it.

The second Temple, which Zerubbabel began to build, was enhanced tremendously by Herod the Great. So magnificent was Herod's structure that it had been under construction for more than 40 years and was still some 40 years from completion. In fact, the second Temple was the wonder of the religious world. Its white marble and richly ornamented gold seemed at times to illuminate the city.

As visiting pilgrims approached the outskirts of Jerusalem, the Temple suddenly came into view, gleaming in the sunlight against the cool green backdrop of the Mount of Olives. The ancient historian Josephus provided a vivid description:

Viewed from without, the Sanctuary had everything that could amaze either mind or eyes. Overlaid all around with stout plates of gold, in the first rays of the sun it reflected so fierce a blaze of fire that those who endeavored to look at it were forced to turn away as if they had looked straight at the sun. To strangers as they approached it seemed in the distance like a mountain covered with snow; for any part not covered with gold was dazzling white.

It seemed inconceivable to the disciples that this grand edifice would ever be destroyed. Yet this was the Lord's prophecy; and in AD 70, Jesus' words were graphically fulfilled.

Jewish discontent with Rome had been growing, and by AD 66 it had erupted into open rebellion against Rome. The final straw came in the person of Gessius Florus, procurator of Judea, who chose a course of cruel repression of the rebellious Jews. His undoing was a raid on the Temple. He removed the Temple funds and massacred many of Jerusalem's inhabitants. The gauntlet was dropped.

After brief attempts at reconciliation and military skirmishing, the full weight of the Roman colossus began to rumble toward Israel. Rome's choice to command the advancing legionnaires was Vespasian, the finest human weapon in the imperial arsenal. He mounted a systematic campaign carefully crafted to demonstrate emphatically the folly of pursuing ambitions of independence from mighty Rome. Shortly before the last desperate struggle for the city, Vespasian left the field for Rome in quest of becoming emperor. He succeeded and dispatched his son Titus to pursue the grim business of placing Jerusalem under siege.

In August of AD 70, the hammer fell on the beleaguered Jews. Of course, they never actually had a chance of deposing their overlord. Yet their tenacity

Artist rendition of Herod's Temple

and valor through the hopeless contest endures as one of the most arresting chapters in the annals of military history.

The siege ended when the Roman legions breached Jerusalem's walls and slowly penetrated the city. After severe and protracted street fighting, they reached the Temple itself. During the deadly struggle, fire broke out in the hallowed sanctuary. Soon the cedar beams and roof were spewing flames and smoke. The very heart of Judaism was being torn from its breast.

By the time the triumphant legionnaires paraded through the streets of Rome bearing on their shoulders the sacred vessels of Jewish worship, the words of Christ had been fulfilled in minute detail. Literally, not one stone was left upon another. As the conflagration's scorching flames lit up the sky, the precious metals that adorned the Temple walls cascaded down between the giant marble blocks—some of which were nearly 70 feet long by nine feet wide. Bands of plunderers reportedly responded by methodically removing the blocks to retrieve the coveted treasure. The destruction was complete.

Today, more than 2,000 years later, the accuracy of Jesus' prophecy concerning the Temple can be seen in Israel. As you follow the ancient street along the remnants of the Herodian wall, you come upon a heap of stones piled up where they fell when the Roman legionnaires cast them down. To be able to reach out and touch them is a present-day, personal encounter with the very words of our Savior, spoken so many years ago.

DESOLATION

Without a sanctuary and with their beloved Jerusalem firmly in the grasp of the Gentiles, the Jewish people began their 2,000-year-long trek across the pages of history. After the city fell, multitudes were taken into captivity.

The final humiliation came when the Jewish people rallied to the side of Jewish leader Simon Bar Kochba in AD 132. This effort was their last fling at liberation. The final uprising was precipitated when Emperor Hadrian, who visited Judea in AD 130, decided to rebuild Jerusalem and change its name. He further proposed to build a shrine to the false god Zeus on the Temple site. The Jewish people were further incensed at his decrees, which forbade circumcision and observance of the Sabbath.

Bar Kochba (meaning "son of a star") offered himself as a military messiah who would banish their adversary Goliath and win lasting freedom for God's people. Sadly, those who had examined and rejected the Messianic credentials of the Prince of Peace were willing to follow Bar Kochba because he strapped on a sword.

Bar Kochba conducted a guerrilla-type campaign that met with initial success.

Jerusalem was recaptured and named the capital and religious center of the new regime. The optimistic leader even minted coins with the inscription "For the freedom of Jerusalem." These coins were dated "Year One," "Year Two," "Year Three." There was to be no "Year Four."

Rome retaliated savagely. As a result, both Jews and Romans suffered enormous losses. Bar Kochba was slain and the insurrection shattered. Jerusalem and its people again awaited Roman retribution, which was both swift and severe. The city was again leveled to the ground. This time the Temple Mount was put to the plow. Rome banished the Jewish people from the city and its environs and forbade them to enter for the next 200 years. Anyone attempting to return and repair his house was to be executed.

Roman vengeance was not confined to Jerusalem. Olive groves for miles around were cut down. In Galilee, noted for its olive production, scarcely a tree was left standing. Villages were burned. For a time, the Romans rigidly enforced a scorched-earth policy, burning and destroying everything. They established slave markets at Gaza and Hebron, as the words of Christ had predicted; and auctioneers sold Jewish people to foreign slavers who carried them to the far reaches of the world. Those who managed to escape Rome's tyrannical grasp packed their tattered belongings and slipped quietly out of the land and into the long centuries of enforced exile. The big dispersion had begun.

A new Roman city, Aelia Capitolina, now replaced Jewish Jerusalem. In its midst stood the objects that were perhaps the most symbolically illustrative elements of the entire, dreadful scene: a statue of the Emperor Hadrian and a shrine to the Roman god Jupiter. They stood atop the Temple Mount over the spot to which Jews had come from every corner of the earth to worship Jehovah.

Eventually, Jewish people spread out around the globe in what later became known as the Diaspora.

Jewish children and adults behind a barbed wire fence after the liberation of the concentration camp in Buchenwald, Germany during World War II.

PRESERVATION

I WILL SEND FAINTNESS INTO THEIR
HEARTS IN THE LANDS OF THEIR
ENEMIES; THE SOUND OF A SHAKEN
LEAF SHALL CAUSE THEM TO FLEE;
THEY SHALL FLEE AS THOUGH FLEEING
FROM A SWORD, AND THEY SHALL
FALL WHEN NO ONE PURSUES.

LEVITICUS 26:36

CHAPTER THREE

The Long, Lonely Road

God's long-standing promises to Moses in Leviticus would now be tested to the fullest. "Yet for all that, when they are in the land of their enemies, *I will not cast them away*" (Lev. 26:44, emphasis added). Amazing words! A numerically insignificant people were to be dispossessed from their homeland and dispersed among the nations. They would experience the intermittent hatred of the people among whom they would settle, have no Temple to preserve their religious continuity, and remain in this condition for nearly 2,000 years. With these facts in view, the ancient prophets' predictions meant one of two things: Either the prophets were mentally unhinged, or they had inside information.

Universally, the inspired penmen made bold assertions concerning the preservation of the Jewish people as a national entity during the coming displacement. These were not shrouded, vague references but bold, clear, repeated predictions that placed the biblical record's reliability squarely on the line.

A passage from Jeremiah illustrates the point:

> Thus says the LORD, who gives the sun for a light by day, the ordinances of the moon and the stars for a light by night, who disturbs the sea, and its waves roar (the LORD of hosts is His name): "If those ordinances depart from before Me, says the LORD, then the seed of Israel shall also cease from being a nation before Me forever." Thus says the LORD: "If heaven above can be measured, and the foundations of the earth searched out beneath, I will also cast off all the seed of Israel for all that they have done" (Jer. 31:35–37).

How dogmatic was Jeremiah about Jewish preservation? If the sun can be extinguished! If the moon can be prevented from influencing the tides! If the stars can somehow be caused to flicker and die! If we can successfully measure the expanse of space about us! If all of the mysteries of the earth can be solved! Only then "I will also cast off all the seed of Israel."

No one in his right mind would venture such statements unless he possessed inside information, and history has demonstrated unequivocally that Jeremiah did. The God of history gave the prophet the particulars hundreds of years before they became historical fact on the stage of human events. No other possibility exists. There is no other satisfactory explanation for how Jeremiah could know the future.

Over the centuries, Jewish people have been hunted like animals, slaughtered, maligned, and driven from nation to nation. No depth of human resourcefulness can account for the fact that these people are still with us today. The only acceptable explanation for Jewry's existence and its tenacious refusal to lie down and die is divine preservation coupled with a divinely infused will to survive.

THE WANDERING JEW

Most of us are at least vaguely familiar with the term *wandering Jew*. It has been bestowed on a card game and a game of dice, as well as on plants. But the principal recipients are the sons of Jacob, whom the medieval church caricatured in an unflattering manner to promote anti-Semitism. The caricature depicted a man who purportedly lived at the time of Christ and was consigned to walk the earth in penitence until the Second Advent because of the so-called atrocities he committed against Jesus at the crucifixion.

The first written record of the wandering Jew comes down to us from the 13th century. It alleges that, after the crucifixion, a Jewish man in Armenia had

Artist rendering of the wandering Jew

been found who had been a personal witness to Christ's sufferings. It claims he had shouted at Jesus, "Go, thou tempter and seducer, to receive what you have earned." The Lord is said to have replied, "I go, and you will await me until I come again." Thus, the legend goes that the Jewish people were condemned to wander the earth until Christ returns.

All stories of this wandering Jew are essentially the same. Perhaps the most universally represented is one that came from Germany in 1602.

> It is related that Paulus Von Eitzen, bishop of Schleswig, in the winter of 1542, when attending church in Hamburg, saw a tall man, dressed in threadbare garments, with long hair, standing barefoot in the chancel; whenever the name of Jesus was pronounced he bowed his head, beat his breast, and sighed profoundly. It was reported that he was a shoemaker named Ahasuerus who had cursed Jesus on his way to the crucifixion. On further questioning he related the historical events that had taken place since. He conversed in the language of the country he happened to be visiting. This version shows "Ahasuerus" was a fully-fledged personification of the Jewish people, incorporating the themes of participation of the crucifixion, condemnation to eternal suffering until Jesus' Second Coming, and the bearing witness to the truth of the Christian tradition. The description of the person suggests the well known figure of the Jewish peddler.[1]

And so the tone is set with the Jewish people portrayed as perpetual vagabonds among the nations of the world. While some may find this fanciful generalization of the Jewish condition quaint, there is nothing quaint about what these people have experienced at the hands of the Gentiles during the long years of their pilgrimage.

INSTRUMENTS OF TERROR

Footsteps in the hallway or a sudden knock on the door have caused Jewish people great apprehension in many parts of the world. The catalog of satanic instruments fashioned to inflict pain and humiliation on them is almost beyond description. Even worse is the fact that these instruments are used over and over again. Regardless of how many decades or centuries elapse, the conspiracy of evil continues.

As unpleasant as some of these things are to remember, we must remember. Too many people want to rewrite history and erase the truth. In light of current developments and the trend toward a new wave of militant anti-Semitism, we should all be aware of the evils apt to confront us.

POGROMS

A small Jewish family shared a simple evening meal together in their home in Odessa, Russia. The year was 1905. For some weeks political turmoil had been the central topic of conversation throughout the town. Much of the talk was frightening, with threatening overtones. News had filtered in of vicious attacks on Jews in surrounding communities. The youthful husband bravely tried to avoid communicating his fears to his wife and two small children.

Suddenly, the clatter of horses' hooves sounded across the yard. He sprang toward the door. The gruff voices of booted intruders were now clearly audible. Without so much as a command ordering the occupants to let them in, the Russian intruders battered in the door. The husband's efforts to protect his family proved pitifully inadequate. He was cut down with a single thrust of a sword.

The terror-stricken mother was torn from the desperate grasp of her children and forced through a door into another room. The children's deaths would be painful but quick when compared to the protracted and cruel torment their mother would endure before she finally died. The ordeal ended as the intruders loaded up the family's humble belongings and moved on to another Jewish family. They murdered 300 Jewish people, and thousands of others received wounds that would serve as lifelong memorials of the infamous event.

Pogroms originated in Russia and were, by definition, attacks. They were a swift, localized form of brutality that had as its major ingredients looting, destruction, rape, and murder. Pogroms were carried out extensively in Russia between 1881 and 1921, resulting in the murder of 70,000 to 250,000 innocent Jews.

During the Russian Revolution and Civil War (1917–1921), 1,236 such attacks took place in more than 500 Ukrainian towns. The result was an estimated 60,000 dead and many more left wounded and homeless.

Unfortunately, pogroms were not confined to Russia. Germany, Romania, Austria, the Balkans, Morocco, Algeria, Persia, and other areas also used them as a means of torturing and killing innocent people solely because they happened to be Jewish.

EXPULSIONS

Of more general and far-reaching consequences were the periodic expulsions from various cities and countries. We have touched on the Jewish expulsions from Israel by the ancient empires, namely Assyria and Rome. Rome further afflicted the Jewish people by periodically expelling them from the capital city. In AD 19, for example, Tiberius ordered all Jews who would not renounce their faith to leave Rome.

During the 15th and 16th centuries, Jewish people were frequently expelled from towns in Germany and northern Italy. Naples, Prague, Genoa, the Papal State (Italy), Moscow, and Vienna were among the localities that bear the distinction of sending Jewish people packing at some time in their history. Often these homeless people had nowhere to go and died trying to find a country that would take them in.

During the years of the Black Death, the plague that swept through Europe from 1348 to 1350, the Jews were blamed for the disease. They were accused of poisoning wells and other sources of water and, as a result, were massacred and banished from regions in Spain, France, Germany, and Austria.

The year 1492 is particularly significant. Americans celebrate it as the year Genoese sailor Christopher Columbus discovered America. It is also enshrined in the memories of the Jewish people, but for quite another reason. It was in 1492 that Spanish monarchs Ferdinand and Isabella decreed that all Jews should be exiled from Spain. This edict dealt a severe blow to the Spanish Jewish community, the largest in the world at the time, which had prospered greatly and contributed significantly to the betterment of life in that country.

It was a disastrous epoch for Abraham, Isaac, and Jacob's posterity in other areas, as well. Between 1492 and 1497 Jewish people were also denied a place in Sicily, Lithuania, and Portugal. These expulsions followed on the heels of enforced exiles from England (1290) and France (1306 and 1394). Consequently, for some time after 1492, no acknowledged Jews lived on the European coast of the Atlantic Ocean, which was the center of world trade at the time.

Other events also inflicted a variety of miseries on the People of the Book. Among other things, they suffered from forced sales, confiscation of their property, and loss of income from being compelled to leave behind uncollected debts. Disease, hunger, and the ever-present danger of ruthless highwaymen also plagued them as they wandered from place to place in search of hope, rest, and peace. A vivid description of their miseries has been preserved. The following comment is from a victim of the expulsion from Spain:

> We ate the grass of the fields, and every day I ground with my own hands in the house of the Ishmaelites for the thinnest slice of bread not even fit for a dog. During the nights, my stomach was close to the ground—and my belly my cushion. Because of the great cold of the autumn—we had no garments in the frost and no houses to lodge in—we dug trenches in the refuse heaps in the town and put our bodies therein.[2]

Jewry was a fluid entity during those unsettled years of searching for a place of security, one to call home. The deprivation and suffering the Jewish people endured bring to mind the solemn words of Moses: "And among those nations you shall find no rest, nor shall the sole of your foot have a resting place; but there the LORD will give you a trembling heart, failing eyes, and anguish of soul (Dt. 28:65).

BLOOD LIBELS

The preposterous allegation of blood libel has ranged the globe from ancient days to today. It repeatedly rears its ugly head to afflict the Jewish people, accusing them of ritual human sacrifice, using human blood for the Passover ceremony, and cannibalism. It is believed the blood libel was employed by the infamously cruel Seleucid ruler Antiochus IV Epiphanes—a forerunner to the last-days Antichrist—as a pretext upon which to justify his desecration of the Temple and brutal slaughter of Jewish men, women, and children.

Although these allegations of blood libel were repeatedly documented as false and even declared false by such prominent people as an emperor and a pope, they were too convenient a tool of destruction to be laid aside. We do not know how many Jewish people have suffered and died because of the blood libel fiction, but we do know it was used regularly by anti-Semites in Russia as late as the 1870s. The most terrifying example of its destructive evil is witnessed in Adolf Hitler's unabashed use of it against hapless European Jewry during the Holocaust.

Although the blood libel traditionally accuses Jewish people of using Christian blood, a new twist has emerged in recent years. In November 2015, *The Times of Israel* ran a story about a leader of the terrorist organization Hamas in Gaza accusing Israelis of killing Palestinian children in order to use their blood to bake Passover matzoh.

Salah Al-Bardawil said on Hamas TV the Jews have "ancient biblical beliefs, which instructed them to kill children and collect their blood, in order to knead it into the bread that is eaten on Passover."[3] He revived the old blood libel, reported *The Times of Israel*, "which dates back to the Middle Ages in Europe and which often was used as a pretext to commit atrocities against Jewish communities. The false allegation is still believed in some Arab cultures and is occasionally cited by officials and public figures."[4]

This preposterous lie refuses to die and continues to assail Jewish people even today.

THE PROTOCOLS OF THE ELDERS OF ZION

Many of us have viewed some form of the document titled *The Protocols of the Elders of Zion*. It accuses a so-called elite element, the Elders of Zion, of joining in a clandestine effort to take over the world by controlling finances and dominating key political positions in various countries. It is interesting that the people who rail on the Jews for their involvement in banking, deeming it a Jewish conspiracy, are the same sort who, in the Middle Ages, literally forced Jewish people into the lending industry by refusing to let them make a living by any other means.

It is well known that the church had prohibited its members from engaging in usury (lending money at interest). Jews, therefore, were allowed to practice what Christians could not. So they became the financiers from whom Christians borrowed money and whom Christians later disliked because of the profits derived from the practice.

Jews, as well as responsible Gentiles, have repeatedly repudiated *The Protocols of the Elders of Zion*. Czar Nicholas II of Russia, although reputed to be anti-Semitic, went on record as branding the version given him as being absurd. But the truth seldom wins over an enormous lie that satisfies the public lust.

The most recent popular version is believed to have been written by a member of the Russian secret police in the hopes of influencing Czar Nicholas. The writer is said to have adapted his version by using excerpts from a French political pamphlet by Maurice Joly that excoriated Louis-Napoleon Bonaparte's (Napoleon III) ambitions for world domination, in part because of his liberal attitude toward the Jewish people. The Russians made the transfer from Napoleon to the Jews and proceeded from that point.

Many have used *The Protocols* as justification for being anti-Semitic. At one time Henry Ford Sr. (1863–1947) sponsored this view in the United States and promoted *The Protocols* in his newspaper, *The Dearborn Independent*. *The Protocols* also was used with telling effect by Russians who hated the Jews; and, of course, Adolf Hitler and his Nazis used it as a reason to justify liquidating the nation in exile.

Today *The Protocols* is being turned against Zionism as justification for the proposed dismemberment of the State of Israel. Gamal Abdel Nasser took this tack when he was Egypt's president (1956–1970), and *The Protocols* has been applauded by many who are attempting to promote a schism between "Jews" and "Zionists," claiming Zionists are only interested in expansionism and the ultimate domination of the Middle East.

In 1935 the presiding justice in a Swiss court scorned *The Protocols* as "libelous," "obvious forgeries," and "ridiculous nonsense." Yet, for all of the reputable sources exposing it as a forgery, it endures as a popular tool to stir up anti-Semitic hate.

Nobel Peace Prize Laureate and Holocaust survivor Elie Wiesel once commented, "If ever a piece of writing could produce mass hatred, it is this one."

The United States Holocaust Memorial Museum in Washington, DC, also had a comment on its website that bears repeating:

> *The Protocols of the Elders of Zion* is the most notorious and widely distributed anti-Semitic publication of modern times. Its lies about Jews, which have been repeatedly discredited, continue to circulate today [America included], especially on the Internet. The individuals and groups that have used the *Protocols* are all linked by a common purpose: to spread hatred of Jews.

That the notorious *Protocols* is receiving five-star reviews from some online purchasers in America is baffling. Here are some comments from people who have bought in to these dangerous and evil fabrications: "This document is spot on." "It cries out in pain as it strikes you!" "We must defend ourselves before it is too late!" "Think! Organize! Do!"

THE BADGE

Jewish people have been marked for persecution most visibly by being forced to wear specific types of apparel. In the Middle Ages the Germanic countries singled them out for humiliation by making them wear pointed hats. In England they were forced to wear a distinguishing badge—Henry III enforced this practice. Edward I decreed the badge should be yellow and larger than previously required. In France the distinguishing mark was a circular emblem. It was to be either yellow, or red and white. Some localities required it to be worn on both front and back. All Jews, beginning as early as age seven, were forced to display it on their clothing.

In Spain it had a name: The Badge of Shame. The order there was not enforced as consistently as in other areas. Fredrick II ordered all Jewish people in the Kingdom of Sicily to wear a blue badge in the shape of the Greek letter T. In addition, men were forced to wear beards as a further means of identification. In Rome in 1360 it was a red cape for men and red aprons for women.

These badges, hats, capes, scarves, aprons, and other devices were used at given intervals over an extended period of time. The reason was clear: They all screamed out, "This is a Jew." The most devastating consequence of being thus identified was during World War II, when European Jews wore on their chests a yellow patch shaped in the form of the Star of David. It was affixed to them as a prelude to their march to the gas chambers.

THE GHETTO

This instrument of confinement was created in order to pen up Jewish people in preassigned geographical areas. It was born in the church councils of the Middle Ages when decisions were made prohibiting Jews and Christians from living together. The ghetto appeared as a permanent institution in Venice in 1516 when Jews "who sought refuge in the city, from which they had been excluded for a lengthy period, were admitted on the condition that they live in a designated quarter, an isolated island among the canals of Venice that could easily be completely cut off from its surroundings by a wall, gates and drawbridges."[5]

This became the established feature that distinguished the ghetto: walled enclosures with gates that could be closed if desired. Some were laid out with only one gate that could be guarded at night to prevent Jewish people from leaving. Ghettos existed in both Christian and Muslim countries in the Middle Ages and later. None, however, equaled the barbarities of the infamous Warsaw Ghetto of the Holocaust.

THE CRUSADES

One of the most lamentable periods in the annals of Jewish-Christian relations was the Crusades (1095–1291), a period in church history that saw successive waves of mail-clad armies move across Europe intent on delivering the Holy Sepulcher from the Saracen (Muslim) infidels. The idea was to establish a Christian kingdom in the Holy Land.

Although there probably were many sincere, devout individuals involved in the Crusades, the cruelty most Crusaders manifested traumatized the Jewish people. As they made their way to the Middle East, bands of Crusaders attacked Jewish communities in German and French towns and massacred the Jews in pogrom-like fashion.

The culmination came with the fall of Jerusalem on July 15, 1099. No amount of romanticism can obscure the grim specter of death that permeated the scene that day. The city was filled with the bodies of those slain by the invaders.

The Crusaders locked Jewish people into their synagogues and burned them alive. They slaughtered them in the Temple area. A Crusader himself gave this account: "They cut down with the sword every one whom they found in Jerusalem, and spared no one. The victors were covered with blood from head to foot."[6] Jewish people have never forgotten the cruelty inflicted on them in the name of Christ, and the Crusades remain a sad chapter in the history of the church.

THE HOLOCAUST

In all of the suffering the Jewish people have endured through the centuries, nothing can equal the singular enormity of the savage attempt to liquidate all of European Jewry during World War II. Adolf Hitler's demonic "final solution to the Jewish problem" will endure as the darkest hour in Jewish history over the two millennia of the dispersion.

Efforts to even begin to provide a dim glimpse into this era will most certainly prove futile. Statistics regarding deaths are inadequate because they are constantly being revised upward as new information emerges. Nevertheless, the United States Holocaust Memorial Museum in Washington, DC, opens a door to the magnitude of this genocide. These figures, provided on its website (ushmm. org), are based on the location of death, including the concentration camps:

Auschwitz complex (including Birkenau, Monowitz, and subcamps)	approximately 1 million
Treblinka 2	approximately 925,000
Belzec	434,508
Sobibor	at least 167,000
Chelmno	156,000–172,000
Shooting operations at various locations in central and southern German-occupied Poland (the so-called Government General)	at least 200,000
Shooting operations in German-annexed western Poland (District Wartheland)	at least 20,000
Deaths in other facilities that the Germans designated as concentration camps	at least 150,000
Shooting operations and gas wagons at hundreds of locations in the German-occupied Soviet Union	at least 1.3 million
Shooting operations in the Soviet Union (German, Austrian, Czech Jews deported to the Soviet Union)	approximately 55,000
Shooting operations and gas wagons in Serbia	at least 15,088
Shot or tortured to death in Croatia under the Ustaša regime	23,000–25,000
Deaths in ghettos	at least 800,000
Other*	at least 500,000

*Other includes, for example, people killed in shooting operations in Poland in 1939–1940; as partisans in Yugoslavia, Greece, Italy, France or Belgium; in labor battalions in Hungary; during anti-Semitic actions in Germany and Austria before the war; by the Iron Guard in Romania, 1940–1941; and on evacuation marches from concentration camps and labor camps in the last six months of World War II. It also includes people caught in hiding and killed in Poland, Serbia, and elsewhere in German-occupied Europe.

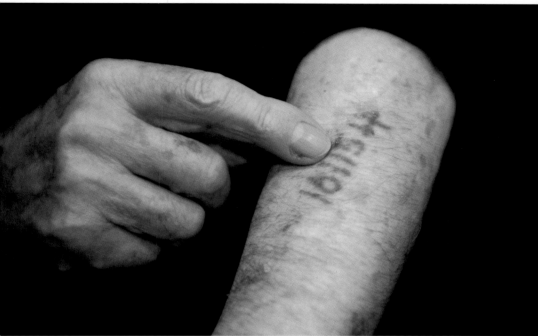

Holocaust survivor showing the number the Nazis tattooed on him in Auschwitz.

The numbers are staggering. They provide a stunning exhibition of what depraved humanity is capable of doing. However, massive numerical summations cannot convey the emotion involved in the fact that the lives of 6 million human beings were snuffed out, and along with them, 6 million very personal life stories. Nor can we compute the mental and physical anguish the survivors must live with for the rest of their days. Every life tells a story, attesting to truths we must never allow ourselves to forget.

The reality of this aspect of life after the Holocaust struck me in a way I'll never forget. Many years ago I sat beside a lovely woman named Nina at a gathering of Christians and Jews at a conference center in Memphis, Tennessee. Nina was the image of sophistication and intelligence. She comported herself with an air of grace that was immediately apparent to everyone around her.

As we chatted, someone sitting across the table asked that something beyond her reach be passed to her. As Nina reached out to comply with the request, the sleeve of her blouse slipped up her arm—and there they were: the faded blue numbers of the Nazis' tattoo. This woman had survived five brutal years in a Nazi concentration camp.

Her father, mother, sister, and rabbi grandfather had all been liquidated. Three thousand Jewish people worked as slave labor in the camp where she was confined. Only 800 survived. To look at her, I never would have known what she had suffered. But the numbers told the story. They spoke of a darker reality, of indescribable horrors and genocidal lunacy that we must never forget.

History is reality. And when accurately transcribed, it provides a record for us to study and, above all, pass down to the younger generations that so desperately need to know the truth.

BABI YAR

What occurred in a ravine near the city of Kiev in Ukraine still endures as a microcosm of the grotesque horror that was the Holocaust. The Babi Yar massacre took place during the German Invasion of Russia in September 1941. As conquering Nazi forces moved ahead, Einsatzgruppen (mobile killing squads) were left behind to deal with the remaining civilian population.

Made up of German SS, collaborating local citizens, and police, these units were tasked with murdering everyone they deemed an intellectual or political enemy of the Nazis, a dangerous radical, or ethnically unfit. Their main preoccupation, however, was to search out and kill every single Jew they could find.

At the time, Jewish people constituted 20 percent of Kiev's population of 160,000 residents. As the Germans approached, approximately 100,000 fled the city. Those left behind were helpless women and children, the infirm, or people incapable of running for their lives. They were left to face the Einsatzgruppen.

Jewish people leaving their homes one September morning in 1941 found an order posted along the streets: "Kikes [pejorative term for "Jews"] of the city of Kiev and vicinity! On Monday, September 29, you are to appear by 7:00 A.M. with your possessions, money, documents, valuables and warm clothing at Dorogozhitshaya Street, next to the Jewish cemetery. Failure to appear is punishable by death."

As Jewish people assembled in a wooded area near the Jewish cemetery, they found themselves facing a large ravine lined with men holding submachine guns. Divided into small groups, the victims were ordered to disrobe completely. Then they were forced to line up before the ravine. Immediately, machine guns began to riddle their bodies with bullets. As people were struck, they collapsed into the pit where executioners waited, pistols drawn, to finish off those who may only have been wounded.

In two days, September 29–30, 1941, approximately 34,000 Jewish men, women, and children were slaughtered for no reason other than they were Jews. In the months following, thousands more Jewish people were killed at Babi Yar, along with Communists, Gypsies, and Russian prisoners of war: a total of about 100,000.

As with those bearing the faded numbers, who are haunted by the atrocities they saw in the death camps, the stains of unremitting terror at Babi Yar cannot be wiped from memory.

Even American Jews born after the Holocaust are still affected by what took place then. Those days of infamy rushed to the mind of a dear friend and colleague as she listened to an interview aired on a CBS *60 Minutes* program in 2015. Here are her words:

I had never heard of Patrick Desbois until October 4, 2015. He's an ordinary-looking man. Wears glasses. Balding. Speaks mediocre English with a heavy French accent and is a Roman Catholic priest.

I'm sure I'll never meet Patrick Desbois in person, and had he not been on the CBS news program *60 Minutes* in October 2015, I wouldn't know he exists. Yet he affected me profoundly as I sat in my living room sipping tea, separated from him by about 4,500 miles and the Atlantic Ocean, because he may have told me what happened to my family during the Holocaust.

As evil as we know the Holocaust of World War II was, it seems new information always surfaces to reveal it was far worse than we imagined. Such was the case in Ukraine. We know that now thanks to Father Desbois.

My mother was born in Ukraine but grew up in Montreal, Canada. She was only a girl when her grandparents practically forced her to board a ship for Canada because they had a premonition that life for the Jews of Ukraine, already bad because of government-sanctioned Jew-killing sprees called pogroms, was about to get worse. She left behind two brothers she adored who couldn't obtain the government's permission to leave.

My mother corresponded with them faithfully until their letters stopped. The last one arrived in Montreal in 1941. By then, my uncles were married and had small children. One of my aunts was pregnant.

My aunts, cousins, and one uncle perished during the war. I had assumed they died in the Babi Yar massacre, a barbaric butchering episode in which the Nazis exterminated more than 34,000 Jewish people in the Kiev, Ukraine, area in only two days. Babi Yar is considered the worst mass murder in history. Then I heard Father Desbois.

Apparently, more Jewish people were murdered en masse in Ukraine than anyone knew. The slaughters were conducted in broad daylight; and watching them was so popular that people ran to them with cameras and chairs as though they were sporting events. "They were fighting to have a good place like for a circus," Father Desbois told Lara Logan of *60 Minutes*.

"When a woman with a baby would approach the pit," one eyewitness said, "they [Nazis] forced her to hold the baby in sight, first they shot the baby and then her."

Others observed, "The pit was barely covered so we could even see their legs and arms."

"We could see the blood bubbling."

"They were screaming, the children were crying. When the pit was full they filled it with a little earth. For three days the ground moved. Some were still alive."

The Jewish people of Ukraine lie by the thousands under cornfields, tomato fields, and houses and in forests and ravines. I have no doubt members of my family are there. The mass graves are invisible, unmarked, and forgotten. Until now.

YET GOD...

And so the heart-wrenching sobs of suffering Jewry rise from the pages of history. Pagans, Muslims, some people who profess to be Christians, and atheists have all joined in the flagellation of the Chosen People. It is indeed a painful fact to contemplate. But there it is, etched in blood, chiseled forever in the granite of the historical tablets.

Yet, above the staccato of man's frenzied efforts to extinguish the Jewish people rise the deep, resounding tones of the eternal Word of God: "Yet for all that, when they are in the land of their enemies, I will not cast them away, nor shall I abhor them, to utterly destroy them and break My covenant with them" (Lev. 26:44).

As we survey the sordid catalog of torture, persecution, and destruction unleashed against the Jewish people over the centuries, we are stunned by man's capacity to afflict his fellow man. The searching query rises, "Why, after all of this, do Jewish people choose to retain their identity? Would it not have been more prudent for them to have slipped quietly away into the anonymity of assimilation?" After all, this is precisely what has occurred to many of Israel's ancient contemporaries. Where are the Hittites, Hivites, Jebusites, and a host of other nations whose existence was recorded in the Bible thousands of years ago? They have long since assimilated and are now all but forgotten. Only occasionally do historians study their place in antiquity. Archaeologists examine physical evidences of their passing tenure in the Middle East; but, in fact, these people have been lost as identifiable entities.

Not so with Israel. The Jewish nation has endured through wearying centuries as great world powers rose, fell, and then lapsed into the musty recesses of time. There can be no doubt about it: The Jews are a miracle people, a people whose story defies analysis apart from divine revelation. Historians and anthropologists have long bent their minds trying to explain the Jewish people. They cannot! How do you explain a people that has survived systematic vilification, persecution, and genocide while scattered around the world?

Israel has been a nation without a country, without a flag, and without a capital—a people who were given no flickering ray of assurance from any human source that they would ever again live sovereignly in the land from which they had been expelled.

THE PEOPLE OF PROMISE

There is but one explanation for the Jewish people's perseverance: God keeps His word. Whatever mysteries lie beyond the grasp of our finite minds, one thing is sure: The God who has pledged Himself to the continuity of this special people has been faithful to His promise. This unchallengeable fact should refresh us to reflect on the biblical foundations upon which Israel's assurance rests.

DIVINE LOVE

Jehovah has assured Israel that His love for the sons and daughters of Jacob is real and enduring: "Since you were precious in My sight, you have been honored, and I have loved you; therefore I will give men for you, and people for your life" (Isa. 43:4).

Through Scripture, Jehovah further reveals that His purpose in establishing Israel is that this people, who "are called by My name and created for My glory" (v. 7), might reflect His love to an errant world. God Himself provides the explanation: "For you are a holy people to the LORD your God; the LORD your God has chosen you to be a people for Himself, a special treasure above all the peoples on the face of the earth" (Dt. 7:6).

DIVINE LOYALTY

God also reveals that this love is not vested in fluctuating, emotional whims but is constant, rooted in His loyalty:

> The LORD did not set His love on you nor choose you because you were more in number than any other people, for you were the least of all peoples; but because the LORD loves you, and because He would keep the oath which He swore to your fathers, the LORD has brought you out with a mighty hand, and redeemed you from the house of bondage, from the hand of Pharaoh king of Egypt (Dt. 7:7–8).

In other words, not one of the promises established through the great covenant transactions between Jehovah, Abraham, and Abraham's posterity will fail. As Israel was delivered out of the suffering and bondage of Egypt by the hand of God, so shall it be delivered from every evil design set against it by its enemies today. The fact is, Israel will not only endure but will one day, as we shall see, emerge totally triumphant with every God-given promise fully delivered.

DIVINE LONGING

At the base of God's program for His Chosen People is the full establishment of all He has designed for Israel to be and do. The Lord will be fully satisfied only when His people are fully devoted to Him. Even during those dark hours of distress, when the Jewish people have questioned God's interest or very presence, His love and resolve have remained unshaken:

> But Zion said, "The LORD has forsaken me, and my Lord has forgotten me. Can a woman forget her nursing child, and not have compassion on the son of her womb? Surely they may forget, yet I will not forget you. See, I have inscribed you on the palms of My hands; your walls are continually before Me" (Isa. 49:14–16).

Divine longing consummates in that future day when all of the processes that have run their course through the nation of Israel's earthly experience will bring about full national reconciliation to God, and God's faithful Word will be accomplished: "They shall be My people, and I will be their God; then I will give them one heart and one way, that they may fear Me forever, for the good of them and their children after them" (Jer. 32:38–39).

Therefore, in the end, the wandering Jew will be transformed into the long-promised "light to the nations."

WHO TAUGHT YOU TENDER BIBLE TALES
OF HONEY LAND, OF MILK AND WINE?
OF PEACEFUL, HAPPY PALESTINE?
OF JORDAN'S HOLY HARVEST VALES?
WHO GAVE THE PATIENT CHRIST? I SAY,
WHO GAVE THE CHRISTIAN CREED? YEA, YEA,
WHO GAVE YOUR VERY GOD TO YOU?
YOUR JEW! YOUR JEW! YOUR HATED JEW!

JOAQUIN MILLER

CHAPTER FOUR

Then There Are Christians

We must frankly acknowledge the fact that much of the persecution that fell on the Jews, particularly in Europe, was inflicted by people who professed to be following Jesus Christ. The Christianized Roman Empire made Jewish persecution official policy. As we've seen, sword-wielding Christian Crusaders hunted down Jewish people. The papacy branded them as "Christ killers," and professing Christians consistently hounded them in the name of the church.

Even as important a figure in Protestantism as Martin Luther adopted a viciously anti-Jewish stance. In 1543 he published two books denouncing the Jewish people, going so far as to encourage their expulsion and the burning of their synagogues; and he tried to persuade authorities to cease distributing their books.

The enduring residual effect has been a deep-seated Jewish resentment and suspicion toward Christianity. Jewish people are well acquainted with what has been done to them in the name of Christ, so much so that it is extremely difficult for them to understand what Christ has done for them.

Christ did not commission the church to perpetrate hatred, death, and carnage. And Jesus Himself was most certainly not anti-Semitic. He was, in the days of His flesh, a Jew. In fact, He was a Jew who spent His life ministering to other Jews. His message of love and life was directed to Jewish people. Here are His own words:

> Do not go into the way of the Gentiles, and do not enter a city of the Samaritans. But go rather to the lost sheep of the house of Israel (Mt. 10:5–7).

> Come to Me, all you who labor and are heavy laden, and I will give you rest. Take My yoke upon you and learn from Me, for I am gentle and lowly in heart, and you will find rest for your souls (Mt. 11:28–29).

> I was not sent except to the lost sheep of the house of Israel (Mt. 15:24).

> O Jerusalem, Jerusalem, the one who kills the prophets and stones those

who are sent to her! How often I wanted to gather your children together, as a hen gathers her brood under her wings, but you were not willing! (Lk. 13:34).

Father, forgive them, for they do not know what they do (Lk. 23:34).

Salvation is of the Jews (Jn. 4:22)

Some Jewish authorities castigate Jesus for His declaration in John 8:44: "You are of your father the devil, and the desires of your father you want to do." One writer refers to this statement as one of the two "cardinal themes appearing in Christian anti-Semitism."[1] Many Jewish authorities contend that Jesus was saying all Jewish people are children of the Devil. But this simply is not the case. Verse 13 clearly indicates Jesus was talking to the Pharisees, who were accusing Him of being satanically motivated and indwelt (cf. v. 48). His accusation was directed toward the religious leaders who had witnessed His miraculous ministry, heard His message, recognized what He was doing and saying, and then deliberately set out to have Him slain.

Jesus' reaction parallels that of a Jewish woman in Jerusalem who had lived through the darkest hours of Israel's 1948 War of Independence. The city was on the brink of starvation because the Arabs had closed the road to Tel Aviv. The Israelis could get nothing through, not even food. In a desperate effort to save the city and the people, heroic Jewish forces cut a road through the hill country, out of the reach of Arab guns.

The first convoy reached Jerusalem on the Sabbath. This woman told how she and other Jerusalemites wept for joy as they witnessed the arrival of the first trucks, driven by men who were at the point of exhaustion. As the trucks began to rumble into the city, a group of ultra-Orthodox Jewish people picked up rocks and began throwing them at the life-bearing convoy. But the next day, these same people were in line to receive the supplies brought by the Sabbath-breakers.

"Oh, how I hated them!" she declared. Hated whom? The Jewish people? Certainly not. In fact, the woman had served for years as secretary to one of Israel's prime ministers. She was proud to be a Jew, and she loved her people. What she didn't love was the superficiality and hypocrisy evidenced by a few. To say her statement branded her as a Jew-hater would be as grossly unfair and untrue as it would be to indict Jesus Christ for His words to the religious leaders of His day, who were cut out of the same cloth as their rock-throwing descendants.

The second of the "cardinal themes appearing in Christian anti-Semitism" is drawn from Matthew 27:25: "And all the people answered and said, 'His blood be on us and on our children.'" A Jewish commentator has stated, "The Jews

Victor Buksbazen

themselves are made to admit their collective responsibility for the crucifixion of the Son of God."[2] Bible scholar Victor Buksbazen provided one of the best comments concerning this verse and its use against the Jewish people:

Many misguided Christians have argued that, with these words, the Jewish people called down God's wrath upon themselves and all the generations that followed and consequently deserve to be punished.

What a perverted and preposterous idea, that God should act contrary to His own righteousness and to all the promises He made to Israel and that He should listen to a frenzied, howling mob and not to His beloved Son, Jesus, who prayed, "Father, forgive them; for they know not what they do" (Lk. 23:34, KJV).

Did this mob really represent all the Jewish people who would ever live, including those who had no part or knowledge of the crucifixion? Of course not!

Should we condemn all the Greeks of every generation for the judicial murder of Socrates? Should we condemn every Russian for the bloody murders of Josef Stalin or every German for the heinous deeds of Adolf Hitler and his henchmen?

For every Jew who shouted "Crucify Him, crucify Him" there were many devout Jewish women who followed Jesus to the cross, weeping. There were also countless thousands of Jews who lived and died for Jesus during the past centuries. Were these Jewish people not more truly representative of Israel in the eyes of God than the ignorant mob in Jerusalem?

It is unfortunately true that many Gentiles have used the wonderful story of God's love to vent their ingrained hatred and unholy wrath on the Jews. These so-called Christians, who make Christ's death an excuse to hate and persecute others, would have readily found some other reason to justify their wickedness.

We also should consider everything the Gospel writer actually recorded. He described the scene in its historical context. He was an eyewitness. It is presumptuous to claim, as some do, that he inserted the statement with a view toward making life difficult for future generations of Jewish people.

Matthew 27:20 says, "But the chief priests and elders persuaded the multitudes that they should ask for Barabbas and destroy Jesus." This verse explains that the crowd was incited by leaders who had already rejected Christ.

WHO CRUCIFIED CHRIST?

In reading the records of Jesus' trial and crucifixion, it becomes obvious that two great representative forces were involved in the events that transpired.

First, there were the ruling Jewish religious leaders. They represented the religious world, and their people were the recipients of all God proposed to reveal through His Word. The great, divine promises had been committed to

Artist rendition of Christ before Pilate (Mark 15)

them with the specific charge to be His witness nation, dedicated to truth, along with the responsibility to disseminate it.

Second, there was Pontius Pilate and Rome. They epitomized the legal and political world. Pilate served on behalf of the emperor, with the responsibility of dispensing the vaunted Roman justice.

Yet both bore equal culpability, as both breached their trusts. Jewish leaders brought trumped-up charges and suborned witnesses against Jesus and were guilty of bribery and inciting simple citizens to cry for His blood. Roman governor Pontius Pilate examined the charges, declared them to be without merit, pronounced Jesus innocent, washed his hands publicly to visualize that innocence, and then still turned Jesus over to be scourged, humiliated, and crucified.

Any contention that the Gospel writers soft-peddled Pilate's role in the crucifixion is totally without justification. To the contrary, it seems they emphasized it. Pilate was not a witless simpleton; he was the emissary of imperial Rome. He was saying, in effect, "In the name of Rome, I find him innocent; take him away and crucify him," fully demonstrating his extreme culpability (cf. Mt. 27:24).

Roman hands fashioned the cross; Jewish voices taunted Jesus along the way. Roman soldiers hammered Roman spikes through Jesus' hands and feet; Jewish lips essentially murmured, "So be it." A Roman soldier thrust his spear into Jesus' side; a Jewish man cried, "He saved others; Himself He cannot save" (Mt. 27:42; Mk. 15:31). Of Jew and Roman alike it is written, "Sitting down, they kept watch over Him there" (Mt. 27:36).

The symbolism drawn from the episode that day just outside Jerusalem's city walls is compelling. Jews and Gentiles, through their responsible representatives, participated jointly. Gentiles were no less guilty than Israel's religious leadership. To attempt to ascribe primary responsibility to one group or the other is blatant hypocrisy. And it is contemptible to give the repugnant designation of "Christ killers" to the Jewish people exclusively. Jesus' crucifixion was a crime of humanity.

Some react to what they see as Jesus' harsh phraseology regarding the Jewish nation's future. They recoil at Jesus' statements of destruction, captivities, and suffering. But we must consider two factors:

1. Christ's pronouncements were no more severe than those of Israel's prophets. It is a matter of record that His statements harmonize completely with those of the Jewish prophets as recorded in the Hebrew Scriptures.

2. Christ's statements, no matter how we may choose to view them, have come to pass. What He predicted has taken place in minute detail. It is inconceivable that any mere human being could make

predictions with such telling, long-range accuracy. His statements came to pass only because Jesus Christ was who He claimed to be: the divine Son of God.

Neither must we forget that while Jesus prophesied of Israel's future suffering, He also unveiled promises of the Jewish nation's future glory, which also certainly will come to pass. He who revealed the Jewish dispersion also announced the return and subsequent establishment of the Messianic Kingdom, when King David's greater Son shall reign "where'er the sun does its successive journeys run," as an old hymn declares.

BIBLE-BELIEVING CHRISTIANS AND JEWISH PEOPLE

An extremely clear distinction must be drawn between biblical Christianity and manifestations of Christianity. Will H. Houghton, a former president of Moody Bible Institute, stated the case generally in a few poetic lines that he penned many years ago:

> Say not a Christian e'er would persecute a Jew;
> A Gentile might, but not a Christian true.
> Pilate and Roman guard that folly tried.
> And with that great Jew's death an empire died!
> When Christians gather in a cathedral, church or hall,
> Hearts turn towards One—the name of Jesus call.
> You cannot persecute—whatever else you do—
> The race who gave Him—Jesus was a Jew!

I surely cannot speak for every Christian or every Jew, and I know some people will disagree with me here. But I do think I can identify a number of general characteristics that usually hold true for evangelicals and some that usually hold true for Jewish people, particularly the more Orthodox. Believe it or not, Christians and Jews do have some beliefs in common.

THE COMMON GROUND

Instead of exploring every area of compatibility, I've chosen four that will demonstrate my point:

1. The authority of Scripture.

2. The Abrahamic promises.

3. The coming Messiah.

4. The future Kingdom.

Christians committed to the Bible firmly adhere to the proposition that "all Scripture is given by inspiration of God" (2 Tim. 3:16). This statement, of course, includes the Old Testament in its entirety. The Bible, therefore, is the only final and reliable source of revelation on which we may place our faith and order our lives.

This being true, it follows that God's promises to Abraham are both literal and permanent. In other words, everything Jehovah has promised to the posterity of Abraham, Isaac, and Jacob will be delivered to them one day. Believing biblicists reject the view that when the Jewish people spurned Jesus' Messianic claims, Jehovah wrote them off forever and then took all of the promises He made to them and transferred them to the church.

This is a form of theological anti-Semitism, and it is utterly foreign to the teachings of the New Testament. The New Testament, in fact, emphatically affirms and assures Israel's future in the economy of God. Most Christians who accept the Scriptures transmitted to humanity via both Old and New Testaments are as committed to the basic aspirations of biblical Zionism as are their Jewish counterparts. We make no apology for being identified as Christian Zionists. Zionism, simply defined, is the belief in the right of the Jewish people to have a national home in Israel on the land God promised to Abraham, Isaac, Jacob, and Jacob's posterity.

REPLACEMENT THEOLOGY

A major error many people make regarding God's promises to Israel is bound up in the term *Replacement Theology (RT)*. More formally, it is called Supersessionism. Here is a brief definition by Dr. James Showers, executive director of The Friends of Israel Gospel Ministry:

> Replacement Theology is the belief that the church has replaced physical Israel (the Jewish people) in the plan of God. Those who hold this view believe the church has become "spiritual Israel" and the inheritor of all the covenant promises God made to Israel. But they say the Jewish people retain all the curses. RT also allegorizes much of Scripture instead of using the literal, grammatical, historical method of interpretation.

An example of the hostility RT can generate surfaced in a statement that appeared in the official Vatican newspaper after Israel declared its independence in 1948 and fought five enormous Arab armies for the life of the state: "Modern Zionism is not the true heir of Biblical Israel, but a secular state....Therefore the Holy Land and its sacred sites belong to Christianity, the true Israel."[3]

All things considered, assigning the term *theology* to the Replacement movement is a stretch. The term is a misnomer. The position is better described as an ideology that is being foisted on the church as a legitimate theology. RT unfortunately has contributed to the persecution and vilification of the Jewish people and now claims Israel has no rights to its land in the Middle East. Rather, it contends that Israel is an oppressive occupier of Palestinian territories. Sadly, some fine evangelicals have been deluded by the errors of this position.

However, no allegorical or fanciful interpretations are capable of diminishing the glory of God's promise of the divine Messiah's future coming, an event that is the great sounding bell of all Scripture in both Testaments. The hope of the world is not another system—social, political, or theological—but a coming Messiah.

Increasingly, Jews and Gentiles are reaching the conclusion that every new political ideology mankind concocts is inadequate. One after another, these mechanisms have proved a failure. We all know why. No matter how diligent our search, we simply cannot find people who are consistently noble individuals.

History's constantly fluctuating uncertainties beckon us back to the Bible. Its message consistently predicts the failure of human ingenuity. Scripture affirms man's acknowledgment that the only valid answer to our problems is the appearance of the One who is qualified to establish a universal domain and execute equity in justice and administration, tempered by divine compassion.

A Jewish friend once expressed to me the rising longing of both Jews and Gentiles as we strolled the streets of Jerusalem. "People," he said, "are looking for a man to come, someone who can take control." Today his statement is being echoed around the world and is fast becoming commonplace. Christian believers know the divine Messiah will come because the Book declares He will.

When He arrives, He will establish a Kingdom that will cover the earth as the waters cover the sea. The capital city from which He will reign has been destined by divine declaration to be Jerusalem. If we believe the Bible to be authoritative, this fact is indisputable. All nations will then turn their eyes toward the venerated soil and dispatch ambassadors to present their credentials in the Holy City.

THE FRIENDS OF ISRAEL GOSPEL MINISTRY

Jewish people and evangelical, Bible-believing Christians have a great deal in common. Rather than being entrenched enemies of Jewry, Bible-believing Christians are actually the best friends the Jewish people and the State of Israel have on this earth. I can say unequivocally that no group of people stands more firmly alongside Israel than do Zionist Christians. This truth is easily documented from both Jewish and Christian sources.

An Israeli historian has gone on record as saying, "Conversely, the role played by the Old Testament in Calvinism led the Puritan sects to identify themselves with the Jews of the Bible and reflected favorably on their attitudes toward contemporary Jewry."[4] These same Puritan sects later carried their views to America, where their beliefs became the foundation on which the traditional American treatment of the Jewish people was established.

The late Rabbi Meir Kahane founded the militant Jewish Defense League in 1968. Kahane was a highly controversial figure—so much so that some hailed him as a "visionary hero of the Jewish people," while others pilloried him as that "criminal racist/Kahanazi." One thing, however, is true: He could hardly be accused of being a Christian sympathizer. For many, therefore, Kahane's statement in *The Jewish Press* is intriguing:

> Israel has within the United States a weapon that itself believes in and can convince others that the United States' true interest is total and uncondi- tional backing of the Jewish State....I refer to the tens of fundamentalist and evangelical Christian Protestant sects, whose members number in the millions and whose leaders have national and international influence.... These are groups who are totally Bible oriented, who believe that the Bible is the literal word of God and to whom the literal prophecies of a return to Zion by the Jewish people and the setting up of a Jewish state are absolute preconditions for the final redemption....The Christian interest is a simple one, the bringing in of God's Kingdom on Earth, and that is clearly done by supporting not only the Jewish State unconditionally, but also opposing any retreat by Israel and urging mass Jewish emigration to the Holy land.[5]

Perhaps the most conclusive comment is found in a declaration concerning the Restoration Movement. The people involved in this movement were Christians in England who labored tenaciously for the establishment and recognition of the State of Israel.

> It should be noted that the idea of a Jewish return to Palestine had long found strong support among prominent Christians in Western Europe, particularly

in England. Eminent men and women lent themselves to what came to be known as the Restoration Movement, which favored the ingathering of Jews to their Homeland on the grounds of Christian doctrine....It is difficult to say to what extent such pro-Zionist sentiments among Christian leaders influenced the Jews, but in all likelihood they helped pave the way for British acceptance of Zionism later on.[6]

Among those identified with this group was Lord Arthur Balfour, architect of the famous Balfour Declaration. This document was the vehicle by which the British officially pledged support for the establishment of a national home for the Jewish people in Palestine. The declaration was later incorporated into the League of Nations Mandate for Palestine, July 24, 1922, and paved the way for the historic vote of the United Nations General Assembly that established the State of Israel in the ancient Jewish homeland.

Others who participated in this movement are referred to in answer to the question "What were the motives of the British Government in issuing the Balfour Declaration?"

In all likelihood the decisive factor lay in the personal and moral convictions of the British statesmen who had the Declaration adopted. Balfour saw in it an historic act of reparation to the much-wronged Jewish people, and a chance for it to develop its great gifts in its own home. Balfour was known as a man of philosophical and detached turn of mind; those close to him found his emotions deeply engaged on only one issue—Zionism. Others like Lloyd George and Smuts were steeped in the Bible, and the concept of the return of the Jews strongly appealed to their faith and sense of tradition.[7]

In 2018, 100 years after the Balfour Declaration was adopted, Israeli journalist Elliot Jager stated the following in his outstanding book *The Balfour Declaration: Sixty-Seven Words—100 Years of Conflict:*

One hundred years ago, providence placed Lionel Walter Rothschild in partnership with a small group of other men and women, including David Lloyd George, James Arthur Balfour, Chaim Weizmann, and Vera Weizmann. Together they made it possible for the Zionist enterprise to achieve its chief goal of creating a Jewish homeland in Palestine. Like all human endeavors the outcome of their efforts has been imperfect. Yet, this can in no way detract from the magnitude of their accomplishment.[8]

One more name should be mentioned in this section: Sir Edmund Allenby.

David Lloyd George (left) and Chaim Weizmann (right)

General Allenby was the British commander of the Egyptian Expeditionary Force in 1917. He was a superb general. Of much greater significance, however, is the fact that he was also a devout Christian. To General Allenby fell the task of delivering Jerusalem from the Turks. At the root of his strategy lay his reverent regard for the City of David. He refused to allow his forces to attack or fire on the Old City. Instead, he circled north in order to isolate his enemies and force them to capitulate.

Upon his approach to entering Jerusalem, Allenby dismounted and walked reverently over the streets his Lord had trod. We do well to contrast Allenby's conduct with that of the Crusaders. It provides a vivid example of the difference between true, devout Christians and people who merely profess Christianity.

All of these people—Allenby, Balfour, the Weizmanns, and multitudes of others—were not whimsical dreamers; they were visionaries. And that vision of the land grant of a legitimate Jewish homeland in Palestine was lifted directly from the pages of God's Word.

THE NEW BIRTH

I must emphasize here that evangelical Christians try to bring the saving message of Jesus Christ as Messiah-Savior to all people without distinction: Jews and Gentiles. The person of Jesus, of course, is the central issue dividing Judaism and Christianity. True believers in Christ must never bring the Good News of salvation (evangelize) to anyone with sword, stone, or dungeon but, rather, with love and a sincere desire to share the knowledge of the One who imparts light, life, and peace. After all, it is a Jew who can transform our lives through faith in Him.

I know what I'm talking about because I remember vividly what happened to me. My story mirrors that of countless others. Reared in a non-Christian environment, I led a life of ordinary activity—but something was missing. Everything changed when the gospel and my need of a personal, new birth through Jesus Christ were explained to me. A key element on my road to redemption was a sermon by Jewish-Christian evangelist Dr. Hyman Appleman. His message was simple and crystal clear. He spoke of my sinful position before a holy God, explained God's gracious provision, and told me new life was available through Christ's redeeming sacrifice on Calvary.

When I accepted the invitation to become a believer, everything changed in an instant. I had peace with God, joy that He had found me, and a never-before-known love for Jesus. The new birth was literally a life-transforming experience. Today, some seven decades later, I can thank Christ for His love worth finding, to borrow a phrase from my late friend Dr. Adrian Rogers.

I've been asked countless times over the years about my love for the Jewish people and Israel—a love totally foreign to me before I encountered Christ. My answer is simple: "I met a Jew one day who changed my life. His name is Jesus. Since I met Him, I've never been the same, and I owe Him everything."

There is a single issue dividing Judaism and Christianity: the identity of the Messiah. When we agree on that point, all will be settled.

Israeli Army first aid crew during the 1948 War of Independence.

RESTORATION

IF YOU WILL IT, IT IS NO DREAM.

THEODOR HERZL

CHAPTER FIVE

Back From the Dead

FRESH WINDS BLOWING

An Israeli immigrant stood on a small hill near his kibbutz (collective farm) home. Beside him was a friend from abroad who had come to Israel for a brief visit. Their eyes swept the barren country being developed by the kibbutzniks. "What possessed you to leave the good life in America for these rock-strewn fields?" asked the visitor.

The Israeli thought for a moment then tapped the center of his chest with a forefinger. "Something in here said, 'Go home!'"

That "something in here" is not new to the Jewish anatomy. As long as there has been an Israel, Jewry's heart roots have gripped its soil to the south of snow-capped Mount Hermon. While it is true that significant portions of the Jewish population have spent time outside the land, it is equally true that the land has never been out of the Jewish heart. Ancient exiles gave voice to the fact as they sat on the banks of the river Chebar in faraway Babylonia:

> By the rivers of Babylon, there we sat down, yea, we wept when we remembered Zion. We hung our harps upon the willows in the midst of it. For there those who carried us away captive asked of us a song, and those who plundered us requested mirth, saying "Sing us one of the songs of Zion!" How shall we sing the LORD's song in a foreign land? If I forget you, O Jerusalem, let my right hand forget its skill! If I do not remember you, let my tongue cling to the roof of my mouth—if I do not exalt Jerusalem above my chief joy (Ps. 137:1–6).

During the protracted exile of the most recent dispersion, generations would hear their Jewish fathers intone during the solemn Passover observance, "Next year in Jerusalem!"

This undying hope is memorialized today each time a Jewish person raises his or her voice to sing the Israeli national anthem:

So long as still within our breasts
The Jewish heart beats true,
So long as still towards the east
To Zion looks the Jew.
So long our hopes are not yet lost—
Two thousand years we cherished them—
To be a free nation in our land,
The land of Zion and Jerusalem.

One writer expressed it this way: "Upheld and fortified in dispersion by the Messianic vision of an ultimate return, the Jews never forgot or forsook their ties with the Homeland. This imperishable hope of redemption gave them fortitude to endure discrimination and persecution."[1]

Until the late 1800s, returning to their homeland remained nothing more than a fond hope for the majority of Jews. But then a freshening breeze began to blow. It was drifting toward the land; and with it rose a strange urgency, telling Jewish people in the Diaspora, "The time has come. Let's go home."

To Bible believers, Jewish and Gentile alike, there was never any doubt that a return to Israel was finally coming to pass. Going home was never a matter of if, only a matter of when. The weeping prophet, Jeremiah, visualized it and wrote through his tears:

"Therefore behold, the days are coming," says the Lord, "that it shall no more be said, 'The Lord lives who brought up the children of Israel from the land of Egypt,' but, 'The Lord lives who brought up the children of Israel from the land of the north and from all the lands where He had driven them.' For I will bring them back into their land which I gave to their fathers. Behold, I will send for many fishermen," says the Lord, "and they shall fish them; and afterward I will send for many hunters, and they shall hunt them from every mountain and every hill, and out of the holes of the rocks" (Jer. 16:14–16).

Of course, the fullness of the prophet's words will not be experienced until the age of the Messianic reign. However, we cannot deny that the initial sickle thrusts of the final harvest-home movement were made near the turn of the 20th century.

Theodor Herzl was among the first to interpret and assimilate the quickening breeze of the impending Jewish return. Herzl, a Jewish journalist from Vienna, had doubts about the quality of the hospitality Jewish people were receiving from the Gentile nations. His suspicions were confirmed when he witnessed the humiliation of Alfred Dreyfus in Paris in 1894. Dreyfus had chosen a career

Captain Alfred Dreyfus

in the French military and had risen to the rank of captain. He was appointed to the general staff of the French army—the only Jew to serve in this position.

However, he later was falsely accused of treason. He was tried, convicted, and sentenced to life in prison on the infamous Devil's Island in 1895. After two more trials and four years in prison, Dreyfus was exonerated of all charges. However, the anti-Semitic furor that the Dreyfus Affair generated shocked Herzl and European Jewry and convinced Herzl that the future of the Jews of Europe was extremely dark.

There is an interesting sidelight. The Scriptures declare that even the wrath of the most ungodly of men is often turned toward accomplishing God's purposes. Karl Lueger served as mayor of Vienna in the 1890s. He was openly anti-Jewish and made his views part of his political platform. His anti-Semitic oratorical outbursts enraptured Adolf Hitler when Hitler went to Vienna to study.

It was this same Karl Lueger whom Herzl thought of as he watched Alfred Dreyfus being railroaded and degraded in Paris. He concluded that if anti-Semitism could prevail in the two most enlightened cities in Europe, it could no longer be considered merely a temporary manifestation of Jew-hatred. It was deep-seated; and though it lay dormant for a while, it was sure to resurface with a vengeance.

Although Lueger willingly made his contribution to the impending Holocaust, he also unwittingly helped set the stage for the reestablishment of the State of Israel.

FIRST ZIONIST CONGRESS

It must have seemed strange to the people of Basel, Switzerland, to see Jewish people in frock coats and white ties moving through the streets to attend the opening session of the First Zionist Congress in 1897. Herzl had insisted that the delegates' attire befit that of officials of state. Most of the world did not give notice to this first assembly of Jews with a dream.

Indeed, even many Jewish people not only ignored it but outright opposed it. Some of Herzl's own friends confided that he had gone quite mad. They went so far as to counsel him to see a psychiatrist. Opposition also came from rabbinical forces in Germany, who officially advised Jewish people to shun Zionism.

However, Herzl and his like-minded contemporaries were not deterred. For Theodor Herzl, the only realistic, long-term option open to them was an autonomous state for the Jewish people. At the close of the historic gathering, he recorded in his diary his belief in the solemn significance of the First Zionist Congress: "At Basel I founded the Jewish state."[2]

Max Nordau drafted a document that explained Zionism's goals. The opening statement is a concise summary of what Zionism involves: "Zionism seeks to establish a home for the Jewish people in Palestine secured under public law."[3]

By the time the final session drew to a close, Zionists had created a political forum, an official press, and a bank. The dream nation also had an ensign. "It is with a flag that people are led to wherever one desires, even to the Promised Land."[4] The now-familiar design incorporated two blue stripes and the Star of David on a white field.

Theodor Herzl with his children in his Vienna study.

WHICH WAY HOME?

Jewish people would go home. The question was "Where would home be?" As surprising as this might seem to us today, it was a serious consideration. Early efforts to deal with the Ottoman Empire, which controlled Palestine, proved futile. The Ottoman Turks would not agree to an independent Jewish state in the area.

North America and Argentina were suggested as alternatives. The British offered African Uganda, and a special commission was dispatched to explore the proposal's feasibility. Ultimately, the Uganda scheme was rejected. Cyprus and El Arish in the Sinai Peninsula were also viewed as prospective areas for settlement.

However, none of these were to be. The Jewish people had a homeland: *Eretz Yisrael.* The land's magnetism would prove irresistible. God's divine hand had removed them from their land; and His hand would guide them back: "Then the LORD your God will bring you to the land which your fathers possessed, and you shall possess it. He will prosper you and multiply you more than your fathers" (Dt. 30:5).

THE ASCENDERS

While the official struggle for political status in Palestine continued, "practical Zionists" proceeded on the assumption that their rights to Israel were self-evident. They would win back their homeland with "another cow, another dunam [one-quarter acre of land]." These early waves of immigrants were known as *Olim* (Hebrew for "Ascenders"). They were making *Aliyah* (Hebrew for "going up") to the Holy Land.

By 1903, the close of the period that has officially been called the First Aliyah, Jewish people had purchased 90,000 acres of land in Israel, and approximately 10,000 new Jewish settlers had immigrated. The Second Aliyah (1904–1914) brought some 40,000 new immigrants. By 1914 the Jewish population in the land had reached 85,000.

The tactic was simple. Settlers would buy land wherever it became available. Financing was provided by foreign patrons—most notably Baron Edmond James de Rothschild. Settlements were established, and Jewish people began to develop the newly acquired areas.

At that point, no one seemed to care that the Jews were buying land because most of the land made available to them was considered worthless. The owners sold it to the Jewish people at exorbitant prices. They were all too happy to get rid of the wasteland and Malaria-infested swamps that they considered good for nothing—and they were making a hefty profit to boot.

The founding fathers of Tel Aviv meet in the sand dunes near the Mediterranean Sea.

But the Jews had a vision, and they were willing to work themselves to death if it meant they could be back in their own land. They slaved away draining the swamps and cultivating the dry, barren soil that one day would produce the verdant farms gracing the countryside around the Sea of Galilee. During this period, the famous kibbutz concept was implemented.

The result of their toil was a beginning. Although there had always been a Jewish presence in Palestine, generations of Jewish people had gone to their graves without realizing the hope of this new day. Others had despaired and gave up believing that returning to Israel could ever become a reality. But something was happening. Jewish people were back in the land in significant numbers. The same weighty hand of persecution that had driven them away now appeared to be driving them back.

As these immigrants went about the work of reviving the land and world Jewry observed the phenomenon with growing fascination, clouds began to gather over the planet. Two wars, global in scope, were approaching. Between them lay a time of prosperity, followed by a crushing depression that destroyed financial empires and imposed crippling poverty on the industrialized nations. These tumultuous years would see the face of Europe altered and new political forces set in motion.

Prophetically, the pace was quickening, and the people who knew what to look for biblically were carefully watching these events that seized the attention of the international community.

THE BALFOUR DECLARATION

The first long step in the establishment of modern Israel was taken when the British government officially recognized Zionist aspirations and voiced its support in the Balfour Declaration in 1917. The declaration itself was named for Arthur James Balfour, one of the initial advocates of a national Jewish home in Palestine. At the time, he served Britain as foreign secretary.

Other prominent people associated with the document were David Lloyd George, the British prime minister, and Chaim Weizmann, later to become the first president of the fledgling State of Israel.

The declaration itself amounted to a statement of sympathy with Zionist goals. Balfour communicated the text of the decision to Lord Rothschild in a letter dated November 2, 1917.

Dear Lord Rothschild,

I have much pleasure in conveying to you, on behalf of His Majesty's Government, the following declaration of sympathy with the Jewish Zionist aspirations which have been submitted to, and approved by, the Cabinet.

"His Majesty's Government view with favour the establishment in Palestine of a national home for the Jewish people, and will use their best endeavours to facilitate the achievement of this object, it being clearly understood that nothing shall be done which may prejudice the civil and religious rights of existing non-Jewish communities in Palestine, or the rights and political status enjoyed by Jews in any other country."

I should be grateful if you would bring this declaration to the knowledge of the Zionist Federation.

Yours sincerely, Arthur James Balfour

Arthur Balfour (left) and Lord Rothschild (right)

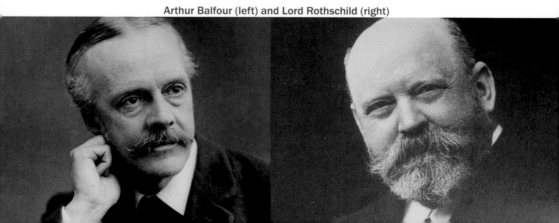

From the practical and human side, several factors motivated the British to produce the declaration. Field Marshal Jan Smuts, a member of the British war cabinet, summarized these factors in a speech he gave in London in 1919. "It would rally Jewry on a worldwide scale to the Allied cause," he said.[5] He further listed moral and religious factors as major considerations; and Balfour, of course, held biblical views on the subject.

An additional point of leverage was the personal contribution Dr. Chaim Weizmann made to the British war effort. Weizmann was a brilliant biochemist and aided materially in the development of military weapons.

Influential Arab leaders also were favorably disposed to the idea of a Jewish state at this time. King Hussein, who became king of Iraq and Transjordan, wrote,

> We saw the Jews...streaming to Palestine from Russia, Germany, Austria, Spain, America....The cause of causes could not escape those who had the gift of deeper insight; they know that the country was for its original sons, for all their differences, a sacred and beloved homeland.[6]

In January 1919, King Hussein's son Emir Faisal, chief Arab delegate to the Paris Peace Conference, and Dr. Weizmann concluded an agreement endorsing the Balfour Declaration. The Jews received pledges that a Jewish state would be recognized and accorded diplomatic relations, conditioned by French consideration of Arab interests in other territories.

As Baron Rothschild scanned the historic document, he must have been taken with a sense of standing in the full flow of onrushing history. Balfour's note was the harbinger of larger events that loomed on the horizon.

WORLD WAR I

For 400 years (1516–1917) the Ottoman Turks ruled Palestine as part of their greater kingdom. Before them, a succession of sovereigns had aspired to possess the land permanently. The Roman occupation had endured from 63 BC through AD 395. Then came the Byzantines. They supplanted the Romans and stayed until the Arabs deposed them in 636. The Arabs were set upon and put to flight by the Seljuks in 1099, only to be chased themselves by the menacing Mamelukes in 1291. The Mamelukes would fare no better than their predecessors. They fell prey to the Ottoman Turks in 1516.

Doggedly each group came, seeking to possess the land of Abraham, Isaac, and Jacob. But as certainly as they entered, they would be spewed out. While this game of imperial musical chairs was going on, the divine program for Israel was slowly unfolding. Events were taking place that would order circumstances

Allenby enters Jerusalem in 1917.

and create the opportunity for Jewish people to return home.

It was 401 years after the oppressive Ottoman reign began that Sir Edmund Allenby stood viewing the walled city of Jerusalem. His expeditionary force had successfully rolled through Beersheba, Gaza, and Jaffa. Now he was about to possess the pearl. On December 11, 1917, General Allenby, as the official emissary of the British crown, strode through the streets of the Old City of Jerusalem in a ceremonial gesture, marking the end of Ottoman rule.

THE BRITISH MANDATE

The ouster of the Turks ushered in a period that would see the foundations laid for the reestablishment of Israel. The Mandate for Palestine (July 24, 1922) called for British oversight of the area. Incorporated into the Mandate was the Balfour Declaration, recognizing the Jewish people's rights to establish a state.

The next 30 years of British rule were characterized by accelerated differences and growing tension that ultimately matured into open hostility that eventually influenced the British to withdraw in May 1948.

When the British defeated the Ottomans, they received a mandate from the League of Nations, the precursor to the United Nations, to govern Palestine and three other former Ottoman provinces. The French received a mandate to govern what is now Syria and Lebanon. The people in these lands had not governed themselves because they had been ruled as part of a greater empire. The idea of the mandate was to give administrative control to a more advanced nation until the provincial population was considered capable of taking over. The British created Iraq from the three provinces. That left Palestine, which was supposed to be granted to the Jews:

> The Principal Allied Powers have also agreed that the Mandatory should be responsible for putting into effect the declaration originally made on November 2nd, 1917, by the Government of His Britannic Majesty, and adopted by the said Powers, in favor of the establishment in Palestine of a national home for the Jewish people, it being clearly understood that nothing should be done which might prejudice the civil and religious rights of existing non-Jewish communities in Palestine, or the rights and political status enjoyed by Jews in any other country.[7]

Originally, the Mandate extended over both sides of the Jordan River and encompassed 45,560 square miles (118,000 sq. km.), an area slightly smaller than the state of Pennsylvania. But in 1922 the British divided the territory into two sections, giving 77 percent to the Arabs to create Transjordan (now

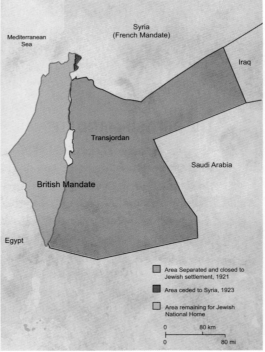

British Mandate

Mediterranean Sea

Syria (French Mandate)

Iraq

Saudi Arabia

Egypt

0   80 km
0   80 mi

1922: Separation of Transjordan

Mediterranean Sea

Syria (French Mandate)

Iraq

Transjordan

Saudi Arabia

British Mandate

Egypt

☐ Area Separated and closed to Jewish settlement, 1921

■ Area ceded to Syria, 1923

☐ Area remaining for Jewish National Home

0   80 km
0   80 mi

Jordan). That left the Jews with a mere 23 percent—10,478 square miles, of which 4,500 square miles were desert.

To exacerbate the situation, British policy on immigration fluctuated during these years. At times Jews were allowed to enter British Palestine, and at other times the British would severely restrict their immigration. They were also forbidden to purchase land. The final straw was the announcement of the White Paper of 1939. Under its provisions, only 75,000 Jews would be allowed to enter British Palestine over the next five years. Then immigration would be closed to them.

These years, however, would be the most traumatic that European Jews would face, as the Nazi Holocaust would wash over them like a tidal wave of terror. To close the doors to the very land the League of Nations and United Nations (UN) had designated for a Jewish national home when Jewish people were trying desperately to get out of Europe seemed cruel and inhumane to both Jews and compassionate Gentiles.

By now a significant segment of the decimated nation in exile was convinced of the necessity of having a place to go. The inner urge had turned into a settled conviction that could no longer be denied. The Jewish people would go home. They would have it no other way.

A NATION REBORN

The post-World War II world reeled under the impact of the disclosure of the indescribable horrors of the Holocaust. That 6 million Jewish men, women, and children could be systematically exterminated by a country that boasted intellectual and theological enlightenment cast a pall of stunned silence over a war-weary planet.

The world had become aware of the Nazi atrocities in the summer of 1943. As a result, the British and United States governments and the Jewish Haganah in British Mandatory Palestine undertook efforts to facilitate the flight of Jewish refugees. Approximately 41,000 Jews reached Palestine between 1943 and 1945.

At war's end, the British again pursued a repressive course that hindered Jewish people attempting to leave the horrors of Europe behind them. Ships carrying refugees were impounded or turned back to their points of embarkation. Many Jews were placed in internment camps and detained indefinitely. Still they persisted in trying to get back to the land. Between 1945 and 1948, 65 immigrant ships embarked for Palestine. Some were intercepted before they could deliver their human cargo. Others were purposely run aground and the passengers unceremoniously discharged.

At Ashdod in 1947, a vessel named the *Shabbetai Lozinski* ran aground. As

British officials began to converge on the scene, local residents rushed to the water's edge and quickly began to mingle with the incoming refugees. By the time the British arrived, it was impossible for them to distinguish between immigrant and resident.

One of the most climactic incidents involved the *Exodus,* a ship crammed with 4,515 Holocaust survivors. It arrived off the coast of Palestine in 1947. The British rammed the ship and boarded it. An altercation broke out between members of the crew and the boarding party, and the melee that ensued left three dead and 28 injured. All passengers were quickly transferred to three other vessels and transported back to France, from where it had set sail.

Upon their arrival, French officials found shiploads of Jews who adamantly refused to disembark. They had boarded the *Exodus* with intentions of going to Israel, and Israel it would be. The French conferred and decided not to remove them against their will. So the ships were directed to—of all places—Hamburg, Germany, where authorities were less disposed to consider the passengers' desires. These poor, displaced, powerless specimens of humanity, who had been victims of Nazi terror, were forcibly evicted from the ships and moved to two internment camps inside Germany.

The event stirred up a hornet's nest for Britain. International opinion turned against British immigration policy at the sight of pitiful Holocaust survivors being forced back into camps in Germany. From then on, the British stopped sending the immigrants back to Europe and instead interned them in detention camps on the island of Cyprus.

The Haganah ship *Exodus* with 4,515 Holocaust survivors on board in the Haifa Port

Inside Mandatory Palestine, Jewish people were mounting organized opposition to British domination. British policy now clearly favored Arab interests. Consequently, the British were caught in the jaws of both Jews and Arabs. Jewish people, desperately seeking refuge after the torment they endured in Europe, were becoming increasingly militant; and the Arabs were becoming ever more demanding.

Jewish residents settled on two firm objectives: (1) force an end to the British Mandate and (2) open the shores of the Mediterranean to Jewish refugees. Resistance organizations began to harass the British. The Haganah followed the directive of official Jewish bodies. Other groups, most notably the Lehi and Irgun, acted independently. By 1947 the sorely tried British were ready to turn the entire matter over to the United Nations.

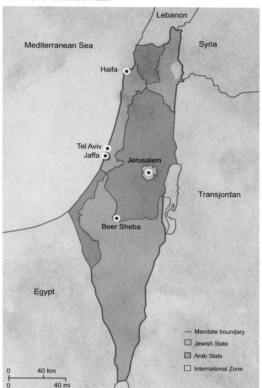

1947 UN Partition Plan

Lebanon

Mediterranean Sea

Syria

Haifa

Tel Aviv

Jaffa

Jerusalem

Transjordan

Beer Sheba

Egypt

— Mandate boundary
☐ Jewish State
☐ Arab State
☐ International Zone

0   40 km
0   40 mi

The UN commissioned representatives of 11 member-states as a UN Special Committee on Palestine. Their recommendation partitioned Palestine into independent Jewish and Arab states. In other words, now the mere 23 percent of the land that was still designated for a Jewish state was reduced even further. These two states were to share economic union, and Jerusalem was to be placed under international control.

On November 29, 1947, the delegates of the UN General Assembly gathered at Flushing Meadows, New York, to consider the committee's recommendation. The dramatic roll call recorded 33 in favor, 13 opposed, and 10 abstentions. Israel was reborn!

The response was immediate and global. Jewish people danced in the streets, wept in their synagogues, and dreamed grand dreams for the future. They joined hands, so to speak, with their brethren of long ago:

> When the Lᴏʀᴅ brought back the captivity of Zion, we were like those who dream. Then our mouth was filled with laughter, and our tongue with singing. Then they said among the nations, "The Lᴏʀᴅ has done great things for

November 1947, Jews dance in Hasenhecke, Germany, after the UN decision to establish a Jewish state in Israel

them." The LORD has done great things for us, and we are glad (Ps. 126:1–3).

Jewish people everywhere seized hold of the euphoric realization that it would be their generation that would stand on the majestic, prophetic pinnacle. It would be for them and their children to sing, "Two thousand years we cherished them—to live in freedom in the land of Zion and Jerusalem." It was no longer the stuff of dreams; it was historical fact. It was a dream come true.

WAR OF INDEPENDENCE

Dov Joseph, military governor of Jerusalem during the War of Independence, summed up his emotions during the climactic vote of the UN Security Council in November 1947: "The voting itself took only three minutes, but it seemed to stretch the length of the exile." His words could well represent the feelings of the majority of biblically oriented Jewish people the world over.

The journey had been long and arduous, but the miracle nation had now arrived at a point unparalleled in history. Israel would be a one-of-a-kind phenomenon. It would wear the crowning distinction of being the only ancient nation ever to be resurrected and restored as a national entity.

A companion miracle would be the revival of an ancient language—Hebrew. The world had never seen such a wonder. An ancient nation returns to its land, along with its language. Today, if an ancient Israelite were to stroll through Zion Square in Jerusalem, the words passing the lips of young Sabras (native-born Israelis) and elderly immigrants would quickly assure him he was home and among his own.

Unfortunately, the UN decision was just that: a decision. Israel was still a nation on paper only. The Mandate would continue in force for another six months. The Arabs rejected the Partition Plan and immediately began violent operations against the Jews. Strikes, riots, and armed attacks all followed. Though the British presence restrained the Arabs from launching all-out military assaults, the Arabs still initiated devastating, localized assaults to which the British turned a blind eye.

As a matter of fact, during the months of hasty preparation for the impending War of Independence (November 1947–May 1948), the British rigidly enforced prohibitions against the Jews importing arms. The Arabs, however, were allowed to amass as many weapons as they wanted and mobilize for the conflict to come.

As the day of the British withdrawal drew near, many people who had supported the resolution in the UN began to waver. It appeared the handwriting was on the wall. How could Israel possibly hold out against the Arabs, who were far better equipped and vastly more numerous?

On March 19, 1948, the United States withdrew its endorsement of the plan. The withdrawal was authorized by the State Department, led by then-Secretary of State General George Marshall, without the knowledge of President Harry Truman who was reportedly infuriated when he learned of it. Only weeks earlier, the president had spoken with Chaim Weizmann, assuring Weizmann of his support for an independent Jewish state. The president expressed his bitter disappointment, as reported by then-White House Counsel Clark Clifford: "The State Dept. pulled the rug from under me today....The first I know about it is what I see in the papers!...I've never felt so low in my life."

Marshall, who was committed to a delay and to placing Israel in a trusteeship under the UN, rather than supporting statehood, counseled his friend David Ben-Gurion to bide his time until a more favorable political climate developed. Perhaps the general thought arrangements could be made whereby the UN could play an active role in implementing the plan.

Ben-Gurion reflected on the general's advice:

> Here, then, was the counsel of a friend and the military appreciation of our situation by one of the world's outstanding soldiers. On the face of it, such advice could not be dismissed lightly. Yet it could not deflect us from our chosen course. For Marshall could not know what we knew—what we felt in our very bones: that this was our historic hour; if we did not live up to it,

David Ben-Gurion reading the Declaration of Independence of the State of Israel in the Tel Aviv Museum on Rothschild Boulevard.

through fear or weakness of spirit, it might be generations or even centuries before our people were given another historic opportunity—if indeed we would be alive as a national group.[8]

In fact, General Marshall, along with State Department officials who had strong pro-Arab leanings, pressed for a UN-established trusteeship over Palestine that would continue until a suitable agreement could be reached. This proposal was categorically rejected. There could be no turning back now. Israel would face whatever prospects lay in store for it.

On May 14, 1948, the National Council, which was destined to become the provisional government for the new state, adopted a Declaration of the Establishment of the Jewish State. This Declaration of Independence closed with a plea:

We appeal to the Jewish people throughout the Diaspora to rally round the Jews of Eretz Israel in the tasks of immigration and upbuilding and to stand by them in the great struggle for the realization of the age-old dream—the redemption of Israel.[9]

After the National Council signing ceremony, Ben-Gurion rose to his feet and announced, "The state of Israel has risen!"

Sir Alan Cunningham, Britain's final high commissioner of Palestine, boarded a destroyer in Haifa harbor at midnight and left the Holy Land. The next day, May 15, British forces withdrew. The British Mandate was officially over. With its demise the stage was set for the tiny Jewish nation's struggle for survival.

TRUMAN SAYS YES

Essentially, there were two schools of thought among members of the Truman administration regarding Israel's independence: One school argued that a Jewish state would constitute the first stable democracy in the Middle East. The other argued that Israel probably wouldn't survive. Discussions on this subject were often so acrimonious and heated that they permanently fractured long-standing relationships.

White House Counsel Clark Clifford, Assistant Secretary of State Richard Holbrooke, and others advocated for independence. They believed a stable Israeli democracy would benefit both the United States and the West. On the other hand, General Marshall and his anti-independence supporters focused on the Israelis' drastic numerical inferiority, expecting that the fledgling state would be quickly overwhelmed by superior Arab forces and would probably lead to Arab hostility toward the United States for backing the Jews.

Caught in the middle of the fracas was President Harry S. Truman. The final decision rested on the shoulders of the man who sat behind the Oval Office desk bearing the famous wooden sign with the inscription "The Buck Stops Here!" Clark Clifford sized up Truman, the individual who would make the decision that would alter the course of history:

From our many talks over the past year, I knew that five factors dominated Truman's thinking. From his youth, he had detested intolerance and discrimination. He had been deeply moved by the plight of the millions of homeless of World War II, and felt that alone among the homeless, the Jews had no homeland of their own to which they could return. He was, of course, horrified by the Holocaust and he denounced it vehemently, as, in the aftermath of the war, its full dimensions became clear. Also, he believed that the Balfour Declaration, issued by British Foreign Secretary Arthur Balfour in 1917, committed Great Britain and, by implication, the United States, which now shared a certain global responsibility with the British, to the creation of the Jewish state in Palestine. And finally, he was a student and believer in the Bible since his youth. From his reading of the Old Testament he felt the Jews derived a legitimate historical right to Palestine, and he sometimes cited such biblical lines as Deuteronomy 1:8: "Behold, I have given up the land before you; go in and take possession of the land which the LORD hath sworn unto your fathers, to Abraham, to Isaac, and to Jacob."[10]

Minutes after David Ben-Gurion made the declaration in Tel Aviv, the world heard from Washington: "Statement by the President. This Government has been informed that a Jewish state has been proclaimed in Palestine, and recognition has been requested by the provisional Government thereof. The United States recognizes the provisional government as the de facto authority of the new State of Israel."[11]

President Truman had said yes.

The lead up to Truman's momentous decision seems straight out of Hollywood. Jewishhistory.org tells the story in a blog titled "President Harry Truman, Friend of the Jews":

Enter one of the strange stories of history. President Truman had served as an artillery captain in World War I, and one of the members of his battalion was a Jewish man named of [sic] Eddie Jacobson. After the war, the two of them went into an unlikely partnership and opened a haberdashery store in Kansas City. The store went bankrupt after three years, but Truman and Jacobson remained loyal friends, which is unusual in itself. Partners who undergo bankruptcy don't usually enjoy each other's company afterward.

The Zionist leader Chaim Weizmann, who was by then old and half-blind, traveled to the U.S. to try and see Truman to get him to reinforce American support of the partition plan. Truman refused. The Jewish leadership put on whatever pressure it could, but to no avail. Truman would not see Weizmann.

Then the Jews sent in Eddie Jacobson. It's been written in Truman's memoirs and many, many other places. Jacobson said, "Mr. President, Harry, you've got to do me this one favor. See this tired, old man. He's come halfway across the world to see you. Just give him a few minutes of your time." And Truman reluctantly agreed.

Weizmann was a great diplomat. He told Truman, and [sic] "You have the opportunity of the ages. If you'll stay strong now, you'll go down in history for all eternity." And Truman was impressed by it, and he called Warren Austin at the UN to inform him of American policy. For added drama, when the call came, Austin was in the middle of a speech about how America was backing

Truman (left) holds the Torah scroll given to him by Weizmann (right).

out of the partition plan. But when he returned from the phone call, he said, "President Truman has instructed me that the United States supports in full the partition plan as adopted by the United Nations and will work to see it implemented." When that happened, the situation turned. The state was declared on May 15, 1948. And not two weeks later, Weizmann presented Truman with the traditional gift Jews give to heads of state: a Torah scroll. When Truman saw it, he said, "I always wanted one of those."

THE FIGHTING

Israel did not return from the dead without a struggle. It would fight battle after battle over the next 13 months. Immediately following the British withdrawal, Arab armies rolled into the country, determined to destroy it. Egyptians, Syrians, Iraqis, the Transjordanian Arab Legion, and the Liberation Army all tried to kill the little Jewish state as it was emerging from the grave.

But God had other plans. He had promised through the prophet Ezekiel that He would bring Israel's dry bones back to life: "Thus says the Lord God: 'Behold, O My people, I will open your graves and cause you to come up from your graves, and bring you into the land of Israel'" (Ezek. 37:12).

For a month war raged up and down the land. Hard-pressed Jewish forces—initially without a tank, fighter plane, or field gun—suffered heavy casualties. The Haganah fought desperately to maintain a corridor from the coast to Jerusalem. This proved to be a formidable task, which the Arabs finally succeeded in making impossible. Jerusalem was besieged.

Inside the Old City, the Jewish Quarter came under heavy assault by contingents of the Elite Arab Legion. Jewish resistance was no less than heroic. The Jews defended the area street by street and building by building. At one point, Palmach forces managed to penetrate through the Zion Gate and make contact with the Jewish defenders. They could not maintain the advantage, however, and surrendered the quarter on May 25, 1948. The Jews were expelled from their homes and places of worship, and it would be nearly 20 years before they could return.

Elsewhere, military supplies were barely trickling into the country, and the prospects of the Arabs accomplishing their purpose began to look promising. During this time the UN Security Council was calling for a ceasefire. Israel was agreeable, but the Arabs were not. Finally, they relented; and a truce was called that went into effect on June 11.

The truce expired on July 9, and fighting resumed. However, with the resumption of hostilities, the Arabs faced a drastic turn of events. During the 45-day lull, the Israelis had managed some incredible feats in securing and

War of Independence. In the photo, a patrol of the IDF's "Samson's Foxes" unit in the south.

transporting vital military supplies into the country. It was now the Arabs who were to feel the lash.

The Egyptians were first in line. On July 8, the day before the truce expired, Egyptian troops renewed attacks in the south. Their goal was to cut off the Negev. But the Israelis were prepared. Strong fortifications and mobile commandoes, dubbed "Samson's Foxes," met the attackers head-on. Within 10 days the Egyptians found their assault shattered, their casualties high, and much of their equipment in Israeli hands.

During those 10 days, Arabs were falling to the same fate in other sectors, as well. Israeli troops took Ramleh, Lydda, and Nazareth. The main body of the Liberation Army was driven back into Lebanon. In the air, Jewish bombers began making runs over Cairo and Damascus.

A new cease-fire was proposed. Now the Arabs were listening, and the Jews were the reluctant party. The new truce went into effect on July 17 in Jerusalem and the next day in the rest of the country.

Fighting would again break out in mid-October. This round saw the Israelis take Beersheba in the south and a number of villages on the Lebanese border. They secured vital roads and new supply routes. All hostilities were concluded by January 7, 1949. The War of Independence was over.

Israel was now a fact, but the price had been high: 4,000 soldiers and 2,000 civilians had lost their lives. The financial cost of $500 million seemed astronomical to the tiny nation with so few resources. But the state was intact, albeit without Old Jerusalem. Other strategic areas also remained in Arab hands. Jerusalem was designated as the capital of the nation. Headquarters were opened in the Jewish Agency. Chaim Weizmann spoke at the opening meeting of the Provisional Council of State:

> This is a great day in our lives. Let it not be regarded as undue arrogance if we say that it is also a great day in the life of the world. Tidings of encouragement and hope go forth at this hour from this house, from this Holy city, to all the persecuted and oppressed the world over who strive for liberty and equality. There is recompense for a righteous struggle. If we, the suffering and wretched people, impoverished and downtrodden, have been privileged to celebrate this occasion, there is hope for all those who aspire for justice and righteousness.[12]

THE STATE OF ISRAEL WILL BE OPEN
TO JEWISH IMMIGRATION AND THE
INGATHERING OF EXILES. IT WILL DEVOTE
ITSELF TO DEVELOPING THE LAND FOR
THE GOOD OF ALL ITS INHABITANTS.

ISRAEL'S DECLARATION OF
INDEPENDENCE, MAY 14, 1948

THE LORD YOUR GOD WILL BRING
YOU BACK FROM CAPTIVITY, AND
HAVE COMPASSION ON YOU, AND
GATHER YOU AGAIN FROM ALL THE
NATIONS WHERE THE LORD YOUR
GOD HAS SCATTERED YOU.

DEUTERONOMY 30:3

CHAPTER SIX

On Eagles' Wings

David Ben-Gurion's proclamation in 1948 brought to life God's cherished promise to return His people to the Holy Land. The news sounded throughout the nations where Jewish people awaited their summons to come home. From the far corners of the world they began the long trek back to the land. In Jewish terminology, it was the "ingathering of the exiles."

Implementing the prophetic word soon became a national obsession. In 1950 the Israeli government established the Law of the Return, granting every Jew everywhere the automatic right to become an *Oleh* (immigrant) and make his or her home in Israel. The Citizenship Law, adopted in 1952, granted all Jewish immigrants instant citizenship the moment their feet touched Israeli soil.

Like bands of Jeremiah's "fishermen" and "hunters" (Jer. 16:16), agencies moved out to ply the highways and sea lanes in quest of Jewish people to woo homeward. From May 15, 1948, through the close of 1951, 684,201 immigrants had found their way back to the land of their forefathers. At the peak of the initial wave of immigration, 1,000 people a day were streaming through the reception centers. Twenty-five thousand came from the internment camps on Cyprus where the British had held them after denying them entrance into Israel.

Hard on their heels were another 70,000 Holocaust survivors from Germany, Italy, and Austria. In the first year following independence, Jewish immigrants from 42 countries had made their way to the old-new land, as Theodor Herzl had called it. In some instances, entire communities moved. A few countries found their Jewish populations almost entirely gone. Here are a few examples:

Iraq	121,512 of 130,000 Jewish people emigrated
Bulgaria	37,000 of 45,000 emigrated
Libya	30,500 of 35,000 emigrated
Poland	103,723, two-thirds of the Jewish population, emigrated
Romania	118,940, one-third of the Jewish population, emigrated
Yemen	Almost all of Yemen's Jews emigrated.

New arrivals from Eastern Europe disembark at Haifa.

During this phenomenon, a story was being written. It was told in the faces of emaciated Jewish mothers clutching infants as they walked off ships to touch the sands of Israel's beaches. After enduring an ordeal too horrendous for words, they had survived. Even more important, the generations to follow would have a place to call home.

Not only was Israel a dream come true, it was also an indispensable necessity. Where would these people have gone had there been no Israel? Where would they go today in the event of another Holocaust?

Pogroms. Expulsions. Persecutions. Genocide. That has been the history of the Jewish people. Anti-Semitism has dogged them for thousands of years and is again reaching epidemic proportions. Where will these people go if not to a land of their own? There are more than 50 Muslim-majority nations in the world today. Why is it unreasonable for the Jewish people to have one nation of their own and to establish that nation on the land God promised to give them forever?

To argue against Israel's legitimacy is irrational. It is also symptomatic of the unrelenting anti-Semitism plaguing this planet. Anti-Semitism is growing rapidly, and it often masquerades as so-called anti-Zionism. But make no mistake: The two are one and the same. In a January 2018 opinion piece for *Newsweek* titled "Anti-Zionism Is Just Anti-Semitism by Another Name," Israeli diplomat Dani Dayan wrote the following:

> It is the increasing acceptance and elevation of anti-Zionists across the world that is cause for particular concern. Those who deny the Jewish people, and only the Jewish people, the right to live in freedom and security in their homeland are routinely paraded as the picture of progressive politics.... The inalienable right to self-determination is the one guarantee that Jews can never become victims to genocidal regimes again. Anti-Zionism is an ideology which perpetuates the political oppression of Jews, and by doing so legitimizes and encourages violence in Israel and the Diaspora.[1]

A PREVIEW OF THE FINAL INGATHERING

The prophet Isaiah peered down the long prophetic corridor and inquired, "Who are these that fly like a cloud, and like the doves to their roosts? Surely the coastlands shall wait for Me; and the ships of Tarshish will come first, to bring your sons from afar" (Isa. 60:8–9).

When the Bible gives us end-times scenarios, it occasionally treats us to tantalizing previews of ultimate fulfillment. Although Isaiah was not privy to the identities of the modern-era returnees to the land, he did hint at how they would get back—by sea and air.

Former Yemenite and Iraqi Jews illustrate magnificently what the prophet was seeing.

Some people believe the Yemenite Jews had been out of their homeland in Israel since the days of Solomon, Israel's third sovereign. No one can say why they would have left Israel for Yemen, which is located on the southern tip of the Arabian Peninsula. One tradition has King Solomon dispatching Israelites there in hopes of mining silver and gold to be used in the Temple. Another theory involves a different time sequence and has the Jewish people fleeing Jerusalem before the destruction of the Temple in AD 70.

Whatever the case may be, these Yemenite Jews, despite their long tenure in Yemen, never regarded it as a permanent home. With the coming of Israeli independence, a surge of Messianic fervor gripped the Yemenites and told them it was clearly time to return home, to a land they had never seen yet had held in their hearts throughout their long sojourn in another country.

Consequently, thousands began making their pilgrimage south toward the seaport in Aden on foot. They carried with them all of their earthly possessions, and they would never look back.

Upon learning of the mass migration, Israeli officials began negotiating with Yemen and the British authorities in Aden to facilitate an orderly exodus. An agreement was reached in May 1949, and Operation Magic Carpet began.

Israelis watched in wonder as an assortment of American and British aircraft swept into the skies and banked in graceful arcs toward the southeast. Before the operation was completed, the transports had logged some 380 flights. Their mission: to transport Yemenite Jews "on eagles' wings" (Ex. 19:4) home to Israel.

By the time the operation came to a close, some 47,000 Yemenite Jews had deplaned in Israel. No more than a few hundred remained in Yemen.

"Who are these that fly like a cloud, and like the doves to the windows?" At least 47,000 of them were Yemenite Jews!

One year later, a repeat performance took place, this time with Iraqi Jews. In March 1950, the Iraqi government announced a "Special Law Authorizing the Emigration of Jews." To qualify, the Jewish people who wanted to emigrate had to renounce their Iraqi citizenship and leave everything behind. No one was allowed to take more than $16 out of the country, and children were allowed even less.

All Jewish people over 20 years of age were eligible. Since all proceeds from land and personal property sales had to be left behind, these people became penniless refugees, leaving with the clothes on their backs and little else.

Israeli workers help Jewish Yemenites board a plane for Israel as part of Operation Magic Carpet.

This time the Jewish Agency decided on a more biblical name for the operation: Operation Ezra and Nehemiah. Over the next 18 months, Israel flew 121,512 Iraqi Jews to Cyprus, then on to Israel by sea and air, bringing them home.

"Who are these that fly like a cloud, and like the doves to their roosts?" At least 121,512 more were Iraqi Jews.

IMMIGRATION

These spectacular events emphasize the importance of immigration to the nation. Israelis view the *Olim* as the lifeblood of the state. For a time, reduced immigration was becoming a problem. Worldwide efforts were undertaken to encourage Jewish people to move to Israel.

From May 1948 through the period after the 1967 Six-Day War, there were four major waves of immigration:

May 1948 through 1951	754,800 entered the country, doubling the population
1955 through 1957	Large numbers of Jewish people from Morocco, Tunisia, Poland, and Romania became the core of new arrivals
1961 through 1964	215,056 came from Eastern Europe and North Africa
Soon after the Six-Day War (1967)	262,000 *Olim* arrived, principally from North and South America, Western Europe, and the Soviet Union.

Perhaps the most intriguing story of immigration to the old-new land involves the Ethiopian Jews. Theories of their origin are many and varied, but none proves conclusive. A prominent conjecture is linked with the storied relationship of Israel's King Solomon and the Queen of Sheba.

Though the question of how a form of Judaism was being practiced by tribal people in remote Ethiopia remains clouded in mystery, the existence of the Falash Mura (Ethiopian Jews) is undeniable. Varying from Orthodox Judaism in significant ways, major tenets of the faith remain in evidence. For example, Ethiopians practice Kashrut (Kosher laws) and ritual bathing. Furthermore, they would not eat food prepared by Gentiles. In addition, the Falash Mura exhibited their affinity, as did Jews of the Diaspora, for Israel as their Holy Land.

Therefore, when a great famine engulfed Ethiopia in the 1980s, causing thousands to seek refuge in the squalid refugee camps of South Sudan, Israel obtained the aid of U.S. Vice President George H. W. Bush and launched

Operation Sheba, airlifting 1,200 malnourished Ethiopian Jews to Israel.

In 1985 another massive airlift, Operation Moses, began. In this undertaking, approximately 8,000 Jews were flown out of Ethiopia in Israeli and American-supplied aircraft.

In 1991, the Communist Ethiopian Mengistu regime was on the verge of being overthrown. In exchange for money and a promise of asylum for regime officials, the government permitted Operation Solomon to begin. In 36 hours, Israeli Air Force C-130s and El Al passenger aircraft flew 14,325 passengers to Israel.

On May 24, 1991, a single, stripped-down Boeing 747 carried 1,122 passengers from Sudan to Israel. This world record for the number of people jammed into one aircraft was made possible largely because the malnourished refugees weighed so little. Immigration continued throughout the '90s and into the first decade of the 21st century at a rate of about 3,000 to 5,000 per year.

To spend time, as I did, at the old Diplomat Hotel outside Jerusalem, which was being used as a reception center for Ethiopians fresh off the planes, raised a bevy of questions. How could Israel, a thriving, progressive society, hope to assimilate a people confronting so many adjustments to life? Their lives in Ethiopia didn't resemble life in Israel in any way whatsoever, not to mention they didn't know the language.

The standard response to that query, if posed to an Israeli, went something like this: "Oh, give us a couple of days." Not quite a couple of days to be sure, but in record time.

With the beginning of mass immigration from Ethiopia in 1984 and the collapse of the Soviet Union in 1991, the number of immigrants increased dramatically.

More recently, the rise in radical anti-Semitism in parts of Europe, the Middle East, and the West has been motivating Jewish people to move to Israel.

France alone has seen 40,000 Jews emigrate since 2006, according to Agence France-Presse. And although that number slowed somewhat by 2017, Ukraine and Brazil saw dramatic increases in immigration to Israel. All of which portends significant growth spurts as international political volatility and anti-Semitic extremism increase.

In the years since Israel's independence, the country has experienced a fivefold population increase. Between May 1948 and May 1973, the overall population rose from 650,000 to 3,240,400. By 2017 it stood at well over 8 million, with 6.58 million being Jewish. Viewing current population trends, experts believe by 2025 Israel's population will top 10 million. It is significant to note that of the 14 million Jewish people estimated to be in the world in 2018, a full 43 percent reside in Israel, according to Israel's Central Bureau of Statistics.

All immigrants are required learn Hebrew. They can do so rather quickly by attending an *ulpan*—a special school that teaches an intensive, six-month course in the language.

In the early days, *Olim* were housed in comparatively primitive quarters—many even lived in tents. Today they are taken immediately to new homes or absorption centers.

These periodic bursts of mass immigration do pose some formidable problems when it comes to cultural integration. Bridging this cultural gap is a major thrust of the Ministry of Immigration and Absorption. The scope of this problem may be seen by comparing the extreme differences in cultural backgrounds of Jewish people from Muslim countries, such as North Africa and Asia, and those coming from America and Europe. Vast differences exist socially, politically, and technologically. Fully assimilating immigrants into Israeli life is one of the greatest domestic challenges Israel faces.

But Israel is tackling it with the same skill and determination it tackles everything, and thousands upon thousands of *Olim* are now fully integrated. They have become full-fledged Israelis, and many have given birth to children who are Sabras.

THE LAND

If you go to Israel today, you'll see a breathtakingly beautiful land bursting with vitality. Not so in the 19th and early 20th centuries. Travelers to what then was either Turkish or British Palestine were struck by the barrenness of the land. Most people saw little to be desired there apart from the historical attachment to religious holy places. It was a desolate area that caused visitors to pose a question that Moses had anticipated 3,000 years earlier:

> The foreigner who comes from a far land, would say, when they see the plagues of that land...and...it is not sown, nor does it bear, nor does any grass grow there..."Why has the Lord done so to this land?" (Dt. 29:22–24).

The American writer Mark Twain declared,

> It is a hopeless, dreary, heartbroken land....Over it broods the spell of a curse that has withered its fields and fettered its energies...desolate and unlovely... where thousands of men once listened to the Saviour's voice and ate the miraculous bread , sleep in the hush of a solitude that is inhabited only by birds of prey and skulking foxes....Palestine is no longer of the workaday world. It is sacred to poetry and tradition—it is dreamland.[2]

The barren land outside Kibbutz Beeri with the first furrows ploughed across in preparation of reclamation.

We can understand why people made such statements. For centuries, calculated destruction had afflicted the Holy Land. A succession of armies had warmed themselves by fires built from Israel's woodlands. The hills were so badly denuded they could offer no fuel to imperial encampments. The animals of wandering Bedouins foraged among the same hills for what sparse greenery remained. Attempts at agricultural pursuits were a thing of the past. As foreigners raised their questions about the underlying causes of this condition, a wasted land awaited the return of its native sons.

Mark Twain and his fellow travelers would most certainly have furrowed their skeptical brows at the prophet Isaiah's confident prediction:

> The wilderness and the wasteland shall be glad for them, and the desert shall rejoice and blossom as the rose; it shall blossom abundantly and rejoice, even with joy and singing. The glory of Lebanon shall be given to it, the excellence of Carmel and Sharon. They shall see the glory of the LORD the excellency of our God (Isa. 35:1–2).

Isaiah's words primarily apply to the glory of the coming Millennial Age. However, we must also be aware of our privilege at being allowed a preview of coming events. If the transformation that has taken place in Israel is merely the bud, what must the full flower of fulfillment hold in store? It will be glorious indeed.

It is doubtful that any other nation in history has taken such long steps in so short a time. If Mark Twain and his traveling companions could see Israel today, they would be hard-pressed to believe they were in the same land. The Malaria-infested swamps and arid deserts have given way to lush farms brimming with fruits and vegetables.

Northern valleys are carpeted with greenery. Hillsides abound with maturing forests. Jerusalem pine, tamarisk, eucalyptus, and acacia now thrust their branches skyward on hills the length of the country. To the south, desert lands stand deep in ripening grain. The Jordan Valley yields abundant harvests of succulent produce. Dates, bananas, avocados, and mangoes hang in abundance from trees along the coastal plain. The coastal areas and hill country are dotted by emerald citrus groves.

Tobacco, cotton, sugar beets, groundnuts, and vegetables of all varieties spring from the soil, while hothouses grow millions of blooms for export and domestic use. Roses, gladioli, tulips, and chrysanthemums are familiar names among floral producers.

From Dan to Beersheba, from the Jordan to the sea, the land has taken on a new look.

Before statehood, the Jewish people had reclaimed 11,120 acres. Between 1948 and 1971, the total escalated to 119,293 acres in the hill country and Negev. Another 110,456 acres were claimed by draining swamplands.

Much of the recovered area is watered by irrigation. Water sources are almost exclusively the Jordan River and Sea of Galilee. Maintaining an adequate water supply has been a constant source of vexation for Israeli agricultural planners. While the northern region benefits from sufficient rainfall, the near-desert areas to the south are not so fortunate. Rain there is a scarce commodity. To distribute available water, Israel developed a national plan for irrigation that used 90 percent of accessible water to irrigate more than 453,700 acres of land.

To accomplish this feat, a prodigious project called The National Water Carrier was developed. This carrier provides a central artery through which water is pumped from the Sea of Galilee and then transported by canal and tunnel, pulled mainly by gravitational force, all the way down to waiting fields in the Negev.

Providing water for irrigation is a priority for Israeli technologists and scientists. The most promising solution rests with the development of satisfactory methods of desalinating vast quantities of sea water. Other advances include Israel's ingenious drip-irrigation system now in use the world over, which distributes miserly but precise amounts of water to sustain growth and produce abundant crops.

In the early days, kibbutzim (plural of kibbutz, collective farms) dotted the face of the land. Nearly 500 new villages and settlements were established between 1948 and 1972. At first, they were primarily agricultural settlements, but many soon adopted industrial facilities. Westerners are somewhat familiar with the kibbutz, where property is owned by the commune. Less familiar, but much more popular, is the *moshav*. Under this arrangement, each family owns and manages its own farm. The cooperative principle is retained, with produce being sold and equipment purchased through a central cooperative agency. By 1986 there were 448 *moshavim* (plural of *moshav*) employing about 157,000 people.

Israel now produces enough fruit, vegetables, poultry, eggs, milk, and dairy products to meet all national demands and supply foodstuffs for export, as well. A variety of grains must still be imported in significant quantities; but even in this area, Israelis satisfy approximately half of the national demand.

INDUSTRY

Industrial growth has kept pace with other segments of national development. The textile industry supplies an abundance of industrial exports. High among the heavy hitters in the Israeli economy is the diamond industry. For years Israel vied with Belgium for the distinction of being the diamond center of the world. Other industries the government encourages and assists are furs, clothing, leather

Members of Kibbutz Urim working in a potato field.

goods, agricultural implements, machinery, die casting, and medical equipment.

Between 1950 and 1972, industrial production in Israel increased by an average of 10 percent a year. Industrial exports grew at an average rate of 20 percent per year during the same period. Today Israel's global dominance in the high-tech industry has vaulted the country from its early days' dependence on Jaffa orange sales to recognition as a "Silicon Valley" player on the world stage.

Israeli versatility in advancing industry was featured in an article touting Israel's "top 45 greatest inventions of all time" on the website israel21c.org, which wrote, "One of Israel's sources of pride is the enormous number of inventions and innovations that have taken root on its soil...despite challenges of geography, size and diplomacy. The ever-churning Israeli mind has brought us drip irrigation, the cherry tomato, the electric car grid, the Disk-on-Key, and much more."

Yes, much, much more. For example, if you need an endoscopy, you can swallow Medtronics' PillCam that takes hundreds of pictures as it travels through your gastrointestinal tract. The facial-recognition technology used in Apple's iPhone X was developed in Israel. In fact, American investor Warren Buffett thinks so highly of Israeli technology that he has invested billions of dollars in Israel. "Israel is the best place to invest," he said, "because of its people. There is no other place with such high quality people, with the motivation and abilities [that Israelis have]."[3]

It is a miracle that a nation born of extreme adversity in 1948 is today a world-class wonder, touching almost every one of us in multiple ways. Surely, God's hand is at work in our midst.

MINERALS

Israelis have often lamented their lack of large quantities of oil. Although the country produces some oil, the amounts are extremely meager when compared with some of Israel's Middle Eastern neighbors. However, when it comes to minerals, Israel is no pauper.

Deuteronomy 8:9 calls Israel "a land whose stones are iron and out of whose hills you can dig copper." The Timna copper deposits seem to have borne out the accuracy of the Mosaic statement. Archaeological discoveries have dated the mines to the 10th century BC—the time when King David and then his son Solomon reigned in Israel. University of Tel Aviv archaeologist Erez Ben-Yosef was quoted in *National Geographic* as saying, "Until recently we had almost nothing from this period in this area. But now we not only know that this was a source of copper, but also that it's from the days of King David and his son Solomon."[4]

Geological surveys have revealed that much of the nation's mineral wealth rests beneath the sands of the Negev. Large deposits of phosphates have been discovered there—chemicals important to the production of fertilizers. Construction products are produced from an enormous stone supply suitable for quarrying and crushing. Limestone is used for commercial marble and building. Cement is another essential product available in abundance. Gypsum is quarried and shipped in from an area near the Gulf of Suez.

The greatest concentration of Israel's mineral wealth is found in the Dead Sea—the lowest exposed place on Earth—an incredible 1,300 feet below sea level. The Dead Sea is some 34 miles long and 1,400 feet deep.

It is unique in that it has an inlet but no provision for egress. For thousands of years the Jordan River has emptied its flow into the Dead Sea. High year-round temperatures cause the deposit of huge quantities of concentrated minerals that amounts to a vast, natural mining system. Over the centuries, the Dead Sea has stored enticing reserves against the day when Jacob's heirs would return to recover them.

In total area, the Dead Sea covers some 393 square miles. The average salt concentration hovers around 34 percent, which makes it one of the saltiest bodies of water on earth—more than nine times saltier than the ocean, which is why tourists delight in floating in it without effort. It contains billions of tons of magnesium chloride, common salt, potassium chloride, magnesium bromide, and calcium chloride.

Theodor Herzl was fully aware of the Dead Sea's strategic value and wrote of its importance in 1902. He specifically mentioned potassium, bromide, and

An evaporation pool at the Sdom potash factory in the Dead Sea.

magnesium and saw great promise for the future extraction of these minerals.

Another interesting aspect of Herzl's vision was not only his fascination with the value of the mineral deposits but, as he wrote in his 1902 book, *The Old-New Land* (*Altneuland*), the canals contributing hydroelectric energy to meet the needs of the future Jewish state.

Herzl's canal imperative implies that access to water was vital to develop the parched lands that lay within his view. There is a desperate need to replenish the Dead Sea, which over the years has been threatened by evaporation and water extractions from the Jordan to nourish agriculture and quench the thirst of rapidly growing communities.

WHEN HISTORY MIMICS SCRIPTURE

On December 9, 2013, in Washington, DC, Israeli, Jordanian, and Palestinian Authority officials signed a historic memorandum of understanding committing to an $800 million program to bring to fruition the long-delayed and much-debated Mediterranean-Dead Sea Project (Med-Dead).

Med-Dead is designed to bring hydroelectric power, fresh water in abundance, and massive desalination facilities to these areas. Through a series of tunnels, the Med-Dead would also deliver a flow of water terminating in the Dead Sea, thus raising the water to sustainable levels in the region.

Long before the Med-Dead Project was a gleam in the eyes of such notables as Herzl or 21st-century Middle East officials, God had something to say through the prophet Isaiah:

> Behold, I will do a new thing, now it shall spring forth; shall you not know it? I will even make a road in the wilderness and rivers in the desert. The beast of the field will honor Me, the jackals and the ostriches, because I give waters in the wilderness and rivers in the desert, to give drink to My people, My chosen (Isa. 43:19–20).

And here are the near euphoric predictions of planners of the Med/Dead project:

> The Dead Sea will be restored to its historic 1960's shoreline level that is approximately 90 feet above the current watermark (filled to -400 elevation). Along the new shoreline, vibrant water projects, marinas, resorts and new cities can be developed. The Dead Sea region's economic development will dramatically increase and enhance the value of this otherwise uninhabited 50+ kilometers of shoreline.

Entirely new industries will emerge as the Dead Sea becomes alive with a seawater ecology, aquaculture and fisheries industry. Resort boating, sailing and more will emerge as the area matures and grows. Dead Sea shorelines will also be developed to create a prosperous inland-sea tourism destination.[5]

Intriguingly, the prophet Ezekiel looked down the corridors of time to the coming Millennial Kingdom and saw in full reality what planners dream of in this age:

Then he said to me: "This water flows toward the eastern region, goes down into the valley, and enters the sea. When it reaches the sea, its waters are healed. And it shall be that every living thing that moves, wherever the rivers go, will live. There will be a very great multitude of fish, because these waters go there; for they will be healed, and everything will live wherever the river goes. It shall be that fishermen will stand by it from En Gedi to En Eglaim; they will be places for spreading their nets. Their fish will be of the same kinds as the fish of the Great Sea, exceedingly many" (Ezek. 47:8–10).

FEARS OF FAMINE

The prophetic Scriptures foretell, and history confirms, that a shortage of two overwhelming necessities, food and water, will grip humanity in the last days. Australian science writer Julian Cribb, author of the book *The Coming Famine,* has stated, "The central issue in the human destiny in the coming half century is not climate change or the global financial crisis. It is whether humanity can achieve and sustain such an enormous harvest."[6]

The harvest reference is based on the estimate that 5 billion more people will enter the food chain over the next half-century. Another source adds, "The UK Ministry of Defence...America's CIA, the US Center for Strategic and International Studies and the Oslo Peace Research Institute all identify famine as a potential trigger for conflicts and possibly even for nuclear wars."

Such warnings of eventual global famine are being sounded with increasing frequency these days. The question is "How long can our speck of Earth continue to supply food for an exploding population?" At some point, fertilizer will become a strategic commodity. Therefore, adequate and readily available supplies will be increasingly important to the great powers.

This gloomy forecast makes Israel, with its billions of tons of chemical assets, a prime target for the great powers seeking relief for their people. Israel's vast reserves of mineral resources may prove to be a prime inducement for end-times intrusions into the Middle East, as foretold by the Jewish prophets.

With this in mind, these statements are attention-getters:

"Israel is one of the few countries in the world possessing deposits of the principle raw materials—phosphates and potash—for the three main types of fertilizers in common use."[7] The fact that Israel produces both potash and phosphate gives the country an advantage among the world's fertilizer producers.[8]

NATURAL GAS

Possibly even more significant than minerals is Israel's enormous natural gas find some 84 miles west of Haifa, in the Mediterranean Sea. *The Wall Street Journal* has called it "the [international] game changer." Israel discovered the gas in 2009 and 2010 in what Israelis have named the Tamar and Leviathan gas fields. They named the Leviathan field after the biblical sea monster because the field is so huge. In fact, it prompted foreignpolicy.com to called Israel "the land of gas and honey."

Three Israeli energy companies, in cooperation with Noble Energy in Houston, Texas, believe the Leviathan field contains 16 trillion cubic feet of natural gas—making it the world's biggest deep-water gas find in a decade, discrediting even more the "peak oil" theories that the planet is about to see dramatic and permanent shortages of oil, gas, and coal. To put the number in perspective, some say the Leviathan field alone would hold enough reserves to supply Israel's gas needs for 100 years.

The Leviathan field is estimated to be nearly twice the size of the nearby Tamar field, which was the largest gas field discovered anywhere in the world in 2009.

In 2018, in a deal Israeli Prime Minister Benjamin Netanyahu called "historic," the partners in Israel's Tamar and Leviathan fields signed two accords with Egypt's Dolphinius Holdings Ltd. for $7.5 billion each for the sale of natural gas over 10 years. The partners include Delek Drilling LP and a unit of Noble Energy Inc., *The Times of Israel* reported in February 2018.

"The deals with Egypt are the first for the fields, and come on the heels of two other accords the partners signed with neighboring countries: Natural gas from Tamar has been exported since the start of 2017 to a Jordanian chemicals manufacturing plant on the Dead Sea, while the Leviathan partners have also signed a deal for the sale of gas to the Jordanian electric company NEPCO," the *Times* said.

Netanyahu said the landmark deal will provide Israel with billions of dollars for health, education, and welfare.

Israel's super-giant natural gas fields may indeed become a game changer because for years, Russia has been the world's second largest producer of natural gas and has exported it to Europe. For energy-hungry Israelis, who have had to import fuel from other countries, including Russia, the tables are turning.

All of these factors may entice Russia and other nations to sweep down on Israel as predators, looking for spoil and prey.

A graphic description of one of these end-times invasions is found in the book of Ezekiel, where the prophet described events that will take place in "the latter years." The revelation clearly identifies the motivation for the incursions into the land of milk and honey. In one instance, invaders come "to take plunder and to take booty" (38:12).

As humanity careens toward the closing phases of the end-times, we are privileged to witness the events God is orchestrating in preparation for the final drama in His prophetic Word. That such a tiny nation as Israel could be the central focus of such a large slice of attention defies explanation. However, it also provokes the question "How and why has this come about?" For the answer, we must go beyond human analytical prowess.

It has been said that little Israel is truly a miracle nation. Located at the center of the earth, "in the midst of the nations and the countries all around her" (5:5), Israel has survived all threats, extermination plots, and unrelenting hate campaigns. The Jewish people even have survived the multitude of satanic attempts to wipe them off the earth by people determined to achieve a "final solution to the Jewish problem."

Looking at Israel's history from a purely secular point of view, it is impossible to explain the continued existence of this miniscule nation. With all the Jewish people have endured, how is it even possible that they are here today? Quite simply, because God loves them and has promised to preserve them. He told them through the prophet Jeremiah, "I have loved you with an everlasting love" (Jer. 31:3), and "'I am with you,' says the LORD 'to save you; though I make a full end of all nations where I have scattered you, yet I will not make a complete end of you. But I will correct you in justice, and will not let you go altogether unpunished'" (30:11).

God also has a warning for Israel's enemies, with an affirmation of affection for the Jewish people, when He describes Israel as "the apple of His eye" (Zech. 2:8).

JERUSALEM

We cannot conclude comments on the Jewish people's return to their homeland without mentioning Jerusalem. It is the spiritual, intellectual, and emotional hub of world Jewry. No people in history have universally yearned to possess a city as the Jewish people have longed for Jerusalem.

To the nations of the world, Jerusalem is a place to conquer. The ancient warriors sacked or embellished it for the glory of their empires or their sovereigns. The Crusaders saw it as representative of their quixotic quest to expel the infidels and establish a Christian kingdom, complete with moated replicas of medieval European fortresses. To Muslims, Jerusalem ranks third religiously, behind Mecca and Medina.

But to the Jewish people, Jerusalem has always been number one—their holiest city on Earth. The world over, Jews pray facing Jerusalem.

Over the long centuries of its history, Jerusalem has been exploited, taxed, mutilated, and subjugated. Now the Jewish people are returning from the Diaspora and strolling the streets of the city that had awaited their coming for what seemed like an eternity. That sacred place, Jerusalem, the eternal capital of Israel.

JERUSALEM WILL BE TRAMPLED BY
GENTILES UNTIL THE TIMES OF THE
GENTILES ARE FULFILLED (LK. 21:24).

JESUS CHRIST, AD 30

WE HAVE RETURNED TO JERUSALEM
NEVER TO PART FROM HER AGAIN.

MOSHE DAYAN, JUNE 7, 1967

CHAPTER SEVEN

We Are at the Wall

On a sultry night in mid-July 1948, David Shaltiel gazed through the darkness at the stately ramparts of the Old City of Jerusalem. The commanding general of Israel's Haganah forces in the city was a bitterly disappointed, frustrated man. He had made promises to his troops and the Jewish people that would not be kept. Youthful officers had listened intently to his words with eyes fixed on the Israeli flag he held before them.

"Tomorrow morning, this flag of Zion will fly from the Tower of David," he said. Some of these same soldiers later heard him rehearse a speech in which he would announce the liberation of all of Jerusalem and its official return to Jacob's sons and daughters.

But it was a speech prepared before its time. The Arabs would brutally repel the assaults his determined forces would make on the Old City. Shaltiel was finally forced to acknowledge that the last opportunity to reach his highest objective had slipped away. The garland he passionately desired for himself and his young, battle-weary soldiers would be reserved for other brows.

MIXED EMOTIONS

Following the 1948 War of Independence, Jewish people were ecstatic over the establishment of the State of Israel. Yet, despite all of their amazing accomplishments, they could never be completely satisfied as long as their beloved city was in the hands of the Jordanians. Israel's heart was being held by another—a condition that would endure for 20 more years.

It is impossible to accurately describe the profound love the Jewish people have for Jerusalem. The Western World has nothing with which to compare it. Suffice it to say Jerusalem is as much a part of Jewry as blood, bone, and sinew are part of the human anatomy. The psalmist said it for all Jewish generations:

Walk about Zion, and go all around her. Count her towers; mark well her bulwarks; consider her palaces; that you may tell it to the generation following (Ps. 48:12–13).

> If I forget you, O Jerusalem, let my right hand forget its skill! If I do not remember you, let my tongue cling to the roof of my mouth—if I do not exalt Jerusalem above my chief joy (137:5–6).

The Jewish yearning for Jerusalem is a phenomenon without historical parallel: The Jews of the far-flung Diaspora never forgot the Holy City.

The years following 1948 proved a trial for Jerusalemites and world Jewry. When the Arab Legion slammed the door of the Old City in the faces of David Shaltiel's soldiers, it remained sealed for two long decades. Jordan held the Old City by force in direct defiance of the United Nations' Partition Plan. Jews were expelled from their homes and denied access to their synagogues.

Most traumatic of all, Jordan (a Muslim country) refused to give the Jewish people access to the Western Wall, their most hallowed spot on Earth apart from the Temple Mount itself. Jordan denied the Jews the right to worship at this most sacred site. To add insult to injury, the Muslims systematically destroyed the synagogues in the Jewish Quarter, many of which had stood for centuries. They defiled and vandalized the Jewish cemeteries, looted Jewish homes, and generally desecrated the entire Jewish section.

The sacred Temple Mount, where Judaism's first Temple had stood for approximately 475 years and where the second had stood for approximately 585 years, was possessed by interlopers. It was here, to the crest of revered Mount Moriah, that Abraham had brought Isaac on a sacrificial pilgrimage long ago. Here David had stood before the avenging angel and stayed a ravaging plague. Later, King David purchased this summit from Araunah the Jebusite as a site for Israel's national house of worship. His son Solomon directed construction of the initial structure that would forever sanctify the Temple Mount as ground most holy.

Solomon's Temple experienced the malicious destruction of the invading Babylonians before being rebuilt on the same foundation by the exiles who returned from captivity in Babylon. Later Herod the Great greatly enhanced the structure, making it so magnificent it beckoned pilgrims from the far reaches of the Roman Empire. Its destruction in AD 70 produced a national state of mourning that endures to this day. No Jewish Temple has stood on the Temple Mount since then.

Without the Old City, the Jewish people became firmly entrenched in what came to be known as the New City of Jerusalem. Israelis built it into a bustling center of official and commercial activity. Yet there was a sense in which they still stood, flag in hand, forlornly viewing the walls and awaiting the opportunity to raise their ensign over the City of David.

THE COMING TEMPLE

Among the great prophetic trumpet sounds of the Old Testament is the announcement of the building of a new Temple in the future. This Temple, Scripture says, will be constructed for the triumphant Messiah during the coming Millennial Age. It will stand as a center of memorial worship of the Messiah's finished work. This house of worship is described at length in Ezekiel 40—44. To this Temple the full manifestation of Jehovah's glory, which had departed before the Babylonian invasion, will return. Ezekiel described the event:

> Afterward he brought me to the gate, the gate that faces toward the east. And behold, the glory of the God of Israel came from the way of the east. His voice was like the sound of many waters; and the earth shone with His glory (43:1–2).

As fervently as some Jewish people desire to rebuild their Temple on Mount Moriah, there are no current plans to do so. The only proper place on which a Temple can be constructed is occupied by the Muslim Dome of the Rock. To be sure, some have sought to assist the prophetic program by attempting to destroy the Dome. There was one reported plot in which members of the Irgun, a contingent of the assault force that attacked the Old City in 1948, had planned to proceed immediately to the Temple Mount and destroy the mosque in order to prepare for the construction of a new Temple. I interviewed many Israeli officials who disputed this story, which was reported as factual in a major publication.[1] Though stories of stones for a new Temple being secretly cut and stored in hidden caves may fascinate many people, they have no basis in fact.

There also has been some confusion about the Great Synagogue adjacent to the Rabbinical Center in the New City. While it was under construction, some conjectured that it might serve as the place for a new Temple; but there was never any intention for this synagogue to serve in such a capacity. Officials explained emphatically that it is a central synagogue and nothing more. There is only one suitable location for a legitimate Jewish Temple, and that is on hallowed Mount Moriah.

THE SIX-DAY WAR

Twenty years after the War of Independence, Arab leaders led by Egyptian President Gamal Abdel Nasser promised to reverse their 1948 losses by annihilating the Jewish state. By May 1967, Nasser had declared that the Arabs were ready to go to war. In the north, his Syrian allies were harassing Jewish kibbutzim by shelling Israeli workers in the fields and planting mines during the night to maim and kill Jewish farmers.

Matters came to a head when the Egyptians ordered UN peacekeepers out of the Sinai and began to amass troops and military equipment across the Suez Canal. By June 4, 1967, Iraq had joined Egypt, Jordan, and Syria in the hope of "rectifying" the error of Israel's existence. Mobilized Arab forces approximated 250,000 troops. They had more than 2,000 tanks and 700 aircraft ready to attack.

As the crisis loomed larger with every passing day, Israel was forced to make a decision. Chief of the General Staff Yitzhak Rabin and Defense Minister Moshe Dayan advised Prime Minister Levi Eshkol that the only advantage the outnumbered and outgunned Israel Defense Forces (IDF) had was the element of surprise. That meant striking first, before their enemies could launch their massive offensive.

On Monday morning, June 5, Israel struck. And in six audacious days the tiny Jewish state changed the map of the Middle East. In their book, *The Six Day War*, Randolph S. and Winston S. Churchill described Israel's preemptive attack in colorful terms: "Israel, like a cowboy in the old Wild West, did not wait for her enemy to draw—she had seen the glint in Nasser's eye."

VOICES IN THE NIGHT

It was nearly midnight when two men stood looking at the night-shrouded parapets of Jerusalem's city wall. They were reviewing what had occurred in the past 48 hours—events that, when fully disclosed to the outside world, would stun everyone. We would have to return to the days of Joshua to find a time that even remotely approached what took place during the Six-Day War. Joshua's famous engagement at Jericho, with its tumbling walls, seemed almost routine by comparison. An observer summarized the final outcome in 1967:

> By a feat of arms unparalleled in modern times, the Israelis, surrounded by enemies superior in quantity and quality of equipment and overwhelmingly superior in numbers, had fought a war on three fronts and not only survived but had won a resounding victory.[2]

After a few minutes discussing their night view of the Old City, Chief Army Chaplain Schlomo Goren looked at Major General Uzi Narkiss, central commander of the Israeli force, and said, "Uzi, you are doing great things now. What is going on in the Sinai and on the Golan Heights is nothing compared to what you are doing here in Jerusalem. I want you to remember this. When you go to the Wall, I want to be with you."

Narkiss told me he replied, "Okay rabbi. Go look for a ram's horn [shofar]!"

Left to right: Moshe Dayan, Uzi Narkiss, Mordechai (Motta) Gur

The next morning the general received one of those elusive second chances so many dream of but so few get. He was to direct the attack that would deliver Jerusalem back to its rightful heirs.

It was difficult for the general to grasp the fact that this was really happening. He found it hard to hide his initial disappointment at orders he received at the outset of the Six-Day War. He was to maintain a purely defensive posture. The Israeli high command's great concern was for the security of the Jewish enclave on Mount Scopus. More particularly, it feared that a determined Arab assault might cut the country in half and divide the Jewish forces. Narkiss' orders were clear: Refrain from all offensive action. Defense was the overriding objective.

No one really expected King Hussein of Jordan to mount an attack along the Jerusalem perimeter. General Narkiss would later comment that perhaps the greatest miracle of the Six-Day War was not the Jewish success in winning the Old City but, rather, the fact that King Hussein attacked Jerusalem. Through the UN, Hussein had received a message from Israel's Prime Minister Levi Eshkol stating that, if Jordan did not attack Israel, Israel would not attack Jordan.

Of course, Narkiss did not know at the time that Jordan's assault would change the nature of his orders from strictly defensive to offensive. Hussein was not expected to attack, but he yielded under two points of pressure:

First, Nasser tricked Hussein into believing the Arab armies were achieving great success and that Hussein would be well advised to enter the fray and share the spoils when victory was complete.

Second, Hussein's military commanders were itching to get into the fight.

Hussein's imprudent decision gave the young Jewish paratroopers an opportunity they had been praying for—and one Uzi Narkiss had fervently hoped for since the War of Independence.

For the general, the chance to succeed in this momentous objective would expunge a frustration that had haunted him for two decades. During the 1948 war, he had been among the assault forces that fought valiantly but futilely to win the Old City. Narkiss was then a 23-year-old leader of Palmach forces in Jerusalem. It was his group that had taken Mount Zion and successfully broken into the Old City through the Zion Gate. Ever so briefly, a corridor was opened to the Jews besieged and starving inside the Jewish Quarter.

In response to his call to David Shaltiel for support troops, Narkiss had received an assortment of bakers, shopkeepers, and townspeople who were the best Shaltiel could provide at the time. The young Palmachnik was faced with an agonizing decision: keep his exhausted troops in the city and risk losing everything or withdraw to defend Mount Zion and maintain a strategic advantage. He decided to withdraw, a decision that zealot critics would later denounce. Now, within hours, their caustic denunciations would be obliterated from Israeli memory; and Uzi Narkiss would step into a very select circle of Jewish luminaries.

The official order to take the Old City was issued at 6 a.m. on Wednesday, June 7, 1967. The deputy chief of staff, Major General Haim Ben Lev, phoned Narkiss with the order. Narkiss, in turn, called a brigade commander, Colonel

Israeli paratroopers gaze at the Western Wall for the first time after Israelis take the Old City in June 1967

Mordechai "Motta" Gur, and charged him with the historic responsibility of taking Jerusalem.

One of those strange quirks of war had brought Gur and his brigade of reservists to Jerusalem. On Monday, these paratroopers had been assembled at an airfield ready to board aircraft for a drop in the Sinai. Instead, they were ordered to Jerusalem and their appointment with destiny.

Gur's work in the morning involved two objectives: secure the Mount of Olives and take the Old City. With their backs exposed to Arab rifles positioned on the city walls, the paratroopers rushed headlong up the side of the Mount of Olives. The sheer boldness of their assault sent the Jordanian defenders reeling. Shortly after 8:30 in the morning, the brigade commander stood before the InterContinental Hotel on the summit. Before him, shimmering in the brilliant rays of the morning sun, lay the City of David. The domes of al-Aqsa and the Mosque of Omar dominated the view against the white esplanade of the Temple Mount.

To the right and beyond stretched the ancient quarters: Christian, Jewish, Muslim, and Armenian. Farther still, nearer the horizon, Gur's comrades could see the familiar skyline of the New City. The Old City's ageless walls, so solidly constructed by the stonemasons of Suleiman the Magnificent, framed Old Jerusalem with a grandeur that moved the young soldiers to a depth of feeling none could fully communicate. Their hearts quickened as they grasped the fact that today, the two Jerusalems would become one.

It was to be a rare day in history, a day for making historic statements. Gur called for his wireless transmitter and summoned the attention of all battalion commanders. Tension rose in his voice as he spoke: "The Temple Mount, the Western Wall, the Old City. For two thousand years our people have prayed for this moment. Let us move forward—to victory."[3]

The race was on. Jewish battalions converged on the city with a collective obsession—to be the first inside and the first to reach the holy places to which they had been denied access for 20 years. It was a scene reminiscent of King David's mighty men storming the walls of the old Jebusite stronghold long ago.

Colonel Gur joined the chase. Leaping into his command half-track, he excitedly flung an order at his hefty, bearded driver, Ben Tsur. He ordered Tsur to get to the ancient city walls as quickly as possible. No soldier in history has responded to a command with more daring abandon than did Gur's driver.

Impervious to danger, Tsur sped down the Mount of Olives and pushed the accelerator to the floor as they began the ascent to the walls. As they careened around lumbering tanks and past hurrying infantry, the commander shouted, waved encouragement, and urged his men onward. When the half-track reached St. Stephen's (the Lions') Gate, Tsur pushed the vehicle unceremoniously through the doors and into the narrow street. A dazed Arab sat beside the road, stunned by the sight. Before them stood another gate in front of which a motorcycle sat squarely in the center of the road. Scorning the possibility of it being boo-by-trapped, they ran right over it and through the gate. Mordechai Gur and Ben Tsur had reached the Temple Mount. It was 9:50 a.m., Wednesday, June 7, 1967.

Soon the commander was surrounded by his victorious soldiers. Again he opened his transmitter. "The Temple Mount is ours. Repeat: The Temple Mount is ours."

Other hard-running paratroopers had eyes for another objective—the Western Wall. As they surged through the approaches to the area, they were met by Arab legionnaires with upraised hands. The Israelis ignored the would-be prisoners as a cry went up from the lead soldier, "The Western Wall! I can see the Wall!" Soon the official word came affirming what Jewish people the world over had long waited to hear: "We are at the Wall."

Once again Jews were assured of lifting their voices before the ancient stones beside which they had prayed for centuries.

At 10:15 a.m., General Narkiss came through the Lions' Gate in his Jeep. On the way in, he came upon Rabbi Goren, who was walking along the side of the road. In the crook of one arm the rabbi held a large Torah scroll. In his other hand he firmly gripped the shofar (ram's horn) the general had suggested he secure the night before.

I spent much time with Uzi Narkiss on one of my many trips to Israel. He told me he halted the Jeep that day and called, "Rabbi! Come, get into the Jeep and ride with me."

"No," replied Rabbi Goren. "Two thousand years we have waited. Now I am not going to the Wall in a Jeep. I'll walk."

When the commander reached the scene, he experienced strange reactions. He recalled, "It was as though I was in another world—in a cloud of happiness....I felt a part of the whole Jewish people who, for 2,000 years, had longed for this. It was an emotion far bigger than myself, bigger than the whole generation."

For 2,000 years non-Jews had controlled the holiest sites in Judaism. No longer. Now, by God's grace, they would be controlled for the most part by the sovereign State of Israel.

Along with his overwhelming emotions, General Narkiss awakened to the realization that he was not prepared in any way for the occasion. "I stood there before the Wall and I didn't know what to do," he told me. "There I was, but what should I do? Memories of [British General Edmund] Allenby's entry into Jerusalem [in 1917] passed through my mind. I remembered how he had waited for several days until he received instructions from his superiors. Then the entire day was given to ceremonies surrounding his entry into the city. But

Left to right: Narkiss, Dayan, and Chief of Staff Yitzhak Rabin enter the Old City through the Lions' Gate.

me, I did not know what to do. When the rabbi arrived, he knew what to do. He prayed and blew the shofar. I then seized myself and led in the singing of the national anthem, and that was all."

It was all for only a fleeting moment. A floodgate had been opened, and the very soul of Jewish joy was gushing forth. Later that day General Dayan came to the Wall, flanked by Yitzhak Rabin and Uzi Narkiss. Dayan's words upon his arrival are momentous: "We have returned to our holiest of holy places, never to be parted from it again." He later enlarged on this statement somewhat by saying, "We earnestly stretch our hands to our Arab brethren in peace, but we have returned to Jerusalem never to part from her again."

David Ben-Gurion, Israel's first prime minister and architect of the modern state, visited the site. As he stood before the giant blocks of the Western Wall, he declared, "This is the greatest day of my life."

So indelible was the imprint of these hours on the minds of Jewish people throughout Israel and the world that intervening years have not dimmed the thoughts and emotions of that special day. An Orthodox Israeli's memories are typical: "I was in my tank, on the way from Jenin to the Jordan," he said. "We had paused to rest and drink some water when someone switched on the wireless. The announcer was reading from the Psalms. 'Our feet shall stand within thy

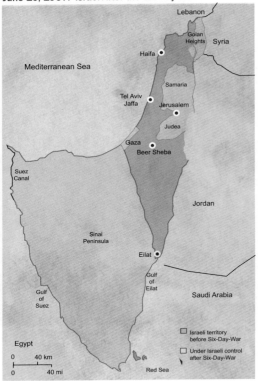

June 10, 1967: Israel After the Six-Day-War

Lebanon

Golan Heights Syria

Haifa

Mediterranean Sea

Samaria

Tel Aviv
Jaffa Jerusalem

Judea

Gaza
Beer Sheba

Suez
Canal

Jordan

Sinai
Peninsula

Eilat

Gulf
of
Eilat

Gulf
of
Suez

Saudi Arabia

☐ Israeli territory
  before Six-Day-War

Egypt

☐ Under Israeli control
  after Six-Day-War

0   40 km

0   40 mi

Red Sea

gates, O Jerusalem' [Ps. 122:2, KJV]. He went on to say our soldiers had taken the Old City and had reached the Wailing [Western] Wall. We had known that our troops were in the city, but to hear it this way brought such a flood of joy I cannot describe. I remember looking at my commanding officer, who was a nonreligious Jew, and the tears were flowing from his eyes and down his face."

On June 27, the Knesset passed bills annexing the Old City. It was now official: Jerusalem was reunified under Israeli control. The flag of Zion would fly over the Tower of David at last. On June 14, a mere 13 days earlier, a quarter of a million Jews from all parts of the country had joined a mass pilgrimage, entering the Old City through the Dung Gate, then on to the Western Wall. It was the largest Jewish gathering there in 2,000 years and was a singular testimonial to the far-reaching implications of the events of the era.

Israel's friends, who literally sat on the edge of their seats in hushed, collective anxiety, breathed a sigh of relief and leaned back to survey the full scope of the incredible accomplishments of those dramatic days. Once again, as David had stood before Goliath, sling in hand, the young nation had faced the colossus and, with precise aim and audacious courage, sent the aggressors crashing down in defeat.

By anyone's standards, this was an astounding accomplishment—almost inexplicable. By and large, the feelings of those touched by this historical lightning shaft is expressed in a simple statement: "God was with us." Perhaps victorious people usually feel this way. Winners instinctively believe God is on their side even though that is not often the case. In this instance, however, there is just cause to ponder the statement.

The prophetic declarations regarding Israel's return to the land in the last days truly reveal living reality. However, there is another fascinating prophecy that bears examining. It was made by Jesus Christ when He spoke of Jerusalem.

Jesus had startled His followers by telling them the splendor of Herodian Jerusalem would soon disappear. The Temple, He said, would be leveled to the ground and the Jewish people sold and driven from the land into the midst of the Gentile nations. Then He added, "Jerusalem will be trampled by Gentiles until the times of the Gentiles are fulfilled" (Lk. 21:24).

Jesus was emphasizing the literal and historical aspects of Jerusalem's deliverance from Gentile domination at His Second Advent. Reunification of the city in 1967 illustrates the historic momentum now moving us toward that great day.

Jesus also made remarkable statements about events that will dominate Jerusalem's future history. These and related circumstances will mark the beginning of the end of Gentile world-supremacy:

◆ Jerusalem will remain under Gentile control for an undetermined time.

◆ Gentile dominance will continue until the closing phase of history as we know it is ushered in.

◆ The Jewish people will become a dominant factor in end-times Jerusalem.

Add four more components to the picture:

1. Christ's prediction of the fall of Jerusalem was fulfilled literally.

2. Christ's declaration concerning the Temple's destruction was fulfilled literally.

3. Christ's prophecy concerning the dispersion of Jewry was fulfilled literally.

4. Christ's references to Israel's return to its land are being fulfilled literally.

COMPUTING THE SUM

It hardly seems logical or possible that, were Christ an imposter and pretender, Jehovah would dignify His prophetic pronouncements with such meticulously precise historical fulfillment. As a matter of fact, one of the ultimate tests of the credentials of someone who claims to be a prophet of God is the accuracy of his long-range predictions. Even the most cunning religious charlatans and well-meaning but deluded "messiahs" have universally failed at this point. God causes it to be so and clarifies this fact through Scripture:

> You may say in your heart, "How will we know the word which the LORD has not spoken?" When a prophet speaks in the name of the LORD, if the thing does not come about or come true, that is the thing which the LORD has not spoken. The prophet has spoken it presumptuously; you shall not be afraid of him (Dt. 18:21–22, NASB).

As touches Jesus Christ, we must remember He claimed that He was the fulfillment of all the Old Testament's Messianic prophecies. There is no mistaking His declarations. He deliberately presented Himself as being one with the Father and being the long-promised Son and Messiah. From that point, He moved on to predict prophetic events that would not take place for centuries.

God did not prevent these prophecies from coming to pass. One by one, they have been fulfilled in every detail. Jesus passed the prophet's test. And He did so beyond question. When we examine these points objectively, we can easily understand why vast multitudes of Jews and Gentiles across the centuries have accepted His Messianic claims.

BUT GENTILES STILL DOMINATE

Yes, Gentiles still dominate the world. The final and full realization of Christ's words are clearly associated with the Messiah's future advent. He came once, and He is coming again. However, what we need to grasp now is the fact that everywhere in Scripture, the Jewish people are in control of Jerusalem during the period called "the last days."

This fact establishes the necessity of the events that have been taking place. We might say that the reunification of Jerusalem was the curtain raiser in preparation of new historical disclosures that will soon come.

We must always be extremely careful not to become so dogmatic in interpreting events that we usurp divine prerogatives. No one knows what tides may yet roll over Jerusalem and the land. Today, as I work on this book in the summer of 2018, Israel is not open to negotiations concerning control of the city. In fact, the United States moved its embassy to Jerusalem in May 2018 and proclaimed to the world that Jerusalem belongs to Israel. But in the realm of politics, things can change in an instant.

If Jewish resolve is any true indicator, it would appear Israelis are ready to die before they would relinquish control of their beloved city. Whether they will be pressured to acquiesce to temporary internationalization of the Old

City remains to be seen. It would seem, however, that the current alignment of nations; the strategic importance of the Middle East, with its vast oil reserves and mineral deposits; and the relative mood trends of the Western nations and imperialistic Russia all point to the fact that we could be witnessing the heralding of the beginning of the end. It is now evident that since June 7, 1967, several important elements have become intensely identifiable, as we'll soon see.

THE YEARS BETWEEN

The years between June 1967 and October 1973 generated a type of national ecstasy in Israel. An aura of invincibility blanketed the land. A Jewish air force sergeant voiced this feeling in 1971. In response to a question about a possible Arab military intrusion, he thrust out a determined chin and declared, "Let them come. We can beat them all!"

Such was the mood of the times. Israelis developed a tendency to see themselves, militarily, as slightly more than human; and much of the world agreed. The Arabs sullenly licked their wounds and faced the disquieting belief that the Israelis had discovered some mystic, super whammy, which they applied whenever Ishmael's descendants mustered up the courage to violate Israel's borders.

All of this would take a sudden turn on a religious fast day late in 1973.

Kibbutz field next to the Gaza Strip

ON ROSH HASHANAH IT IS INSCRIBED
AND ON THE FAST DAY OF ATONEMENT
IT IS SEALED AND DETERMINED HOW
MANY SHALL PASS AWAY AND HOW MANY
BE BORN; WHO SHALL LIVE, AND WHO
SHALL DIE; WHOSE APPOINTED TIME
IS FINISHED, AND WHOSE IS NOT.

CHAIM HERZOG

CHAPTER EIGHT

A Quiet Day in October

If the Six-Day War can be regarded as a modern parallel to the Israelites' victory at Jericho, the Yom Kippur War can be viewed as Israel's modern Ai. Bible readers are well-acquainted with the swift turn of events that befell the Israelites following their resounding victory at Jericho. Because of their success, their enemies trembled in fear before Joshua and his men: "His fame spread throughout all the country" (Josh. 6:27).

Ai, an insignificant-appearing village, was the next obstacle confronting Israel. Joshua sent men to reconnoiter and bring him an evaluation of the enemy's capability to wage war. Their report exuded optimism:

> So the men went up and spied out Ai. And they returned to Joshua and said to him, "Do not let all the people go up, but let about two or three thousand men go up and attack Ai. Do not weary all the people there, for the people of Ai are few" (7:2–3).

In view of the spectacular victory at Jericho, the scouting report given to the commanding general of the Israelite army seemed sound. However, forces were afoot that neither Joshua nor his scouts were aware of, and things did not turn out as they had expected:

> So about three thousand men went up there from the people, but they fled before the men of Ai. And the men of Ai struck down about thirty-six men, for they chased them from before the gate as far as Shebarim, and struck them down on the descent; therefore the hearts of the people melted and became like water. Then Joshua tore his clothes, and fell to the earth on his face before the ark of the LORD until evening, he and the elders of Israel; and they put dust on their heads (vv. 4–6).

Unbeknown to Joshua, the cause of Israel's defeat already lay buried beneath the sands of the Israelite camp. Someone had taken spoil that God had forbidden (vv. 9–21). Consequently, the Israelites had marched confidently toward a rude awakening.

They had been overconfident and ill-prepared and woefully underestimated the enemy. Before the day was over, Israel's vaunted war machine experienced retreat, death, and humiliation. The Israelites fell under a pall of confusion and depression, and the entire affair resulted in a sweeping inquiry designed to ferret out the man who had brought sin into the camp.

Israel at Ai provides a fascinating preview of the Jewish experience during the Yom Kippur War in October 1973. As was true with their ancient forefathers, the Israelis found themselves deluded by overconfidence, unprepared for the conflict, and quite unaware of the enemy's determination. In the war's aftermath, sweeping inquiries were conducted to ascertain who to blame. Sainted Israelis like then Prime Minister Golda Meir and famed General Moshe Dayan became mortals again. The amount of Jewish blood spilled on the Golan Heights and in the Sinai troubled the nation's conscience for years to come. Morale was so badly shaken that it was difficult to view the final outcome as a victory, even though Israel won the war. As Israel assessed the damage, a sense of foreboding replaced the aura of invincibility.

THE DAY OF ATONEMENT

Yom Kippur (Day of Atonement) is the solemnest holy day on the Jewish calendar. It is a day set aside each year as a time of national fasting and repentance. The Jewish New Year (Rosh Hashanah) and the Day of Atonement are separated by 10 days, during which Jewish people are to show deep contrition before God.

The Western Wall in Jerusalem

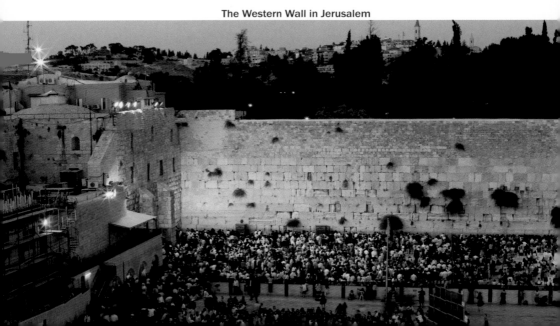

Hence these days are called The Days of Awe or The Ten Days of Repentance. On Yom Kippur people are to give themselves to self-examination and reconciliation with God and their neighbors. The hours of holy observance are marked by complete fasting. Everyone 13 years old and older is expected to observe this solemn fast.

Yom Kippur is the one time when life in Israel nearly comes to a complete standstill. The religiously observant pass the day in the synagogue, wrapped in prayer shawls and imploring Jehovah for forgiveness. The nonreligious stay at home out of respect for the commemoration. No shops or businesses are open. Travel is forbidden. Highways are devoid of both pedestrian and vehicular traffic. Medical doctors and military personnel are the only exceptions to the stricture against travel. Radio and television do not operate on Yom Kippur. It is the one day of the year the media fall silent.

The Day of Atonement is devoted to God. For a few brief hours, Israel stands silent before Jehovah. The very atmosphere seems to be charged with a sense of peace and tranquility. In 1973, however, the day for prayer and fasting became a day for fighting and dying.

IT CAN'T BE WAR

By noon on October 6, it was apparent to worshipers something was amiss. First, they became aware of the whine of jet engines as an increasing number of aircraft passed overhead. This was unusual on Yom Kippur.

Next, eyes were diverted from prayer books as cars were seen moving through the streets. The automobiles, some of which were stoned by religious zealots, were driven by those responsible for alerting military mobilization teams. Buses came later to pick up reservists from their homes for the trip to the Suez front or the Golan region.

Still, Israelis did not believe this could be war. Perhaps it was merely another irritating alert that too frequently called Jews from their civilian pursuits. But a full-scale war? It couldn't be.

Yet it was. Israel had been caught by surprise. Prime Minister Golda Meir, the high command, and the officers manning the garrisons of the Bar-Lev Line (the first line of warning and defense along the Suez Canal) were all stunned when the Arab onslaught began. Many Israelis would die without even grasping the scope of the encounter. Israel was again fighting for its existence.

In the Six-Day War, Israel took the Arabs by surprise and won an overwhelming victory. Now, inexplicably, the Arabs had surprised Israel. Syria and Egypt had launched attacks from the north and south respectively. Contributing to the new offensive against Israel were nine countries that included four non-Arab

Middle Eastern states. Although Israeli intelligence had reported rumblings of an enemy offensive, Golda Meir and Israel's leaders were not willing to prepare a first-strike strategy like the one that had brought them such success in 1967. They believed there would be another war in the future, but they did not believe it was imminent.

For their part, the Arabs had covered their movements as routine military training maneuvers, while in fact 110,000 Arab troops were poised to stream into the Promised Land from the north and south. An armada of tanks and hundreds of aircraft were set to challenge Israeli armor and air strength. The massive assault was launched simultaneously on the Golan Heights and along the Suez Canal. At precisely 2 p.m. on Saturday, October 6, the giant military pincers began to squeeze Israel in yet another attempt to impale the Jewish state.

When the Israelis realized they were involved in a major struggle, they angrily asked their leaders, "How could it happen to us? How could Israel, with perhaps the most astute intelligence-gathering operatives in the world, be caught by surprise? How could preparations for such a ponderous venture be accomplished without activating red warning lights in Israel?" A number of explanations have been advanced.

GOLDA'S CHOICE

Golda Meir and the political leadership were fully aware the Arabs were gearing up for an attack at some date in the future. They were faced with whether and when to employ a first-strike offensive of the type unleashed in the Six-Day War. Israel's preemptive strike in 1967 had been responsible for the astounding military success in that brief but decisive struggle.

However, with the first strike came the adverse flood of world opinion, accusing Israel of being a land-grabbing warmonger. In 1967 Israel decided it had to strike first because it had almost no other options available. Its major population centers had been threatened with almost immediate attack by adversaries in the Gaza Strip, Syrians perched on the Golan Heights, and enemies positioned within minutes of the country's heartland.

The Six-Day War had altered this precarious situation. Now Egyptian cities would be threatened first in the event of new military outbursts. The entire Sinai lay open as a base of defensive maneuver between Israel and Egypt. To the north, the Syrians could be engaged farther away from the Israeli settlements in the Valley of Jezreel. Electronic warning time for the Egyptian Air Force's impending attacks had been stretched from four minutes prior to the Six-Day War to 16 minutes. These considerations weighed heavily on Israel's attitude toward its ability to react when the Arabs decided to take up the fight again.

Golda Meir speaks with the new Chief of Staff David Elazar at Beit Hanassi in Jerusalem.

Consequently, the government decided to let the enemy deliver the first blow. Israel would rely on its counterattack capability to deal with the situation. Thus the world would see clearly who was attacking whom. Even when it became clear that war was brewing, Israel resisted the temptation to launch a preemptive strike. Chief of Staff General David Elazar urged Mrs. Meir, Moshe Dayan, and the War Cabinet to authorize a deterrent strike during the morning of October 6. His request was resolutely denied. Later that morning Prime Minister Meir met with Ambassador Kenneth Keating of the United States. She relayed her intelligence information, which indicated an attack was inevitable, then added, "That is our decision. Israel will not open fire. Moreover, Israel is not mobilizing fully, to prevent such an act being interpreted as provocation."[1] The decision would prove a costly one.

OVERCONFIDENCE

The stunning victories of the Six-Day War became like a tranquilizing opiate to Israel. When I asked a high-ranking Israeli military official what lessons the country learned from the Six-Day War, he replied, "We learned nothing from our victory. The Arabs learned a great deal from their defeat."

While Israeli military commanders felt confident their tanks and planes could handle any future enemy intrusion, their enemies were developing deterrents to both of those weapons, under Russia's tutelage. A carefully constructed umbrella of surface-to-air missiles defused the Israeli Air Force in the opening phases of the war. The Egyptians staged their first assault under the protection of their missile canopy. The success of this strategy was born out by the fact that the Air Force played a minimal role in the war until after the missiles were dealt with. So devastating were the Russian-made projectiles that *Aviation Week*'s December 1973 issue reported that of 114 Israeli aircraft destroyed during the war, only four were lost to aerial combat. All the rest fell to missiles and antiaircraft.[2]

The Sagger antitank missiles, carried by infantry in boxes like suitcases, were brought into the tank battles by both Egyptian and Syrian forces. These weapons had an effective range of one mile. They were steered to the target by trailing wires, which allowed the infantrymen to guide them directly into the targeted tank. These fearful devices, coupled with tidal assaults by tanks, produced enormous problems for Israel's armored units. According to one report, every Israeli tank on the Syrian front was hit at one time or another.

The Bar-Lev Line was another example of Israel's misplaced confidence. The line was composed of a series of fortifications strung along 110 miles of the Suez Canal. These installations were located seven to eight miles apart, with observation posts placed at strategic points between. Tank-firing ramps were constructed along the line from which armored vehicles could concentrate fire on the approaches to the canal.

At the time of the Egyptian attack, 436 Israeli soldiers manned 16 of the 33 strongholds along the line—the rest were empty. General Haim Bar-Lev's creation proved of little effect as Egyptians charged through the undefended openings, bypassing the fortifications. Some Jews have cynically described this defense system as "Israel's Maginot Line."

Another factor that reveals Israel's unrealistic appraisal of the situation was its persistent failure to act decisively on the intelligence information that had projected ominous Arab intentions. An obvious illustration of this point is seen in a report that stated at no time before the beginning of the war "did any element link the Syrian build-up in the north...with the unusual Egyptian activity and concentrations in the south. It was as if the assumption that the Arab armies could not or would not go to war caused a complete black-out."[3]

MISINFORMATION MANEUVERS

In an interview after the war, Egyptian Chief of Staff Saad a-Din Shazli remarked, "I never believed that the enemy could be led astray."[4] Neither could the rest of the world. Nevertheless, prior to the Yom Kippur War, the Egyptians had successfully laid the same trap for Israel that the Israelis had sprung on them in the June war of 1967.

For years the Egyptians had labored to lull the Israelis into a state that would allow them to set the stage for a surprise attack. Apparently taking a cue from the Russians, they launched a program of misinformation. They leaked press reports that told of their own military forces' ineptitude and unpreparedness. "Expert sources" would report low morale, waste, corruption, and contention. Such reports, disclosed over an extended time, slowly sedated the enemy. A prime example of this ploy appeared in a December 1972 release by United Press International in Brussels.

> Only 40% of Egyptian weapons and 60% of aircraft are in good working order—according to a secret Egyptian Air Force document in Cairo. Diplomatic sources in Brussels noted, as the main factors, poor maintenance and lack of spare parts from the Soviet Union. According to the report, Egypt has lost 50 Soviet-made fighter planes in training since the end of the War of Attrition. Since reputable sources report Egypt as having 523 aircraft before the War of Attrition, it follows that she now has between 400 and 500, of which only 300 are fit for combat.[5]

Such reports were filtered through press sources around the world. No doubt many of them were factual. However, the disciplined and determined offensive waged in the early stages of the war belie their general accuracy.

In preparing for the resumption of hostilities early on, Egypt's President Anwar Sadat settled on a program of frequent, large-scale military exercises designed not only to train his own troops, but also to lure Israel into a state of complacency. For three years the Egyptians drilled soldiers in canal-crossing procedures. When they finally crossed the canal on the opening day of the war, they did it in precisely the same way Israeli observers had seen it practiced many times before.

In the spring (April–May) and again in September 1973, the Egyptians held large-scale maneuvers to which Israel was forced to respond by placing armed forces on alert. When the attacks never materialized, the Israelis became weary of mobilizing their troops unnecessarily every time the Arabs conducted training exercises.

Israel's adversaries rightly concluded that the Israelis would be reluctant to call up their soldiers immediately prior to political elections because they would want to promote a sense of security. Furthermore, in October Israel would be observing its high holy days. So officials would hesitate to disrupt the observance without certain cause to do so.

As the fateful hour of the invasion approached, the Arabs watched and waited as Israel swallowed the bait.

In the final analysis, no one can truly explain why Israel was surprised. It does seem there was an inexplicable, partial blindness on the part of the country's leadership—a blindness that, when lifted after Israel's final recovery and subsequent victory—would give way to a vision with solemn dimensions.

DEATH AT THE WATERLINE

The fury of war pounced suddenly on Israel from both the Syrian and Egyptian fronts. Along the Suez Canal, 2,000 Arab guns spewed 3,000 tons of devastation on Israeli fortifications in the first 53 minutes of battle. It is estimated that in the first 60 seconds of the bombardment, 10,500 shells pounded Jewish positions.

At the same time, 70,000 men prepared to storm the Sinai while thousands of tanks were warming their engines. In preparation for the assault, giant Egyptian water cannons systematically carved gaps in the 130-foot ramparts the Egyptians had constructed to hide their preparations from prying Israeli eyes. Within minutes, pontoon bridges and assault boats were in the water; and soon Egyptian infantry and armor were pouring across the canal Moshe Dayan had once called the best antitank ditch in the world.

Eight thousand infantrymen made up the first wave of invaders, while a mere 436 Israelis occupied positions on the Bar-Lev Line. The Israelis were outnumbered 18.5 to 1. Within 24 hours, five Egyptian infantry and armor divisions would be in position three miles east of the canal. In the air, 240 Egyptian planes flew over the bridgehead to rake Israel's airfields and missile installations in the Sinai.

The young Israelis manning the fortifications on the line fought with the tenacity and raw courage that has so distinguished the soldiers of modern Israel. It was soon apparent, however, that their situation was militarily hopeless. Herculean efforts were made to rescue those who were besieged in the fortifications. But Israel's Phantom and Mirage jets systematically fell to the enemy's missiles. Tanks and half-tracks attempting to reach the Israeli soldiers were set ablaze by the surface-to-surface missiles. Some of the men finally managed to escape to the safety of Israeli lines; others died defending their positions. Those who remained faced the uncertainties of captivity. Only one of the Bar-Lev strongholds managed to survive the assaults.

For what seemed an interminable 48 hours, the Israelis fought a frantic holding action while they awaited the arrival of mobilized reserves. Problems arose in moving troops and armor to the front. The massive Egyptian invasion did not allow for much preparation or organization. Israeli units were thrown into the fight as soon as they arrived on the scene. The intensity of those early hours of the struggle caused an Israeli officer, Colonel Amnon, to exclaim, "The whole of Sinai was on fire."[6]

The Egyptian army that crossed the bridges into the Sinai was a new model. It was tenacious, disciplined, and well led. It fought courageously in the face of determined Israeli opposition. Wave after wave of infantry and tanks swept into the teeth of Israeli weaponry. Even after their attack faltered, the Egyptians mounted five to six new attacks daily in an attempt to dislodge the Jewish forces.

When the first day's casualty figures were tabulated, the Israelis began to understand the gravity of their situation. Five hundred of its sons were dead and 1,000 more were wounded. Scores of others were taken prisoner. In the Six-Day War, 850 fell during the entire struggle on all fronts. It was soon apparent that Israel was facing its severest test in 25 years of independence. A writer graphically summed up the situation:

> In less than 24 hours, Israel was transformed from a military power, even in global concepts; from a state with an army the fame of which had become a model to the world; from a country which—six short years ago—had won the most brilliant victory in the history of modern warfare; from a state with, according to her leaders' declarations, "an army that has never been in a better state"—to a country fighting with clenched teeth for its very existence. A country living under the shadow of extermination.[7]

Israeli soldiers pray in Sinai during the Yom Kippur War.

By October 9, Egyptian forces had reached the high-water mark of their drive into Sinai. By then Israel was fully deployed and prepared. The armies faced each other along a front that had been established some five to seven miles from the Suez Canal. On October 10, it was decided that Israeli forces should cross the canal. It would be the most effective way to upset Egypt's strategy and allow Israel's tank force to employ its famous flair for speed and maneuverability. Preparations began for the crossing into Egypt.

On Sunday morning, October 14, the Egyptians launched an attack that set in motion one of the largest tank battles in the history of warfare. Approximately 2,000 tanks would be engaged along the length of the front. The Egyptians struck in orderly fashion, which allowed the Israelis, with their superior-range weapons, to wreak havoc on them. The first Egyptian tank brigade was destroyed, costing Egypt 93 tanks. In this incredible battle, not one Israeli tank was lost to Egyptian fire. The Twenty-First Egyptian Division saw 110 tanks destroyed. Major portions of Egypt's Third and Fourth Divisions met as grim a fate. By day's end, 264 Egyptian tanks lay smoldering in the desert. Only six Israeli tanks were knocked out. The tide had turned.

In the late hours of October 16, Jewish paratroopers stood in the moonlight looking down on the waters of the Suez Canal. Ten days after Egypt had started the war, Israel was ready to launch an invasion of its own. Israel's crossing into

Former Chief of Staff Haim Bar-Lev (center left) consults with Maj. Gen. Ariel Sharon (with bandage) during the Yom Kippur War.

Egypt would alter the entire situation and trap Egypt's Third Army.

The Israelis destroyed missile installations along the canal, which gave the Israeli Air Force mastery of the skies over Sinai. These triumphs would prove to be Israel's chief bargaining weapon after the ceasefire. By October 29, Jewish troops were threatening to enter Cairo, sealing off the dejected Third Army and holding 16,000 square kilometers (6,177.6 square miles) of Egyptian territory. It was now clearly time for the Russians and United Nations to save Egypt once more.

IN THE VALE OF TEARS

Hundreds of disquietingly eerie "cats'-eyes" danced through the moonlight falling on the Golan Plateau. The "cats'-eyes" were infrared lights attached to the sides of the Syrian tanks that rumbled in orderly procession toward the Israeli positions on the Golan Heights. It was now apparent that the Syrians, who had launched their attack earlier in the day, had no intention of allowing hard-pressed Jewish troops any respite during the night. The situation facing the IDF's Northern Command was perilous.

Hours before, a UN observer positioned on a road between the territories held by Israel and Syria had witnessed a startling sight. It appeared to him as though a veritable sea of Russian-made, Syrian-manned tanks was approaching his outpost. As the tanks neared the observation position, they veered away north and south. One segment moved toward Kuneitra, roughly in the center of the Israeli defense line. The other column sped to the south in the direction of the village of El Al in the southern sector of the defense line. What the astonished UN observer was actually seeing was but two segments of the three-pronged Syrian offensive. The prearranged destinations of these armored vehicles were the bridges across the Jordan in the fertile Hula Valley. Syria's plan was to dissect the Israeli defenders, slash the region into three isolated segments, and then hammer each segment into submission.

The Golan Heights lie immediately south of Mount Hermon and northeast of the Sea of Galilee, extending to the Yarmuk Valley in the south and to the Ruqqad Stream in the east. The Golan Plateau is a volcanic elevation rising from 600 feet in the southern extremity to 4,000 feet in the north. The land area of the Golan Heights totals some 480 square miles.

These heights rise sharply from the valley floor adjacent to the Sea of Galilee. The incline is so abrupt that only a few roads permit access to the upper elevation. Israel considers it imperative that it possess the area overlooking the Galilee in order to protect the Israeli villages below. Prior to 1967, it was from these heights that the Syrians shelled Israeli farmers in the fields.

Of the main approaches from the heights, one runs through El Al. The other, a more historic route from northern Galilee to Damascus, crosses the Jordan River at the Benot Yacov Bridge (Bridge of the Daughters of Jacob). This road runs through Kuneitra on the main route to Damascus.

Militarily, the problems of defending the Golan Heights differed drastically from the problems the forces in the Sinai faced. From the Suez Canal to Israel's population centers lay 125 miles of desert, which allowed for defensive retreats while waiting for reservists to mobilize and deploy. However, only 17 miles of virtually unbroken plain, with no naturally defensible barriers, stood between the Syrians and the steep cliffs descending from the heights. Israeli and Syrian troops were separated by a no-man's-land approximately one half to one mile wide running the length of the Purple Line, which marked the ceasefire line established following the 1967 war. UN observers occupied posts along the main routes between the opposing forces.

Israel had established 17 fortifications, each manned by 15 troops, along the Purple Line. These fortifications ran from Mount Hermon to the Yarmuk River. The installations were well entrenched, protected by mines and wire obstacles. Behind these a detachment of tanks was stationed. The system was designed to block a Syrian advance until reserves could be mobilized. The Israelis assumed that intelligence information would give them adequate time to prepare and mobilize. This would not be the case. They also assumed massive air support would be available to bolster the holding action during the initial phases of hostilities.

The Jewish outpost on Mount Herman was a key factor in defending the Golan Heights because it was an electronic observation station that stood at 6,600 feet on the side of the mountain. From it, Israelis commanded a view of the entire battle area. Losing this position and its sophisticated equipment in the early stages of the fighting dealt a major blow to the Israeli effort.

When the fighting began, matters were further complicated by the presence of civilians who lived in 15 settlements on the plateau. Eleven were within a few miles of the ceasefire line. At some point, women and children were evacuated. However, the men had remained and were there when the attack came. Evacuating them impaired the combat units' effectiveness during the early hours of the war.

The 300 Syrian tanks that had startled the UN observer moved ponderously about their appointed tasks. As the column divided and swung toward their respective targets, another 400 tanks moved up from the south along the road to Raphid. Israel's 176 tanks braced to meet the armada's onslaught. The massive Syrian force caused one Israeli to exclaim, "I never knew there were so many tanks in the whole world."[8]

Syria's plan called for a 55-minute artillery barrage, followed by an armored assault. The Syrians calculated that their sheer weight of numbers would

Prime Minister Golda Meir and Defense Minister Moshe Dayan (seated next to her) speak to troops on the Golan Heights during the Yom Kippur War.

overwhelm the Jewish defenders as the attackers moved toward the bridges on the Jordan.

Of the bridges spanning the river in this area, the Syrians apparently planned to cross two in what they intended to be their triumphal entry into Israel. One was the Benot Yacov Bridge, by way of Kuneitra. The other was the Arik Bridge that spanned the river just north of the tip of the Sea of Galilee. The invaders envisioned destroying all Israeli opposition on the Golan Heights by Tuesday, October 8.

Israel's Barak Brigade and contingents from the 7th Armored Brigade met the Syrians' southerly thrust. On the morning of October 6, the brigade commander found members of his command absorbed in fasting and praying. The group was being visited by an Orthodox Hasidic group whose zeal had persuaded even the nonreligious soldiers to join in the solemn rituals. As he listened, the brigade commander was moved by the prayer being recited by his troops: "On Rosh Hashanah it is inscribed and on the Fast Day of Atonement it is sealed and determined how many shall pass away and how many shall be born; who shall live, and who shall die, whose appointed time is finished, and

Pres. Efraim Katzir awards the Medal of Valor to Zvika Greengold for his heroism in combatting a Syrian tank force in 1973. Left to right: Defense Minister Shimon Peres, Katzir, and Prime Minister Yitzhak Rabin. Rabin succeeded Golda Meir in 1974.

whose is not."[9]

Over the next few days, 90 percent of the tank commanders in the Barak Brigade were killed or wounded. Israeli tank commanders directed action from partially exposed postures with hatches open and upper bodies in the open. The saga of the Barak Brigade is one of singular heroism in the face of overwhelming odds. By the time the first day and night of fighting ended, the Barak Brigade had been reduced to a force of 15 functioning tanks. Still the soldiers repeatedly flung themselves into the path of 450 Syrian tanks.

Acts of individual heroism abounded. Among the most conspicuous were the exploits of a young Israeli, Zvi "Zvika" Greengold. The freckle-faced, blond lieutenant made his home on a kibbutz in western Galilee. He was on leave when news of the fighting reached him. Hitchhiking north, he arrived at the command headquarters at Nefekh and asked for a command. The request was granted, and he was given four tanks, three of which had to be repaired before they were fit for action.

His group was named Zvika Force and was sent into the fray. Over the next

30 hours, Zvika would wreak havoc on the enemy. When the other tanks in his command were destroyed, he fought alone, engaging one of the main thrusts of the Syrian advance. Opposing forces outnumbered him 50 to 1. Through the night he darted in and out among the hills to destroy enemy tanks and then quickly melted into the night.

At one point, Zvika's tank was hit and set on fire. Zvika flung himself to the ground, wounded and suffering burns on his face and arms. Recovering from the initial shock of his wounds, he commandeered a passing tank and, scrambling into the hatch, continued his war. When he finally dragged his battered body from the tank, he muttered an apology to his superior officer. "I can't anymore," he said. Zvi Greengold, son of Holocaust survivors, had single-handedly destroyed 60 Syrian tanks.

Despite such heroic efforts, the Syrian assault moved on. It took up a position on the outskirts of El Al, one of its objectives on the road south. The Syrians apparently were stunned by their success. They had broken Israeli resistance. At the moment, the bridge on the Jordan was wide open to them. Strangely, however, at this point, they stopped. No one can explain why. Perhaps, as with the Egyptians, their success had made them fear the Israelis had baited a trap for them. It could be they went only as far as initial strategy had outlined and then stopped to await further instructions.

When they halted the advance on the night of October 6, their lead tanks were within four to six miles of the Jordan River. By the time they prepared to continue the offensive, Israeli reserves were on the scene and ready to block the advance. Viewing the situation, an incredulous Israeli soldier quipped, "The Syrians simply stopped in midstream, and didn't start again. Why? We'll ask them sometime, if we have the chance."[10]

To the north, successive waves of assaulting armor hammered the 7th Brigade. This brigade was born in the deadly battles of Latrun during the War of Independence. The 7th had long been one of the IDF's premier fighting units. Its immediate task was to block the Syrians' attempt to penetrate the Damascus to Kuneitra road—the most direct route to the Benot Yacov Bridge.

The Syrians' first attempts to cross the antitank ditch the Israelis had prepared were repulsed. Although the Israelis were satisfied with the performance of their armored forces in this encounter, they were deeply concerned over the enemy's persistence and the number of forces driving into the central sector. As successive columns of Syrian tanks exploded under the impact of Israeli shells, the Syrians simply kept coming in what appeared to be an endless procession.

Syria had chosen a 2.5-mile swath across a valley between Hermonit Hill and a ridge called The Booster. The 7th Brigade was well positioned defensively at this point. In military terms, it had chosen an ideal killing ground. However,

Yom Kippur War Cease-Fire Lines: October 24, 1973

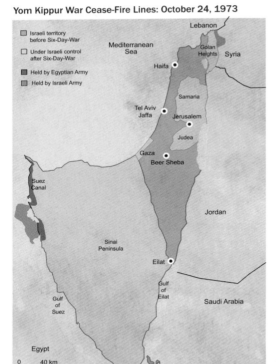

☐ Israeli territory before Six-Day-War
☐ Under Israeli control after Six-Day-War
☐ Held by Egyptian Army
☐ Held by Israeli Army

Lebanon
Mediterranean Sea
Golan Heights
Syria
Haifa
Samaria
Tel Aviv
Jaffa
Jerusalem
Judea
Gaza
Beer Sheba
Suez Canal
Jordan
Sinai Peninsula
Eilat
Gulf of Eilat
Gulf of Suez
Saudi Arabia
Egypt
0   40 km
0   40 mi
Red Sea

the odds weighed heavily on the side of Syria to say the least: 500 Syrian tanks led by Russian-made T62s, the most modern on the field, against a mere 70 Israeli tanks. Interspersed within Syria's armada were infantrymen carrying antitank bazookas.

Jewish and Arab forces became locked in a life-and-death struggle that raged through the night of October 7, with attacker and defender often firing at each other from point-blank range. In fact, tanks and infantry from the two armies became intermingled in the darkness, and the battlefield became a nightmare of destructive confusion. Finally, the Syrians broke off the attack and retreated in order to regroup for a new thrust.

As morning light crept across the valley, Israelis saw the curtain rising on a ghastly scene. No fewer than 130 Syrian tanks lay destroyed and abandoned before them. Wrecked personnel carriers and mangled human bodies added to this dreadful portrait of death and destruction. Exhausted Israelis spoke for themselves and their adversaries when they named this sector of the struggle for the Golan Heights The Valley of Tears.

Yet this was not the end. These men fought on for days without respite. Sleep and food were luxuries they could ill afford. When tanks were not rolling toward them, artillery and rockets were raining down on them.

Before the battle-drained Jewish warriors saw the columns of dust rising from the tracks of the retreating Syrians, hundreds of men breathed their last in the graveyard of the Golan Heights. Not only here, but also across the entire Golan lay the remnants of the battle that had threatened Israel's very existence. General Raful Etyan, who commanded all Jewish forces on the Golan Heights, spoke by way of wireless radio to Colonel Avigdor, commander of the 7th Brigade, as Avigdor looked down on the valley. Etyan said, "You have saved the people of Israel."[11] That commendation would be handed to all the courageous young soldiers who fought on the Golan Heights.

By war's end, the Israelis had successfully defended themselves from an attack by Jordanian and Iraqi forces. They had enlarged appreciably the land they controlled on the Heights and had positioned their columns well down the road to Damascus. At a considerable loss of life, the Golani Brigade wrested the strategic observation post on Mount Hermon from the Syrians in the waning hours of the war.

The storied Golani Brigade embodied the indomitable spirit exhibited by Israeli troops during the difficult battle for the Golan Heights. Formed three months before the outbreak of the 1948 War of Independence, the Golani Brigade had a reputation of being the unit consisting of rejects from other army groups—some would say misfits. However, after fighting many battles and losing many comrades, the Golani soldiers earned the distinction of being among the fiercest fighters in the IDF.

When Syrian tanks and infantry stormed across the Golan Heights, initially routing the understaffed Israelis manning defensive positions, it was the determination of two Golani soldiers who turned the tide.

Gideon Pick, publisher of the online magazine onjewishmatters.com, explained:

> I once read the memoirs of an Israeli general who fought in the Yom Kippur War in the defense of the Golan Heights. In his memoir, the general described how the Israeli army was running away in panic on the first day of the war when the Syrian army launched its surprise attack. Everyone was fleeing the Golan Heights to take shelter in Israel. The general tried to stop them and set up a defense line, but confusion and panic took over. Then he saw two Golani soldiers with a machine gun; the soldiers set up their machine gun on the narrow asphalt road, pointing it toward the advancing Syrian army. They were ready to face the entire Syrian army themselves if needed. Two soldiers, one machine, and a Golani attitude; this was how the Israeli general begun setting up his defense line.[12]

Israel managed to hold on to the Golan Heights. When the full tally was taken, it became obvious that Israel, north and south, had forged a remarkable victory. It was a triumph, however, that no one felt like celebrating.

THE AFTERMATH

As the brutal statistics of the war began to be tabulated, Jewish people the world over went into mourning. Although the scope of Israel's victory was obvious, so was the cost in lives.

The Syrians and Egyptians are estimated to have lost approximately 16,000 men. Combined Arab forces, which included not only Syrians and Egyptians but Iraqis and Jordanians also, saw 2,000 tanks and 450 planes destroyed. Israel lost 800 tanks and 104 aircraft. Coupled with the land gained during the conflict, Israel's accomplishment was exceptional.

However, it came it an enormous cost. More than 2,500 Israelis were killed in the fighting, while approximately 7,000 more were wounded. This was more than three times the number lost in the Six-Day War.

These figures may not seem high to Americans, but they were enormous to Israel. The death toll was equivalent to the United States losing 160,530 soldiers in battle—almost three times the number of American soldiers who died in the Vietnam War. The losses threw the Jewish nation into shock, anger, and bewilderment.

Moshe Dayan referred to this period as "a time when heroes were deposed." National illusions were shattered. For the first time since independence, many Israelis lost confidence in their leadership. Grieving mothers would spit at Dayan when they passed him in the street. The Israeli military establishment, long lauded for its unparalleled preparedness, suddenly became suspect.

Questions began to arise over the commitment of Israel's allies abroad—particularly those in Europe who had offered Israel no help. These factors and others converged to plunge the nation into a prolonged depression that endured without appreciable letup until Israel's daring rescue of Jewish hostages being held in Entebbe, Uganda, in 1976.

A Jewish woman articulated the mood to me in late 1975. "We are only now beginning to realize," she said, "that we actually won the Yom Kippur War, that it was a victory rather than a defeat." These were days when the words of the prophet Jeremiah forced their way once again into the minds of the Jewish people: "Is it nothing to you, all you who pass by? Behold and see if there is any sorrow like my sorrow" (Lam. 1:12).

Perhaps Israel's distress and extended lament were in part a release of pent-up tensions that had strained minds and emotions for years. No nation had lived under the threat of potential annihilation as had Israel. The Arabs' belligerence and seemingly uncompromising dedication to the Jewish state's destruction were almost certain to affect the national nervous system eventually. Living under constant threats, acts of terrorism, harassment, and recurrent mobilization to meet potential attacks all contributed to the situation.

As Israel gathered the bodies of its young after a war its enemies callously began on the highest of Jewish holy days, the full measure of the nation's frustration, fear, and anger burst from people's hearts. Depression, suspicion, and economic hardship became the lingering legacies of the Yom Kippur War, which produced three distinct results:

Uncertainty: Israelis were not sure any longer. Their sense of invincibility had vaporized. A psychologist accurately phrased the mood: "This war dispelled Israel's seeing themselves as supermen and the other side as permanently inferior and destroyed their ideas of security."

Futility: Every new fight, even those they won, only presaged more battles ahead. Though the Israelis were not ready to quit (after the war Jewish leaders feared the Arabs might misinterpret the mood and commit the error of launching a new offensive), they sensed the horrible fact that war seemed to be an inevitable fact of Israeli life.

Isolation: Most significantly, Israel settled into the awareness of being slowly isolated. It was surrounded by hostile neighbors, a tiny island in the midst of a giant sea. There had been only one hand of help extended during the days of trauma. Maj. Gen. Chaim Herzog noted in his forceful book, *The War of Atonement,* "Only the United States appreciated the significance of Israel's struggle."[13] The sight of major European nations cowering before Soviet blustering and Arab oil sheiks caused justifiable consternation.

INVENTING HISTORY

Around 1990, attacks on Israel changed from focusing exclusively on military campaigns to focusing on propaganda. Sensing they may not win on the battlefield, Israel's enemies launched a different type of war—a war of lies. They started to make preposterous statements, such as claiming the Jewish people have no history in Palestine. If they couldn't defeat the Jews with weapons, they would beat them with words by inventing a new "history" and changing world opinion. Enter the revisionists.

Revisionists claim no credible evidence exists that Jewish Temples ever stood on Mount Moriah in Jerusalem. Never mind that archaeology, Scripture, and world history completely contradict these lies. But truth never matters when it comes to propaganda. The bigger the lie the better; and the more you tell it, the more people are duped into believing it. So the lies became enormous, and people began to believe them because of their pitiful lack of knowledge of true history.

Among the first proponents of reinvented history was Yasser Arafat, founder of the Palestine Liberation Organization (PLO) and president of the Palestinian Authority. He turned heads by claiming Jesus was a Palestinian freedom fighter and martyr for the Palestinian cause.

In a conversation with U.S. President Bill Clinton following the failed Camp David Summit in July 2000, where Clinton tried to get the Arabs and Israelis to make peace, Arafat reportedly astonished the president by asserting, "The Jews never had a historic presence in the land." Equally astonishing is the fact that such an absurdity is the majority Palestinian position to this day.

If that were not enough, Arafat and company's big reinvention of history is being promoted, rather than repudiated, in many international circles, including the United Nations. Where such lies are not accepted as historical reality, the presence of hard-core revisionists tones down any positive declarations of the Jewish people's bona fide rights to their own country.

Of course, in addition to all of the confirming archaeological evidence on the Jewishness of Jerusalem, there is also a set-in-stone witness in faraway Rome. It is displayed on the triumphal Arch of Titus celebrating the emperor's conquest of Judea in the Jewish Wars in AD 66–70. The relief depicts legionaries carrying booty from the Temple in Jerusalem—the table of shewbread, silver trumpets, and the golden menorah.

WHEN TRUTH BECOMES A CASUALTY

Rejecting biblical, moral, ethical, and spiritual values is a serious issue. The problem is accelerating rapidly today and threatens the stability of America and other Western democracies. The result is the developing all-out war against true Christianity and the Judeo-Christian underpinnings of Western culture.

Tragically, the invasion of revisionist ideology has plunged a dagger into the heart of truth. History is inviolable; it doesn't change. To ignore it or attempt to refashion and manipulate it for ulterior purposes ensures a bad result. The campaign waged by the Palestinians and others who are like-minded qualifies as a "big lie." It is dangerous and designed to achieve Israel's destruction and slander the Jewish people.

It follows the strategy of master Nazi propagandist, Joseph Goebbels: "A lie told once remains a lie," he said. "But a lie told a thousand times becomes the truth." When the masses can't tell the difference between lies and truth, everyone suffers the consequences.

The years between the end of the October Yom Kippur War and the dawn of the 21st century have seen few things change. The UN continues to flaunt international law by casting Israel—a legal, democratic state and member of the UN—as an inhumane occupier of Palestinian lands and the world's chief enemy of peace. And though the issue of dependence on Arab oil has changed in recent years, Europe has not altered its consistent pro-Arab, anti-Israel bias.

For their part, the Palestinians continue their campaign of denial penned at the Khartoum Arab League Summit held in the aftermath of their crushing defeat in the 1967 Six-Day War. The Khartoum resolution featured three nos: no peace with Israel, no recognition of Israel, and no negotiations with Israel.

Thus, while some things have changed, the fundamental issues have stayed the same. The Khartoum doctrine has echoed through all of the declarations Palestinian leaders have made from Yasser Arafat to his successor, Mahmoud Abbas, to many other Arab notables. Never recognizing Israel as a Jewish state is the consistent mantra of Palestinian hard-liners.

Two bloody intifadas (Palestinian uprisings), terrorist indoctrination of Palestinian children, more than 2,604 rockets shot into Israel from Gaza by 2018, home invasions, suicide bombings, threats of war and nuclear annihilation, stabbings, bus bombings, demonstrations, and attempts to instill fear and disrupt lives have all been part of the Palestinian crusade. The Arab agenda is not bent on forcing peace through inflicting pain. It is bent on destroying Israel and driving the Jewish people into the sea.

A young Sabra, the daughter of an Israeli foreign-service officer, captured the nation's feelings when she answered a question about what she felt American youth could do to help Israel. Her poignant response was, "Tell them to believe it is important for us to survive."

A MAN MUST COME

A Jewish historian wrote that when Jews pass through times of trouble, two themes historically manifest themselves: The first is a longing to return to the ancient homeland. The second is a corresponding revival of Messianic expectation. The historian was in precise agreement with the prophets of the Bible. They prophesied of a time when Israel will find itself isolated—all alone, with no human hand of help. No political system, military combine, or resolution of self-determination will be able to stay its bloodthirsty enemies.

Almighty God referred to this period when He said, through the prophet Zechariah, "And it shall happen in that day that I will make Jerusalem a very heavy stone for all peoples; all who would heave it away will surely be cut in pieces, though all nations of the earth are gathered against it" (Zech. 12:3). This developing isolation will culminate in a unified national outcry for the Messiah.

Following the Yom Kippur War, signs of Messianic expectation began to materialize. They appeared not only in predictable religious sources but in secular ones, as well.

On the religious side were Orthodox groups, one of which was Gush Emunim. Gush Emunim (meaning, a faithful bloc or a group of believers) is a settlement movement that arose after the Yom Kippur War. The majority of its adherents were religiously zealous Jews who were actively preparing for the day when their *Moshiach* (Messiah) would appear.

Their explanation of basic beliefs is illuminating. I had an opportunity to interview someone within the movement, and this is what he told me: "When we saw how bad things became during the Yom Kippur War, we were convinced that the coming of the Messiah must be very near. So while other Jews were depressed over the outcome of the war, we were encouraged. We believe that this was the beginning of the redemption of Israel. Our belief is quite simple, really. We believe when we possess all of the land historically held by the Jewish people, the Messiah will come. How will He come? Hasidic Jews expect Him to come suddenly, miraculously, seated on a cloud. We do not believe this. Our belief is He will come to Jerusalem in a lowly manner, riding on a colt of an ass."

Secular Israelis have made similar statements, although they would not claim religious bias for doing so. When speaking privately with Jewish people from various walks of life, it is easy to discern a tone that seems to indicate a realignment of thinking—a conclusion that the hope for the future is not to be found in another system. Rather, it is to be found in the appearance of a man who can provide leadership that no one so far has adequately delivered.

For example, I was in the home of a publisher one evening in Jerusalem when his family and other guests were discussing politics and current problems. At one point in the conversation, one of the guests, a historian, rose to his feet and declared, "America has not produced a philosopher in 50 years. A man must come, one who can take control. A man who towers above all the rest." The Jewish people there generally agreed this was the ultimate answer.

A few days later, I had lunch with a friend who holds a doctorate from the Hebrew University and was working for one of Israel's Zionist agencies. I brought up the subject of Messianic expectation. He replied, "No. I don't believe there is much hope of a revival of that kind of thinking in modern Israel." Moments later, on our walk back to his office, he offered this observation: "You know, I can't explain it, but there is great trouble ahead. I believe we will have another war, a big war with Russia. Things will be bad for a while, but then it will be all right. Don't ask me how I know it, but I am certain it will happen this way."

Without realizing what he was saying, this young man detailed the prophetic future of the Chosen People. There will be two climactic intrusions into the Middle East. One great power in the end-times will unsuccessfully try to invade Israel from the north, the region currently identified as Russia. Then a belligerent confederation of nations will follow shortly thereafter and run headlong into the Messiah!

The Six-Day War is reminiscent of Joshua and his triumph at Jericho. Ai and the Yom Kippur War are compatible comparisons of humiliation and frustration, ancient and modern. But we must not stop here. If we move through Joshua's historical account, we will soon arrive at yet another battle—one that involved not one adversary but, rather, a confederation of belligerent kings who banded together hoping to crush Joshua and the Israelites (Josh. 10:5–15). When the dust of that battle settled, Israel had won the day; and the inspired penman wrote, "There has been no day like that, before it or after it, that the LORD heeded the voice of a man; *for the Lord fought for Israel*" (v. 14, emphasis added).

Israel's last great confrontation will once again see the day when the Lord will fight for His Chosen People.

CHAPTER NINE

The Stalking Bear

A fascinating look into the climactic battles of the end-times is conserved for us in the writings of the prophet Ezekiel. They mark what might be called the beginning-of-the-end preparations for the Messiah's return to establish the Millennial, or Messianic, Kingdom. Here prophecy and history converge, and the preview seems so contemporary that we cannot fail to take notice.

In a succinct chronology, Ezekiel identified the time, location, and motivation of the battles; the annihilation of the military juggernaut moving against a regathered Israel; and the divine consummation of events.

Time: in the latter years. "In the latter years you will come into the land of those brought back from the sword and gathered from many people on the mountains of Israel, which had long been desolate; they were brought out of the nations, and now all of them dwell safely" (38:8).

Location: from the far north. "Then you will come from your place out of the far north, you and many peoples with you, all of them riding on horses, a great company and a mighty army" (v. 15).

Motivation: to take spoil. "You will say, 'I will go up against a land of unwalled villages; I will go to a peaceful people, who dwell safely, all of them dwelling without walls, and having neither bars nor gates'—to take plunder and to take booty, to stretch out your hand against the waste places that are again inhabited, and against a people gathered from the nations, who have acquired livestock and goods, who dwell in the midst of the land" (vv. 11–12).

Annihilation: destroyed on Israel's mountains. "You shall fall upon the mountains of Israel, you and all your troops and the peoples who are with you; I will give you to birds of prey of every sort and to the beasts of the field to be devoured" (39:4).

Consummation: God to be glorified. "Thus I will magnify Myself and sanctify Myself, and I will be known in the eyes of many nations. Then they shall know that I am the LORD" (38:23).

THE PERPETUAL ANTAGONIST

Although we are not privy to the precise identity of the future political power fitting Ezekiel's description, we do see striking similarities to the region's occupants throughout history. Whether they be Czarist, Communist, or post-Soviet Russia, the characteristics remain constant. Expansionism, anti-Semitism, and aggression have all typified the great power from the north.

These characteristics were clearly displayed during the 1973 war. The Yom Kippur War would not have occurred had Russia not cooperated in the venture. Following the Arabs' catastrophic losses in the Six-Day War, then-President Anwar Sadat of Egypt hesitated to begin a new escapade against Israel until he knew he could deter the threat of Israeli deep-penetration bombing. The Soviets provided this assurance.

The Soviets supplied Egypt with surface-to-surface missiles in March 1973. These Scud missiles could deliver high-explosive or nuclear warheads at a range of 180 miles. They confirmed Egypt's ability to reach Jewish population centers in the heart of Israel. Bolstered by this capacity for devastation, Sadat, who succeeded Nasser in October 1970, decided to launch the war. So the determination to attack Israel actually belonged to the Soviets, who placed the Scuds in Sadat's welcoming hands.

An unconfirmed report even suggested it was the Kremlin that chose the very day hostilities should begin:

> The French Weekly *Le Nouvel Observateur* later reported that the ex-head of the Soviet military mission in Egypt, General Vassil Vasilevitch Okolkoniev, was the man who chose Yom Kippur as the appropriate time to surprise Israel: "The Russian general read that the radio is silent in Israel on the Day of Atonement and so he thought up the idea."[1]

In the dramatic UN sessions following the Six-Day War, Israel's Minister of Foreign Affairs Abba Eban read lists of Soviet military equipment that had fallen unscathed into Israeli hands. It was unmistakably clear the Soviet Union would not rest until the sting of the 1967 humiliation could be assuaged.

Immediately after the hostilities of the Six-Day War ceased, the Soviets got to work rebuilding the Arab war machine. On June 11, 1967, the Kremlin had urged Egyptian President Nasser not to quit, assuring him all of the aid necessary to recoup his losses. Mere weeks afterward, a Soviet mission arrived in Egypt to evaluate the situation and establish a plan to rebuild the Egyptian military force. A three-part program was implemented.

Reequipping: Russia replaced what Egypt had lost to Israel within the brief span of six months. The ultimate Soviet goal was to create an Egyptian army that would number 800,000 troops. This time around, Russia would supply equipment designed to deal with the two most formidable weapons the Israelis had at their disposal: the plane and the tank. Missile systems and the surface-to-surface antitank projectiles were the result of their efforts.

Training: It would not be enough for the Soviets to supply the weapons for a new war; they would also take the responsibility for fashioning a new breed of soldier. Russia would train the new Egyptian army. Every Egyptian missile installation, brigade, and battalion had its own Russian advisor who kept tabs and filed reports on the Egyptian officers.

Soviet arrogance and thinly veiled contempt for the Egyptians soon created a deep-seated resentment among members of the Egyptian army. This growing attitude of hostility toward the Russians became so pronounced that Anwar Sadat, in a short-lived fit of pique after an unhappy set of exchanges with the Kremlin, asked the Soviets to withdraw its advisors and troops from Egypt. No one applauded more enthusiastically than the Egyptian officers whom the Russians had belittled. The Russians, however, had no intention of letting their clients shake off the yoke; many advisors and instructors never left the country.

Before long the differences were patched up and the spirit of the Treaty of Friendship and Cooperation was again operational. This treaty was a 15-year agreement whereby the Soviets pledged aid to Egypt to rebuild its socialistic society.

The Russian objectives for the armies of both Egypt and Syria were admirably successful. The one insurmountable difficulty they faced was an inability to teach the Israelis how to lose.

Manning the Hardware: To further ensure there would be no repeat of the 1967 fiasco, Russia decided to provide more direct forms of assistance, as well. In certain instances, Russians reportedly manned the hardware they supplied.

During the War of Attrition (1969–1970) that Nasser initiated in an attempt to take back the Sinai Israel had won in 1967, Egypt hit the Israelis with massive artillery bombardments along the Suez. Israel responded by sending its air force on deep-penetration bombing sorties against Egyptian targets. In the process, Israel wrecked the network of Sam 2 missiles that had been carefully erected to circumvent the very thing the Israelis were accomplishing.

Nassar sent out a hurried S.O.S. to the Kremlin. The response was eagerly forthcoming. Russia sent 1,500 Soviet personnel to accompany the Sam 3 missiles sent to replace the old system. These missiles were supplemented by the eventual arrival of an additional 15,000 to 20,000 air defense units, which now bore the brunt of protecting Egypt from Israeli penetration. Of course, this meant Israel would not only be confronting its Arab neighbors but, at times, it would also be directly confronting Russian forces. In fact, before the

An Israeli soldier overlooks the Suez Canal during the War of Attrition.

War of Attrition was over, Israeli jets battled Russian-piloted patrols over the Suez Canal at least once.

During the battle for the Golan Heights in the Yom Kippur War, Soviet advisors were helicoptered to the Israeli position on Mount Hermon that had fallen to the Syrian forces. Once there, they did an in-depth examination of the Israeli equipment the Syrians had captured.

A GROWL FROM THE NORTH

Collapse of the Arab forces brought an impassioned response from the Russians—one that brought them to the brink of direct intervention and brought the world to the edge of nuclear upheaval.

The April 12, 1976, issue of *Time* magazine presented an intriguing scenario of the brush with nuclear conflagration. According to *Time*, Israel assembled 13 nuclear devices during the early stages of the 1973 war, when things looked exceedingly bleak. Here is what *Time* reported:

At 10 p.m. on October 8, the Israeli Commander on the northern front, Major General Yitzhak Hoffi, told his superior: "I am not sure we can hold out much longer." After midnight, Defense Minister Moshe Dayan solemnly warned Premier Golda Meir: "This is the end of the third temple." Mrs. Meir thereupon gave Dayan permission to activate Israel's Doomsday weapons.

The article further stated that by the time the weapons were ready, the crisis had passed, along with any further consideration of using the devices. *Time* and other sources believed Russia probably learned of Israel's nuclear weapons through observation by the Cosmos spy satellite orbiting over the Middle East.

On October 13, 1973, Russia sent nuclear warheads to Alexandria, Egypt, to be installed on the Scud missiles. The United States, however, detected the devices when the ship transporting them passed the Bosporus Strait on October 15. America then issued a military alert, which told the Russians their warheads had been detected.

Some reports indicate the Soviets were prepared to join the fight on the Arab side. As the Egyptian situation deteriorated (Israeli forces had established a bridgehead on the Egyptian side of the Suez Canal, defeating Egypt's armored forces), Sadat issued a plea for joint U.S. and Soviet military intervention.

Russian satellite reconnaissance had verified the situation. The Soviets were ready to intervene, but the United States refused to get involved. A Russian note reportedly sent to American officials by Leonid Brezhnev, the Soviet Union's general secretary of the Communist Party, stated, "I shall state plainly that if the United States rejects the opportunity of joining with us in this matter, the Soviet Union will be obliged to examine as a matter of urgency the question of the unilateral institution of appropriate measures to stop Israeli aggression."[2] Egypt had started the war. But as soon as Israel began winning, it became "Israeli aggression."

The Russians began a buildup that had all the appearances of preparing for a military incursion. They placed Soviet divisions in East Germany and Poland on alert. A full division of Soviet airborne troops was transported from positions close to Moscow to an airfield near Belgrade, Yugoslavia. The staff of this division was then in Syria, positioned just outside Damascus.

Other Soviet units, along with Antonov freighter aircraft, were also removed to Belgrade. Southeast of Cyprus, the Russians were mounting a naval buildup complete with assault boats and helicopter pilots. And if all this were not enough, U.S. reconnaissance over Egypt discovered the deployment of Scud missiles.

The United States reacted with a combat alert. All U.S. troops were placed on standby, awaiting orders. All leaves were cancelled. The alert was worldwide and involved more than 2 million American military personnel.

In concert with the alert, U.S. Secretary of State Henry Kissinger drafted a communiqué to Secretary Brezhnev. It stated that the United States would not abide any intervention by the Soviet Union in the Middle East. Any intrusion by the Russians, said Kissinger, would place world peace in jeopardy. The Russians backed away.

How near the world stood to Israel, Egypt, or the Soviet Union pushing a nuclear button we probably will never know. However, we saw a vivid example of Russia's continuing obsession with expansionism.

WITH EYES TO THE SOUTH

Keeping Ezekiel's prophecy in mind, we can learn much by tracing the development of Russia's southerly thrust, which will eventually spend itself on the mountains of Israel. A quick historical survey illustrates how far we've come, where we stand, and what lies ahead.

Comparing a map of Russia from the late 1500s with the territory Russia held until the Soviet Union collapsed in December 1971 shows that Russia expanded its territory 16 times during those 400 years. The Russians have engaged in an almost continuous program of expansion. After World War II, Russia forcibly annexed six independent Eastern European states having non-Russian populations and 105 million people. Before the Soviet Union's dissolution, 112 million of its 240 million people were not Russian.

In addition, at the heart of Russia's expansionist designs has been its desire to become a world-class naval power. Thus the Russians first moved north to the Arctic, the direction that afforded the least resistance. Next they moved into the area bordering the Baltic, which offered the nearest shore. Peter the Great established a foothold there and began building the first Russian navy. The Black Sea, which the Russians held from the end of the 15th century, provided ice-free ports. But exits into and out of the Mediterranean Sea still eluded them. They were controlled by other nations.

Over the centuries, the Russians systematically moved to secure additional territories in all directions. From the 16th century until it was defeated by Japan in 1905, Russia expanded eastward into Asia. Even after that setback, it scooped up sizable portions in those regions until 1914. The Bolshevik Revolution in 1917 brought a transition that offered Russia's neighbors brief relief. But Communist imperialism was not a liberation movement.

In due time the Soviets became preoccupied with moving toward the south, eventually focusing squarely on the Middle East. A secret agreement concerning the Middle East between Russia and its World War I allies granted Russia control of a significant portion of the land mass held today by Iran. The agreement also ceded Russia a considerable slice of eastern Turkey to the Black Sea and gave it authority over Constantinople (Istanbul) and the Straits into the Mediterranean.

The Russian Revolution negated implementation of the agreement, but the important fact is that Russia had turned its expansionist eyes south and was beginning to move in that direction. At the outset, the Bolsheviks renounced territorial aspirations. By the 1930s, however, they were clearly exploiting their power. The Communists would soon take up where the czarists left off. But before their efforts could know any measure of success, a major change was necessary because after World War I, the Western powers were firmly entrenched in the Middle East.

THE WEST RETREATS

The year 1920 marked the zenith of Western influence in the region. Algeria, Tunisia, Aden, Libya, Egypt, Iraq, Palestine, Cyprus, and the Sudan were all under direct British rule. Oman was under indirect rule; while Turkey, Persia, and what is now Saudi Arabia (except for Yemen) were allied with the British crown.

During the years between 1921 and 1939, a period of retrenchment set in. Egypt became an independent kingdom with certain "reserved points" secured to Britain. Iraq became independent, while Transjordan became an emirate under British mandate. Turkey, Persia, and Saudi Arabia all gained independence. Indeed, by 1940 the Western hold on the Middle East was slipping away.

The years between 1940 and 1971 saw retrenchment turn into a virtual full retreat. Western predominance, especially in the case of Great Britain, all but disappeared. Syria, Lebanon, the Sudan, Morocco, Tunisia, Algeria, Aden, and Libya all joined the ranks of independent nations. Also, Rhodes was ceded to Greece, the Canal Zone agreement was nullified, and the British mandate over Palestine was abandoned.

By 1971 the United States and Britain saw the area virtually swept clean of their military bases. Morocco, Algeria, Tunisia, Libya, Egypt, Iraq, and Aden all issued the West eviction notices. Only Malta and Cyprus remained open for military operations. And while the newly independent nations were breathing the heady air of self-determination, the Soviet Union was already well along in forging its campaign to shackle Arabs and Israelis alike.

RUSSIA MOVES IN

The book *Russia: Imperial Power in the Middle East* explained the following: "In 1940, Nazi Germany proposed that Russia should join the Tripartite Pact (of Germany, Italy, and Japan). The proposal centered around the idea that the three Axis powers would agree in advance to certain Soviet territorial ambitions. The book states the following:

On 25 November 1940, in an official note addressed to Germany, the Soviet Government accepted the proposal in principle and defined "the centre" of Russia's "territorial aspirations" as "the area south of Baku and Batum in the general direction of the Persian Gulf."[3]

Batum is located on the eastern tip of the Black Sea near the Turkish border. Baku is situated on the western side of the Caspian Sea, north of Iran.

Although Russia's alliance with the Axis powers was not consummated, after World War II the Soviet Union made four attempts to implement its desires:

In March 1945 it claimed the right to establish a permanent military base on the Dardanelles because, in its view, Turkey was too weak to deter "foreign powers."

1. The Soviets demanded that Turkey cede a strip on the southeastern tip of the Black Sea, which ran along the Russian-Turkish border south to Iran. Their justification was that they had possessed the area during part of the previous century.

2. During World War II, British and Russian troops had been stationed, by agreement, on Iranian soil. After the British adhered to the timetable and withdrew, Russia refused to evacuate its troops and kept them in the province of Azerbaijan. By the end of 1945, all key government positions in Azerbaijan were held by Communists, who were declaring the province to be independent of Iran.

   When Iranian troops sought to intervene, the Soviets blocked them and denied them entrance. After the matter was brought to the UN twice and pressure was brought to bear, Russia agreed to withdraw providing it received controlling interest in a Russian-Persian oil company that covered all Iranian territories bordering on the Caspian Sea and Soviet Union. The Iranian parliament refused to ratify the agreement after Soviet withdrawal, and the Russians dropped the case.

3. Russia launched a fourth effort in September 1945. The Russians approached the United States, Britain, France, and China with the idea that the Soviet Union be given trusteeship over Tripolitania, a sizable portion of northern Libya adjacent to Tunisia. Their justification was that the Soviet Union needed Mediterranean ports for its fleet.

Russia was turned aside in all of these efforts to seek fortunes in the south.

It was the Western powers, led by a determined United States, that refused to let the Bolsheviks obtain their objectives. Though the United States was denied many of the land bases it wanted, its Sixth Fleet in the Mediterranean became a primary deterrent to Soviet ambitions.

However, tyrants never sleep. Tyranny is an insatiable mania, and failure only breeds a more ruthless determination. History provides no clearer witness to this fact than the Soviet Union at the height of its power. The Russians saw these reverses as temporary frustrations that in no way diminished the Soviet Union's commitment to its broad objective. It would only be a matter of adopting new methods of approaching the problems.

Russia launched its next offensive among the fledgling independent nations in the Middle East. It began a process of leap-frogging the Western powers, alighting amidst the Arab sheiks with a chest full of sumptuous delights that would fill the vacuum left by the West's departure. Indeed, the foundation of the initial intrigues was the newly independent countries' anti-Western mood. The refrain was, "We're enemies of your enemies, so why shouldn't we be friends?"

The Soviets' master plan involved creating dependence on the Soviet Union, establishing Soviet dominance, then moving on to annexation. The first stage was the creation of dependence in three distinct areas—military, economic, and political.

MILITARY DEPENDENCE

Russian objectives at the time became crystal clear with a casual rundown of the arms agreements executed in the Middle East. Note the progression:

DEAL	COUNTRY	TYPE OF SUPPLIER
1955	Egypt	Main supplier
1955	Syria	Main supplier
1958	Iraq	Main supplier
1962	Algeria	Main supplier
1967	Sudan	Main supplier
1967	Yemen-South Yemen	Main supplier
1967	Iran (terrorists)	Partial supplier
1970	Libya	Partial supplier
1971	Lebanon (terrorists)	Partial supplier

Items the Soviets supplied to military arsenals included planes, tanks, artillery, missiles, naval vessels, electronic equipment, small arms, and sundry other

Soviet-made T-54 tank captured during the Six-Day War and refurbished by the IDF.

materials.

And of course, with the acceptance of military supplies, other elements also appeared. Replacements and parts came from the supplier and at the supplier's pleasure. Thus military adventures had to be sanctioned or at least tacitly supported by Russia.

With supplies came the need to import personnel for construction; instruction; and, in the case of the ultra-sophisticated equipment, operation: These Middle Eastern countries needed people to man the equipment they were receiving. This last point accomplished the Russians' most basic aim of all: to establish a presence in the area marked for eventual occupation. A further side benefit was the necessity of bringing local military and technical personnel to the Soviet Union for instruction on military and political matters.

By fostering the Arab-Israeli rift and doing everything in its power to prolong the existing problem, Russia saw a golden opportunity to deepen Arab dependence on the Soviet Union and eventually to create the opportunity to intervene as a benevolent protector.

ECONOMIC DEPENDENCE

Soviet economic programs were initiated in Algeria, Egypt, Sudan, Yemen, South Yemen, Turkey, Syria, Iraq, and Iran. The amount of involvement varied significantly but generally followed a pattern in which the Soviets initiated long-term projects that required extended Soviet participation. Examples are the

Aswan Dam in Egypt (10 years) and the Euphrates Dam (eight to nine years).

Hydroelectric projects were initiated in Egypt, Syria, Iraq, and Iran. Heavy and light industries, ports, roads and railways, irrigation projects, agriculture, fisheries, oil, natural gas, and numerous other ventures comprised the larder from which Arabs were encouraged to draw.

Syria and Egypt became the most heavily obligated to their Soviet mentors. Although definitive figures have not been published, estimates claim that between 1954 and 1971, Egypt accepted some $2 billion in aid, while Syria's take was approximately $750 million.

It is of primary interest that the two countries in which Russia's most determined efforts were being expended were Israel's neighbors to the north and south.

POLITICAL DEPENDENCE

Russian contacts with Arab nations proceeded without regard to how the Communist parties happened to be faring in the individual countries at any given time. Although there was no Arab Communist party operating legally, Communists with Russian orientation were active illegally in Egypt, Syria, Sudan, South Yemen, Turkey, Iran, Jordan, Lebanon, and Iraq. In Algeria, Egypt, Syria, and Iraq, legitimate political organizations had contact with the Soviet Communist Party.

Once again, examining Egypt provides interesting revelation. Here Russia attempted to infiltrate the Arab Socialist Union in an effort to ensure that leading individuals maintained pro-Soviet allegiances. Interestingly, Moscow instructed the Egyptian Communist Party to voluntarily disband, and its members were told to join the Arab Socialist Union. They were then directed to seek key positions, with particular designs on the information media.

In characteristically clandestine Russian operational fashion, secret groups were formed within the Arab Socialist Union to create further mischief. The aim was to tie the knot with Russia much more securely. Anwar Sadat's purges in 1971, instigated to ensure his control of Egyptian fortunes, seemed to decimate this movement.

More productive, in a sense, was the creation of legitimate contacts between the Communist Party of Russia and the various political parties of the Arab states. These contacts allowed Russian spokesmen to inject Communist ideas without running the risk of interfering with the internal affairs of the countries involved. The Soviets attempted to impress the Arabs with their model, which they fondly hoped would produce eventual union.

TIPPING THE BALANCE

While these events were transpiring and the Soviets were treading deftly on the tightrope of détente and UN manipulation, their first priority was to create a military imbalance. The presence of America's Sixth Fleet in the Mediterranean was thwarting Russia's highhanded attempts at expansion. The Soviets' long-standing efforts to achieve naval superiority were no secret, and their inflexible drive for supremacy was viewed as one of the main ingredients in tipping the scale in their favor. Before long, their labors were starting to pay off.

Beginning in 1965, Russian naval presence in the Mediterranean became a constant fixture. The Russians moved into the area the West had vacated. It had established bases from which to operate and duly impress locals with Soviet naval power and strength. The Russians made a concerted effort to establish bases of operation throughout the area. Russia requested permission from Spain to establish a permanent base on the Spanish coast. In Syria, the port city of Lattakia welcomed ships bearing the hammer and sickle. Far to the south, on the Indian Ocean, Aden and facilities on the island of Socotra served as havens for seafaring Soviets from the north.

Some argued that the buildup of conventional weapons systems was simply an exercise in waste, in view of the opposing superpowers' nuclear capabilities. No nation, this reasoning supposed, would move into conventional warfare and run the risk of global holocaust. However, three observations may beg to differ with that reasoning:

Israeli Prime Minister Menachem Begin (left) and Deputy Prime Minister Yigal Yadin (right) visit the U.S. 6th Fleet on the aircraft carrier *Eisenhower* anchored In Israel.

1. Russia apparently had rattled the nuclear hardware in order to accomplish conventional objectives during the Yom Kippur War.

2. A nuclear deterrent is meant to deter nuclear adventurism. Each party can assert decisively what it can deliver should one party initiate a conflagration. However, all pragmatic military thinking takes place one step down—just below the nuclear threshold. Here conventional clout dictates the terms and determines victors and vanquished. The Soviets anticipated a reaction in which the Middle East and the world would raise their hands and say, "Better we be red than all of us dead."

3. According to the prophetic Scriptures, initiating a conflagration is precisely what the Russian hordes will do when they decide to launch a frontal military assault on the Middle East. Their move is seen as a conventional intrusion.

All of the historical background we have examined supports what God told us thousands of years ago would happen.

A SHAKING IN THE LAND

The prophet Ezekiel's account of an eventual Middle East invasion from the north reads like a precise preview of the historical events and intents we have scanned. The only missing factor seems to involve the element of timing. When will it happen? Of course, we cannot say. What we can say is that historical events are consistently flowing in this direction.

A CLASH OF THE GODS

Interestingly, some of the nations joining the fray are familiar to people who read the Bible. For example, the countries include Persia, Ethiopia, and Libya. Bible prophecy expert Dr. Mark Hitchcock delineates the dimensions of the coalition assembled to move against Israel:

> Based on these identifications, Ezek 38–39 predicts an invasion of the land of Israel in the last days by a vast confederation of nations from north of the Black and Caspian Seas, extending down to modern Iran in the east, as far as modern Libya to the west, and down to Sudan in the south. Therefore, Russia will have at least five key allies: Turkey, Iran, Libya, Sudan, and the nations of Central Asia. Amazingly, all of these nations are Muslim nations

and Iran, Libya, and Sudan are three of Israel's most ardent opponents. Iran is one of the "axis of evil" nations that is trying desperately to attain nuclear weapons. Many of these nations are hotbeds of militant Islam and are either forming or strengthening their ties as these words are being written. This list of nations reads like the Who's Who of this week's newspaper. It does not require a very active imagination to envision these nations conspiring together to invade Israel in the near future.[4]

Two objectives will motivate the invaders:

1. **Greed.** "'I will go to a peaceful people, who dwell safely, all of them dwelling without walls, and having neither bars nor gates'—to take plunder and to take booty, to stretch out your hand against the waste places that are again inhabited, and against a people gathered from the nations, who have acquired livestock and goods, who dwell in the midst of the land" (Ezek. 38:11–12).

Although sacking a country that has made spectacular progress and accumulated great wealth and resources since its people returned home is an attractive inducement, it is only a secondary motivation.

2. **Hatred.** The main driving force behind the evil venture is an unequivocal hatred of Israel and its people. These countries share an obsession to finish what others could not: the annihilation of Jewry.

God tells us what will happen: "Then you will come from your place out of the far north, you and many peoples with you, all of them riding on horses, a great company and a mighty army. You will come up against My people Israel like a cloud, to cover the land" (vv. 15–16).

WHEN TO STRIKE?

The timing for this nefarious enterprise is familiar. It will be as it was on Yom Kippur in 1973, when the Israel Defense Forces were standing down and the nation was at worship or rest. Then the hordes of Gog will descend on a totally distracted people:

Thus says the Lord God: "On that day it shall come to pass that thoughts will arise in your mind, and you will make an evil plan: You will say, 'I will go up against a land of unwalled villages; I will go to a peaceful people, who dwell safely, all of them dwelling without walls, and having neither bars nor gates'" (vv. 10–11).

The situation begs a question: Why will Israel be under the illusion that it is at peace and that it is secure when surrounded by massive forces plotting its destruction?

Competent prophetic scholars place this interlude of security during the time when a covenant exists between Israel and the Antichrist, as described in Daniel 9:27:

> Then he shall confirm a covenant with many for one week [seven years]; but in the middle of the week he shall bring an end to sacrifice and offering. And on the wing of abominations shall be one who makes desolate, even until the consummation, which is determined, is poured out on the desolate.

The "he" is the Antichrist.

The scenario also implies that the invasion from the north will occur during the first three years of the seven-year Tribulation forecast in Scripture.

During times of distress and anxiety, when circumstances seem to overwhelm us, we often ask, "Where is God and why doesn't He do something?" The answer is that He is doing something; and in this situation, we have been given intriguing insight. For here we are, privy to seeing both sides of the coin: human intentions and God's purpose.

MY GOD, YOUR GOD

Nearly every war in history has involved more than mortal combatants, or at least the combatants have thought so. Nations take their gods to war with them; thus god is pitted against god. Clans, tribes, nations, and empires have asked their gods to help them win so that they could, in turn, place the garlands of their triumphs on their deities' altars. The process became an integral part not only of war, but of the pursuit of peace, as well.

Aggressors move against those they hope to vanquish with three inescapable ends in view: subjugation, humiliation, assimilation.

Subjugation introduces the sequence. The goal is to force the enemy to capitulate—peacefully, if possible, militarily if necessary.

Humiliation is the objective of phase two. The aim is to make the conquered feel inferior and utterly defeated. They must accept being subjects. The ancients accomplished this phase by insulting and carrying away the vanquished people's gods or implements of worship. In the process, they would defy these gods to do anything about the situation.

Babylon did this, as did Syria. Rome's periodic desecration of the Jewish Temple and sacred Mount Moriah also attest to this system. The sequence is as old as history. The victor basically says, "My god has defeated yours. Your god does not answer. You have been mastered."

Assimilation is the final objective. After the victor dispossesses its enemies of their political ideologies and religious systems, it convinces them to embrace the victor's system, including its god. Of course, religion is the most emotional and unifying factor involved in true assimilation. If genuine religious union can be established—victor and vanquished joining hands in worship at the same temple—then garrisoned troops can be sent home. Both the war and the victory have been won.

Such was not the case when Russian Communism came on the scene. Atheism became the official state dogma. In essence, the state became the god; and instead of trying to assimilate the people they conquered, the Soviets subjugated them as expendable pawns of the system.

Therefore Communism, like fascist Nazi Germany, became the definitive satanic device. It cast aside any pretense of lip service to a deity and blatantly declared war on almighty God. It is important to grasp the enormity of this phenomenon and all it implies. Communism set itself apart as the uncompromising foe of every nation whose people owned allegiance to any god, false or true.

Russia's goal was not to see nations join hands in worship but, rather, to raise the Kremlin as the final realization of the Marxist dream, the state supreme, the system triumphant. In this regard, Communism (and any other ideology like it) is different. It stands as a crowning manifestation of the evolution of satanically dominated political systems. To ideologies like this one, deposing Jehovah is the final atheistic stroke on the way to a new, humanistic Earth.

Consequently, it is natural for satanically inspired imperialists to spill the most noxious venom on the descendants of Jacob. The three greatest religions on Earth (Judaism, Christianity, and Islam) all sprang from Abraham's seed. Mastery over the Jewish people and their land would symbolize planting the banner of defiance of Jehovah on the totalitarian, anti-God summit.

THE FIRST ACT IN THE GRAND FINALE

What we're about to consider may seem somewhat enigmatic at first: It is Jehovah, not the Russians or their Islamic cohorts, who will initiate the move against Israel:

Thus says the Lord GOD "Behold, I am against you, O Gog, the prince of Rosh, Meshech, and Tubal. I will turn you around, put hooks into your jaws, and lead you out, with all your army, horses, and horsemen, all splendidly clothed, a great company with bucklers and shields, all of them handling swords. After many days you will be visited. In the latter years you will come into the land of those brought back from the sword and gathered from many people on the mountains of Israel, which had long been desolate; they were brought out of the nations, and now all of them dwell safely. You will ascend, coming like a storm, covering the land like a cloud, you and all your troops and many peoples with you" (Ezek. 38:3–4, 8–9).

God Himself stirs up in their minds what they passionately hold in their hearts: "Thus says the Lord GOD: 'On that day it shall come to pass that thoughts will arise in your mind, and you will make an evil plan: You will say, "I will go up against a land of unwalled villages; I will go to a peaceful people, who dwell safely, all of them dwelling without walls, and having neither bars nor gates""" (vv. 10–11).

What appears to be the march of Gog and his unstoppable masses against a defenseless few turns into an awesome display of God's pent-up wrath of judgment against His enemies and Israel's tormentors. What will transpire on Israel's mountains represents the beginning of the Lord's steps to settle the score against His enemies.

Next in line for divine judgment will be the Man of Sin (the Antichrist) and his legions. In the aftermath of this encounter, the Antichrist will break his covenant with Israel and proclaim himself God: He will oppose and exalt himself "above all that is called God or that is worshiped, so that he sits as God in the temple of God, showing himself that he is God" (2 Th. 2:4). The power behind the Antichrist, of course, is Satan himself—the archfiend who has motivated the evils assailing humanity since the Garden of Eden.

After fury rises in the face of God; after a great quake shakes the earth; after hailstones, fire, and brimstone devastate the invading host; and after the seven-year tasks of cleaning up, burying the dead, and burning the weapons are finished, Jehovah's perpetual archenemies will go down in defeat.

The Lord says, "I will magnify Myself and sanctify Myself, and I will be known in the eyes of many nations. Then they shall know that I am the LORD" (Ezek. 38:23).

YOUR KING IS COMING TO YOU.

———————

ZECHARIAH 9:9; MATTHEW 21:5

CHAPTER TEN

Trauma and Triumph

At this point we begin examining aspects of God's plan that are almost exclusively prophetic in nature. So I think it will be helpful to look back at the central features in God's program for His Chosen People.

Dispersion, preservation, restoration, and reconciliation. These four factors comprise God's program for Israel and can be plotted on the timeline along which the nation has moved through history. Before us lives a people divinely set apart to be a special testimony to the truth of Scripture. As we look into God's plan, we see two major elements: man at his worst and God in His faithfulness.

MAN AT HIS WORST

The way Gentiles have treated the Chosen People across the long centuries of Jewish suffering should forever dispel the fiction that human beings in their natural state are innately good and if left to their native proclivities will soar to divine heights. That simply is not true.

Israel is surrounded by millions of people who cry out daily for its annihilation. In addition, millions of Christians around the world are being persecuted, tortured, and murdered in horrific ways. Christian persecution is worse in the 21st century than at any other period in history. No moral evolution has surged in the human breast. People are as capable of unspeakable cruelty, suppression, evil, and selfishness today as they were thousands of years ago.

Therefore, we need only to look around and witness the rise of the barbarians around us. A somber example emerged in 2011 from the misnamed Arab Spring that introduced a period of blood-letting almost too terrifying to imagine.

THE ARAB SPRING

Today's travelers to Israel can stand before King Hezekiah's ancient wall and walk through the tunnel he ordered built in his attempt to save Jerusalem from the menacing army of Assyrian King Sennacherib (705–681 BC), who had pledged to destroy the city and ravage its people.

Though thousands of years have passed, nothing has changed. Islamic fanatics like Hamas, Hezbollah, Iran, and ISIS (the self-proclaimed Islamic State) have promised to finish what the Assyrians and other invaders could not. Proof that they're serious can be seen in the bomb shelters dotting Israel's landscape and the giant tunnels Hamas has built to kidnap, attack, and kill innocent Israelis.

The Arab Spring began with a small incident in Tunisia that quickly morphed into uprisings against Arab governments, initially in Egypt, Syria, Libya, and Yemen. What began as a liberation movement was soon commandeered by rabid Islamists (ISIS) whose crusade of barbaric slaughter and mayhem is unparalleled in the 21st century. Their stated aim: to create a global Islamic caliphate, depose existing world leaders, and establish Allah and Islam as supreme.

The scope of ISIS violence has demonstrated its intentions, with attacks in Australia, Algeria, Canada, United States, Saudi Arabia, France, Libya, Lebanon, Egypt, Denmark, Tunisia, Yemen, Afghanistan, Turkey, Kuwait, Bangladesh, and Indonesia.

Syria experienced a few weeks of hope in 2011. "Since then," wrote journalist Patrick Cockburn, "endless catastrophe, defined as a civil war by the UN since mid-2012. Up to 350,000 people have died, 4.4 million are refugees, swathes of the country are controlled by Isis, moderate rebels have been massacred, the Assad regime remains (partly) in place, and intervention by foreign powers—including Russia, Iran, the US, France and the UK—has not slowed the slaughter."[1]

A *Jerusalem Post* report explained ISIS' final objective in an article that quotes the "Al-Naba newsletter identified by the Jihad and Terrorism Threat Monitor of MEMRI (the Middle East Media Research Institute) and shared with *The Jerusalem Post*":

> However, it continues, Islamic State "rejects this 'international order,'" and its war against its enemies "has no boundaries other than those which Allah prescribed on the Muslims in their jihad to make the polytheists submit to Islam's rule—the entire world is an arena for its jihad; all the Muslims are potential soldiers in its army; and all polytheist combatants on earth, and the Jews among them, are legitimate targets for it.

> It continues, "Any threat its leaders [issue against] the Jews emanates from the [promise] from Allah that He will enable them to carry it out. As the [Islamic State of Iraq leader] Sheikh Abu Mus'ab al-Zarqawi said in the past, he and those that are with him fight in Iraq *while their eyes are on Jerusalem*"[2] (emphasis added).

Although the longevity of the Islamic State is in question, it has already made great strides in achieving its objective. This is true particularly in Europe, where militant Islamists have seeded their people among the masses of refugees fleeing the turmoil in the Middle East. Their objective is to turn Europe into an Islamic fiefdom.

Reports estimate that more than 1 million refugees entered Europe in 2015. In the first two months of 2016 alone, a reported 135,000 more came. And while the majority of immigrants come in peace, radicals do not. They have one thing on their minds: conquest in the name of Allah. We know this is true by the spike of terrorist attacks and the growing presence of "no-go" zones dominated by Muslim Sharia-law loyalists. A no-go zone is where a country's government exercises little or no sovereignty, police do not go in, and Muslim Sharia courts exist.

Andre Walker, a news correspondent covering the work of the British Parliament and prime minister, identified the problem facing Europe and, for that matter, the United States: "We tell ourselves nothing can be done about terrorism when we should be honest with ourselves: Terrorism is here to stay in Europe because we allowed it to continue. We have encouraged the problem by discouraging integration, as if you have no duty to act like a European when you move to Europe."[3]

CHRISTIANS BEWARE

The grand objective of global Islamist radicalism is not to assimilate into host countries but, rather, to eliminate the "infidels" (non-Muslims) and possess their lands. And while extremists fight "while their eyes are on Jerusalem," they also fight against the followers of Jesus. These butchers delight in posting online videos of themselves beheading Christians en masse, so everyone can see what they're doing in their quest to make the Middle East Christian-free.

It is a big mistake to underestimate the scope of radical Islam's reach. The persecution of Christians is growing exponentially. According to the U.S. State Department, Christians in more than 60 countries face government persecution and/or persecution from their own communities and family simply because they believe in Jesus Christ.

A report from The Center for American Progress says what is happening to Christians in the region [and elsewhere] indicates what type of society will emerge from the chaos: "If one of the most important religious groups in the world continues to be forced out of the Middle East, this bodes negatively for pluralism, tolerance and the ability of the region's people to live interlinked with the rest of the world."[4]

This is the crucial factor that opens the door to a Christless world—one condemned to chaos, without moral chart or compass, and moving quickly toward an inevitable and fatal apocalypse. The intensity of the animosity now trending toward violence and public alienation of believers in Christ should awaken us to the prophetic perspectives found only in God's Word.

Of course, hostility toward Israel, as well as toward true Christians, is evident to anyone who is realistic. Here is where human delusion and biblical reality part ways. Many people claim the monstrosities of human behavior revealed in the Bible repel them, and they scoff at the apocalyptic portions of Scripture. The fact is, people are more than capable of committing the horrendous acts described in Scripture. Centuries of history have demonstrated that fact over and over again. We should credit the Bible with what can always be said of it: It has always told it like it is—and how it will be. No wishful illusions, no sugar coating, no attempts to make people seem better than they are. The Bible shows us humanity as it is, pure and simple and in need of a heart transplant.

Through prophecy, God allows us to look into history before it takes place. And we must always bear in mind that Jehovah is never the perpetrator of human belligerence. People do that all on their own. We are fallen creatures, every single one of us, since the beginning of time. God is no more the author of anyone's evil actions than He was of the original fall in the Garden of Eden. He simply lets us see ourselves at our worst and, in so doing, allows us to anticipate the future and prepare for it.

GOD IN HIS FAITHFULNESS

Through all of the events recorded for us in Scripture shines one grand design: the reconciliation and establishment of Israel in the glory Jehovah promised through His prophetic Word. While we are allowed to see humanity at its worst, we are also afforded a spectacular preview of God's great purposes for His Chosen People.

We must bear in mind that we are involved in eternal processes. Our time-shaded perspective of history is like a speck of dust on a horizon that is as broad as eternity itself. From the divine point of view, we are moving through an orderly sequence of events that will bring us to the culmination God prepared in eternity past, where all things promised find fruition.

Two portions of Scripture delineate God's unalterable attitude toward the Jewish people. The first comes to us from the prophet Jeremiah: "They shall be My people and I will be their God; then I will give them one heart and one way, that they may fear Me forever, for the good of them and their children after them" (Jer. 32:38–39).

The second comes through Paul, the Pharisee-turned-apostle-of-Christ. It

The Dead Sea Scrolls on display at the Shrine of the Book Museum in Jerusalem.

illustrates the message of both the Old and New Testaments regarding Israel: "I say then, has God cast away His people? Certainly not! For I also am an Israelite, of the seed of Abraham, of the tribe of Benjamin. And so all Israel will be saved, as it is written: 'The Deliverer will come out of Zion, and He will turn away ungodliness from Jacob'" (Rom. 11:1, 26).

Fulfillment of God's program will come in three distinct phases: breaking the Gentile sword, revelation of the Messiah, and the reconciliation and establishment of Israel.

BREAKING THE GENTILE SWORD

Atheistic Communism, Islamist fanaticism, anti-Semitic fervor, and cultural God-hatred are but a few manifestations of persistent Gentile intransigence in the face of Jehovah's right to reign over the affairs of men. The entire flow of the history of Gentile world powers falls into a similar pattern. The prophet Daniel gave us a striking overview of the nations as they are seen from both human and divine perspectives.

On the human level, the successive world empires look like a colossal statue. King Nebuchadnezzar of Babylon dreamed of a "great image, whose splendor was excellent...and its form was awesome" (Dan. 2:31).

In his vision he saw the coming empires as gold, silver, bronze, and iron entities that joined to form a spectacular statue of a human image. The empires represented in the image were later identified as Babylon, Medo-Persia, Greece, and a Roman system that would have both ancient and modern counterparts.

To say the least, the statue was impressive—awe-inspiring even. So much so that Nebuchadnezzar built a huge replica of it in gold and placed it in the plain of Dura as a representation of his royal attributes. He required his subjects to bow down and worship the image or die. This order led to the famous confrontation between the king and the three Hebrew young men who refused to bow to it. The Hebrews were thrown into a fiery furnace yet came out unscathed (chap. 3).

The episode reflects the folly recurrent in Gentile history: seeing the state—both the system and its leaders—as worthy of veneration, while displacing the worship of Jehovah. The empire stands in God's place and demands total loyalty. Often this allegiance takes the form of worshiping gods the nations have created themselves.

The point is, whether men bow to an emperor, a man-made god, or a humanistic philosophy, the result is the same: God is displaced in people's hearts, and they are displaced in God's program.

Even in the world's parade of great images that humankind persistently reveres, the divine finger pens the final word. God says there will not be four empires, but five:

> And in the days of these kings the God of heaven will set up a kingdom which shall never be destroyed; and the kingdom shall not be left to other people; it shall break in pieces and consume all these kingdoms, and it shall stand forever (2:44).

With this declaration, Jehovah injected the concept of a coming divine Kingdom through which He will order affairs on the scene of human events. God gave His prophet Daniel heaven's evaluation of what the king of Babylon saw: "Daniel spoke, saying, 'I saw in my vision by night, and behold, the four winds of heaven were stirring up the Great Sea. And four great beasts came up from the sea, each different from the other'" (7:2–3).

From heaven's viewpoint, these same empires look like voracious animals, preying on one another—stalking, crushing, and devouring those who are weaker than they. The inflexible rule of force dominates all the characteristics of these imperial marauders. And so it has been; the strong survive while the weak are consumed and subjugated.

Within this scheme of things, only two considerations seem valid: either have the strength to dominate or at least fend off the enemy, or possess the will to use force when national interests are at stake. Any other approach to the might-is-right posture of world systems will likely fail.

Once again, at the very heart of the revelation, God lays bare His eventual response to humanity's cherished alternatives to His sovereign rule:

> I watched till thrones were put in place, and the Ancient of Days was seated; His garment was white as snow, and the hair of His head was like pure wool. His throne was a fiery flame, its wheels a burning fire. I was watching in the night visions, and behold, One like the Son of Man, coming with the clouds of heaven! He came to the Ancient of Days, and they brought Him near before Him. Then to Him was given dominion and glory and a kingdom, that all peoples, nations, and languages should serve Him. His dominion is an everlasting dominion, which shall not pass away, and His kingdom the one which shall not be destroyed (7:9, 13–14).

The Bible clearly teaches that before the Messiah's Kingdom is established, the Gentile powers will finally and emphatically be broken.

KINGS' ROW

Scripture gives us a fascinating preview of the national alliances that will hold sway in the end-times—the latter phases of this segment of history. These alliances will congregate under specific leaders:

The King of the North

Daniel used the appellation "king of the North" (11:40) to describe the leader of the region now occupied by Russia and its confederacy. We've already seen that the nations joining Russia are from the north, Europe, the Middle East, and Africa (Ezek. 38—39). They will follow their leader into resounding defeat.

The King of the South

Daniel also said the king of the South will be associated with the invasion of Israel (Dan. 11:40). Apparently, this king initially allies himself with the king of the north, only to be betrayed and overrun. Historically, this leader has been identified as the ruler of Egypt. He will consort with and represent the North African and Arab states that join the southern confederacy. Prophetic scholars viewed with interest the efforts of Egypt's late president, Anwar Sadat, to establish a himself as the dominant leader in the Arab world.

The Kings of the East

Revelation 16:12 tells of a coalition of kings from beyond the Euphrates River who will be involved in the final struggles. These representatives are thought to be the powers of the Far East. Revelation 9:16 sets the number of this invading horde at 200 million troops. Interestingly, The People's Republic of China, run by the Communists, has claimed it can field a land army approximating these figures. Furthermore, China is building a massive military arsenal capable of dominating the Far East and becoming a major force in international affairs.

The Western Leader

The most sinister of all of these end-times personalities will be the leader of the Western nations. Based on Daniel 7 and other texts, major prophetic scholars believe he will lead a form of the revived Roman system—a confederation of states within the boundaries of the old Roman Empire. Some believe the land mass may even exceed that of ancient Rome.

Scripture refers to him by various names; the Beast, the Man of Sin, and the Willful King are but three of the designations. The most prominent title ascribed to him is the Antichrist. It is perhaps the description most consistent with his overall character for he will enter the Temple in Jerusalem, place an image there, declare himself to be God, and demand universal worship (2 Th. 2:4).

In these alliances we see the final form of Gentile powers that will dominate in the last days. It is sobering to note that they are, at this moment, roughly aligned in the positions outlined in the Bible.

A GATHERING IN THE LAND

Both Old and New Testaments teach that the nations in the Middle East will assemble for one climactic end-times confrontation at Megiddo (Zech. 12; Rev. 16:16). It will be more massive than anything humankind has never witnessed. Jeremiah spoke of it as "the time of Jacob's trouble" (Jer. 30:7). Christ referred to it as a time of "great tribulation, such as has not been since the beginning of the world until this time, no, nor ever shall be" (Mt. 24:21).

The Scriptures universally agree that, at this time, the nations of the world will come together to do battle, with Israel again in the middle of the apocalyptic conflict. The prophet Joel put it this way:

> Proclaim this among the nations: "Prepare for war! Wake up the mighty men, let all the men of war draw near, let them come up. Beat your plowshares into swords and your pruning hooks into spears; let the weak say, 'I am strong.'" Assemble and come, all you nations, and gather together all around. Cause Your mighty ones to go down there, O LORD (Joel 3:9–11).

Zechariah also took up the theme:

"Behold, I will make Jerusalem a cup of drunkenness to all the surrounding peoples, when they lay siege against Judah and Jerusalem. And it shall happen in that day that I will make Jerusalem a very heavy stone for all peoples; all who would heave it away will surely be cut in pieces, though all nations of the earth are gathered against it." Behold, the day of the LORD is coming, and your spoil will be divided in your midst. For I will gather all the nations to battle against Jerusalem; the city shall be taken, the houses rifled, and the women ravished. Half of the city shall go into captivity, but the remnant of the people shall not be cut off from the city (Zech. 12:2–3; 14:1–2).

John the apostle voiced agreement through his description:

For they are spirits of demons, performing signs, which go out to the kings of the earth and of the whole world, to gather them to the battle of that great day of God Almighty. And they gathered them together to the place called in Hebrew, Armageddon (Rev. 16:14, 16).

Menacing forces will descend on Israel to initiate a campaign that will, for a brief time, run the length and breadth of the land. The intensity of this struggle, which the prophet Daniel and the apostle John described so vividly, will be unmatched in history. It will affect the entire world. No one will escape

Meggido

it. That's why Jesus said, "Unless those days were shortened, no flesh would be saved; but for the elect's sake those days will be shortened" (Mt. 24:22).

Unparalleled tribulation will afflict the world—the result of satanically emboldened men on the one hand, and Jehovah's judgment on the other. While nations clamor and maneuver to dominate international affairs, God moves in with cataclysmic judgments on humankind. A succession of divinely sent calamities will buffet Earth's entire population. Yet, rather than repent and acknowledge God, people will persist in defying Him: "And men were scorched with great heat, and they blasphemed the name of God who has power over these plagues; and they did not repent and give Him glory" (Rev. 16:9).

These frightful days will be marked by suffering, warfare, and defiance of the Almighty. Pestilence, famine, and persecution will torment the earth, and one half of the world's population will perish. Once again, Israel will be the primary target of Gentile hatred. The heel of oppression will fall heavily on the Jewish people. And it also will fall heavily on anyone who dares to own allegiance to Jesus Christ. The blood of those who acknowledge Christ as Savior will whet the tyrant's sword.

The Middle East will erupt into warfare. And the Antichrist, who earlier had stood with Israel, will turn viciously on the Jewish people and become worse than the sinister, evil creature typified by the ancient Hellenistic ruler Antiochus Epiphanes, who infamously desecrated the Temple in Jerusalem in the second century BC. Jesus called the Antichrist's desecration of the future third Temple the "'abomination of desolation,' spoken of by Daniel the prophet" (Mk. 13:14; cf. Dan. 12:11). It is viewed as the ultimate act of humanity's rebellious, anti-God pilgrimage on this planet (2 Th. 2:4; Rev. 13).

So it is that the world will gather for its Armageddon. All historical byways have directed its pathway steadily toward this battle. Gentile nations will stand poised to do what they've always wanted to do: obliterate Israel and depose Jehovah forever. As Jewry teeters on the brink of annihilation, it will turn its eyes heavenward and behold its glorious Messiah.

REVELATION OF THE MESSIAH

Earlier I spoke of a Jewish historian who pointed out that in times of great national distress, Jewish people long for their homeland and for the coming of their Messiah. This observation coincides with the sequence of events outlined in both Old and New Testaments. When Scripture mentions the final trauma, it inevitably follows up with a passage depicting the coming triumph of the Messiah. Here are some examples:

JOEL'S WORD

Proclaim this among the nations: "Prepare for war! Wake up the mighty men, let all the men of war draw near, let them come up. Beat your plowshares into swords and your pruning hooks into spears. Let the weak say, 'I am strong.' Assemble and come, all you nations, and gather together all around. Cause Your mighty ones to go down there, O Lord (Joel 3:9–11).

These verses tell the nations to gather for war. Yet the next few verses take up the theme of the judgment that will fall on them as a result of this gathering:

The Lord also will roar from Zion, and utter His voice from Jerusalem; the heavens and earth will shake; but the Lord will be a shelter for His people, and the strength of the children of Israel (v. 16).

Restoration and the reign of the Messiah and His people fill out the narrative.

ZECHARIAH'S COMMENT

Zechariah further clarified the matter with his detailed chronicle of events surrounding the Messiah's intervention:

Behold, the day of the Lord is coming, and your spoil will be divided in your midst. For I will gather all the nations to battle against Jerusalem. Then the Lord will go forth and fight against those nations, as He fights in the day of battle. And in that day His feet will stand on the Mount of Olives, which faces Jerusalem on the east....Thus the Lord my God will come, and all the saints with You (Zech. 14:1-2, 3-5).

Then the inspired writer expounded on the establishment and quality of the reigning Messiah's Kingdom-rule. Central to the passage are these words: And the Lord shall be King over all the earth. In that day it shall be—'The Lord is one,' and His name one (v. 9).

JESUS' CONFIRMATION

Jesus followed the sequence. He described the rigors of the Tribulation that will precede His return to Earth, and then said,

Immediately after the tribulation of those days the sun will be darkened, and the moon will not give its light; the stars will fall from heaven, and the powers of the heavens will be shaken. Then the sign of the Son of Man will appear in heaven, and then all the tribes of the earth will mourn, and they will see the Son of Man coming on the clouds of heaven with power and great glory (Mt. 24:29–30).

He went on to describe the establishment of the Messianic reign, then said, "And He will send His angels with a great sound of a trumpet, and they will gather together His elect from the four winds, from one end of heaven to the other" (v. 31).

PAUL'S WITNESS

Paul picked up the same refrain in his message to the Thessalonian church. Responding to a question the Thessalonians had about the "day of the Lord," he talked about the appearance and foul work of the Man of Sin (the Antichrist, 2 Th. 2:3), whom he said will be revealed after the church is raptured and the Holy Spirit's restraint is withdrawn. This will be the time of Jacob's trouble (the Tribulation, Jer. 30:7).

Paul assured the Thessalonians, "And then the lawless one will be revealed, whom the Lord will consume with the breath of His mouth and destroy with the brightness of His coming" (2 Th. 2:8).

In conjunction with this thought, Paul referred to Israel's total restoration following the Lord's return when he wrote his epistle to the church in Rome (Rom. 11: 25–27).

JOHN'S PERSPECTIVE

After the apostle John described the dark days of the Tribulation, with its thunderous judgments, manic tyrants, and suffering saints, he lit the sky with an awesome description of the coming of the Messiah to set things right:

Now I saw heaven opened, and behold, a white horse. And He who sat on him was called Faithful and True, and in righteousness He judges and makes war. His eyes were like a flame of fire, and on His head were many crowns. He had a name written that no one knew except Himself. He was clothed with a robe dipped in blood, and His name is called The Word of God. And the armies in heaven, clothed in fine linen, white and clean, followed Him on white horses. Now out of His mouth goes a sharp sword, that with it He should strike the nations. And He Himself will rule them with a rod of iron. He Himself treads the winepress of the fierceness and wrath of Almighty God.

And He has on His robe and on His thigh a name written: KING OF KINGS AND LORD OF LORDS (Rev. 19:11–16).

John gave us sublime words about the Kingdom Age under the Messiah's sovereignty. Still the sequence holds true—tribulation, revelation, and restoration.

We need to understand that the Messiah's appearance will not be the result of anything people do to create conditions they think will be conducive to the divine King's entrance. No religious, political, or philosophical system will triumph to the point of preparing the way for the Messiah. In fact, the exact opposite will be true. Spiritual, moral, and political conditions will be abysmal. They will deteriorate until the world is brought to the brink of the global conflagration so long feared by responsible members of the world community.

This is what the Bible has always said, even through times of euphoric optimism when people looked to science, education, and technology to usher in a golden age. From our vantage point, we have a more realistic view of the calamities that await Adam's posterity.

In scanning the whole of the Bible on the subject, there can be no doubt that the Messiah is the One who will make a spectacular personal appearance in the future. Attempts to assign the Messianic passages to the nation of Israel or a phantom ideal or anything else simply does not square with the clear message of the Holy Scriptures. Nothing and no one will meet the universal human need that the King of glory alone can satisfy.

For people who believe the Bible, both Jews and Gentiles, the issue settles on the question, "Who is the Messiah?" Christians say He is Jesus; Jewish people say He is not. His identity is the taproot of the division between Christians and Jews who acknowledge the authority of Scripture. On the surface, this statement may seem extremely simplistic. The truth, however, is that this all-important issue is one that is all too often obscured in the heat of peripheral questions. It is the fundamental consideration that all human beings everywhere must honestly face. Who is the Messiah? And who is Jesus?

THE MESSIAH'S IDENTITY

Who is the King of Israel? How can we recognize Him? The answers to these questions are crucial to our personal relationship to God. The Old Testament Messianic Scriptures give us two precise views of the work of the predicted Deliverer: He will be both sufferer and sovereign.

In trying to reconcile how the Messiah could be both, four main interpretations have arisen over the years:

1. There are two Messiahs: one who will suffer and one who will reign.

2. The sufferer will not be a personality but, rather, the nation of Israel in its persecutions.

3. Choose the most desirable manifestation and reject the other.

4. There is one Messiah, with two appearances on Earth.

A COMPOSITE OF THE MESSIAH AS SUFFERER

The keynote comes from God through the prophet Zechariah concerning the coming King:

> Rejoice greatly, O daughter of Zion! Shout, O daughter of Jerusalem! Behold, your King is coming to you; He is just and having salvation, lowly and riding on a donkey, a colt, the foal of a donkey (Zech. 9:9).

Three notes ring out here. The King comes. He comes in humility. He brings salvation. Advent, humility, salvation. Around these distinct considerations God draws His purposes in the Messiah's ministry of suffering. This King would be betrayed into the hands of His oppressors: "Even my own familiar friend in whom I trusted, who ate my bread, has lifted up his heel against me" (Ps. 41:9).

Psalm 22, given to King David by God, is the first in the great trilogy that portrays the full-orbed ministry of the Messiah as suffering Savior, ministering Shepherd, and reigning Monarch. His suffering is described in startling detail:

> My God, My God, why have You forsaken Me? Why are you so far from helping Me, and from the words of My groaning? But I am a worm, and no man; a reproach of men, and despised by the people. All those who see Me ridicule Me; they shoot out the lip, they shake the head, saying, "He trusted in the LORD, let Him rescue Him; let Him deliver Him, since He delights in Him!" I am poured out like water, and all My bones are out of joint; My heart is like wax; it has melted within Me. My strength is dried up like a potsherd, and My tongue clings to My jaws; You have brought Me to the dust of death. For dogs have surrounded Me; the congregation of the wicked has enclosed Me. They pierced My hands and My feet; they divide My garments among them, and for My clothing they cast lots (vv. 1, 6–8, 14–16, 18).

The psalm abruptly turns from suffering and death to resurrection and victory for the Sufferer and the sons of Jacob:

> I will declare Your name to My brethren; in the midst of the assembly I will praise You. You who fear the LORD, praise Him! All you descendants of Jacob, glorify Him, and fear Him, all you offspring of Israel! For He has not despised nor abhorred the affliction of the afflicted; nor has He hidden His face from Him; but when He cried to Him, He heard (vv. 22–24)

Isaiah joined David to complete the portrait.

> He is despised and rejected by men, a Man of sorrows and acquainted with grief. And we hid, as it were, our faces from Him; He was despised, and we did not esteem Him. Surely He has borne our griefs and carried our sorrows; yet we esteemed Him stricken, smitten by God, and afflicted. But He was wounded for our transgressions, He was bruised for our iniquities; the chastisement for our peace was upon Him, and by His stripes we are healed. All we like sheep have gone astray; we have turned, every one, to his own way; and theLORD has laid on Him the iniquity of us all. He was oppressed and He was afflicted, yet He opened not His mouth; He was led as a lamb to the slaughter, and as a sheep before its shearers is silent, so He opened not His mouth. He was taken from prison and from judgment, and who will declare His generation? For He was cut off from the land of the living; for the transgressions of My people He was stricken. Yet it pleased the LORD to bruise Him; He has put Him to grief. When You make His soul an offering for sin, He shall see His seed, He shall prolong His days, and the pleasure of the LORD shall prosper in His hand. He shall see the labor of His soul, and be satisfied. By His knowledge My righteous Servant shall justify many, for He shall bear their iniquities (Isa. 53:3–8, 10–11).

As did David, Isaiah moved from the trauma of suffering to the glories of the Messiah's triumph:

> Therefore I will divide Him a portion with the great, and He shall divide the spoil with the strong, because He poured out His soul unto death, and He was numbered with the transgressors, and He bore the sin of many, and made intercession for the transgressors (v. 12).

On the basis of this justification, Israel is instructed to

> Break forth into singing, and cry aloud....Enlarge the place of your tent....

Your descendants will inherit the nations....Do not fear...For your Maker is your husband, The Lord of hosts is His name; and your Redeemer is the Holy One of Israel; He is called the God of the whole earth (54:1–5).

Again, sequentially, the Messiah's sovereign reign follows His suffering. And there is an excellent reason for this divine progression.

FIT SUBJECTS FOR THE KING

The Kingdom of God, we know, will have a fit King. There can be no true Kingdom until the hearts of the Messiah's subjects are in one accord with Jehovah. This can only be fully accomplished by a program of propitiatory reconciliation, which is beyond our human ability to accomplish. In other words, if we are to be saved—cleansed of sin and made suitable to stand before a holy and righteous God—it will be God who will have to cleanse us.

God is holy, just, and righteous. We are sinners. Israel's entire Levitical system of worship reflected this truth. After earnest Israelites had done their best to abide by the stern strictures of the laws and commandments, they still came with their sacrifices to petition God for mercy. Why?

On the one hand, they were obeying God's command to do so. Yet they also recognized that, for all of their efforts, they were still failures. They were still sinners. If you were an Israelite who had genuine faith in God and were keenly aware of your sin, you could have brought sacrifice after sacrifice over and over and over again. The sacrifice was God's answer to man's need, but it was only a temporary solution. It covered sin; it did not remove it.

In the Messiah's suffering, Jehovah forever met the demands of divine justice. The Messiah, who was fully God and fully human, became the final sacrifice for sin—the only sacrifice capable of removing sin, rather than merely covering it. Once and for all, God, in His incomparable love, provided for man's need. No mere human being could have satisfied God's requirements because all people are sinners. As King Solomon said, "There is not a just man on earth who does good and does not sin" (Eccl. 7:20).

Jehovah has always demanded that every sacrifice brought to Him be perfect. That is why it was imperative that the Messiah be more than a mere human. He could not be a sinner, or His suffering would have been in vain. He had to be God Himself—pure, holy, perfect. The prophet Micah confirmed the one born in Bethlehem would be divine when he said His "goings forth are from of old, from everlasting" (Mic. 5:2). Only God's "goings forth" can be from everlasting.

In the Messiah's suffering, everything that smoldering altars and ministering priests were doing to help people atone for sin was finally delivered. "He was bruised for our iniquities" (Isa. 53:5) that through His suffering we could be healed. "And the LORD has laid on Him the iniquity of us all" (v. 6). If we accept this truth by faith, God ascribes to us the Messiah's righteousness, and He removes our sin (Phil. 3:9).

Only one man in all of history has had the proper credentials to be the suffering Messiah. He was a Jew; a Jew who longed for the redemption of Israel as no one else ever had; a Jew who said and did what no human being ever approached in word or deed; a Jew who still towers above all religious teachers, military men, politicians, philosophers, and educators; a Jew who, when left off the list of the "Ten Greatest Men in History" compiled by a world figure, would receive the supreme accolade: "Oh, I did not include Jesus Christ because He is in a class by Himself. He is incomparable." And because Jesus is God, He had the power to rise from the dead.

Jesus Christ was a Jew who predicted His sacrificial death for sinful humanity and then willingly allowed Himself to be killed. Jesus Christ was a Jew who said He would triumph over death and vacate a tomb; and He did. Jesus Christ was a Jew who offered Himself as the Savior of all who will receive Him, both Jewish and Gentile, and has demonstrated over the centuries in the lives of believers that He is everything He ever claimed to be. Jesus Christ was a Jew who predicted what the world will ultimately come to, and we are witnessing the truth of His words. Jesus Christ was a Jew who promised to return to His Chosen People as a reconciling and reigning Messiah, and He soon shall. Jesus Christ was a Jew who declared that His Kingdom will one day cover the earth as the waters cover the sea and that it will be filled with justice, righteousness, and peace—and we yearn for that day!

WHY DIDN'T ISRAEL'S LEADERSHIP ACCEPT HIM?

Israel's leadership probably rejected Jesus for the same reasons most people today reject Him, namely, pride, power, and preference.

Jesus told the leaders they would have to acknowledge being in need of a redeemer, just like the rest of us. The religious power brokers could not abide such a thing. It was simply more than their religious pride could take. To reduce proud Pharisees or Sadducee Temple dignitaries to ordinary people who needed to be saved was unthinkable to them. Tell the same thing today to people who think themselves religious and watch their reactions. The result will likely be the same.

Jesus taught that power with God was to be found in serving and ministering, not in lording it over the masses. He spoke of bearing burdens and becoming servants, taking the lowly place and being deferential in the way we treat others. Religious leaders reacted negatively to those ideas. The truth is, they almost always do.

This was not a Jewish problem but a human one. Had Christ promised a system that would have delivered power into their hands, they no doubt would have been happy to acknowledge Him. But as history has demonstrated, religious power, untempered by the humility of Christ, can become an instrument of oppression. Of all people on Earth, the Jewish people have witnessed this fact in the persecution brought on them by religious Gentiles.

Finally, given a choice between having a sufferer or a triumphant King, they opted for what they preferred—someone who would handle the Roman tyrant. They had had enough suffering and humiliation. They wanted to hear promises of grandeur and glory. Even Christ's disciples were not immune to this desire. They persistently pressed Jesus for the immediate establishment of the Kingdom and were stunned when He predicted His death and suffering at the hands of their enemies. Actually, the disciples were seeing only what they chose to see in the prophetic Scriptures.

I am not implying that everyone in the religious systems of Jesus' day was corrupt. This certainly was not the case. Many were true worshipers of Jehovah. However, as is often true, the less spiritual had labored successfully to grasp the reins of power.

Christ was so nonpartisan religiously and politically that, in the end, all parties would conspire to destroy Him. His consistent refusal to manipulate or be manipulated was beyond the ken of self-serving interest groups. The rule of God was His obsession; their success was theirs.

RECONCILIATION AND ESTABLISHMENT OF ISRAEL

No more glorious strain runs through Scripture than the revelation of the full establishment of the Messiah's Kingdom on Earth. Zechariah prophesied of the beginning of this fulfilling period: "And I [God] will pour on the house of David and on the inhabitants of Jerusalem the Spirit of grace and supplication; then they will look on Me whom they pierced. Yes, they will mourn for Him as one mourns for his only son, and grieve for Him as one grieves for a firstborn" (Zech. 12:10).

The mourning of embattled Israel will be answered by the appearance of the once "pierced" Messiah-Savior: "And in that day His feet will stand on the Mount of Olives, which faces Jerusalem on the east. And the Mount of Olives shall be split in two, from east to west, making a very large valley;...Thus the LORD my God will come, and all the saints with You" (14:4–5).

Joel identified the great valley that will be opened at the Messiah's return as

Early morning view of the Mount of Olives from the Zion Gate in the Old City of Jerusalem.

the place where the nations will be brought for judgment:

> I will also gather all nations, and bring them down to the Valley of Jehoshaphat;
> and I will enter into judgment with them there on account of My people, My
> heritage Israel, whom they have scattered among the nations; they have also
> divided up My land. They have cast lots for My people, have given a boy as
> payment for a harlot, and sold a girl for wine, that they may drink (Joel 3:2–3).

If you stand on the Mount of Olives and look across the Kidron Valley
toward the walls of the Old City, you can see a mute witness of the major religions' affirmation of faith in these words. Muslims, Christians, and Jews have
all established cemeteries there in anticipation of a future judgment.

THE LEAST OF THESE MY BRETHREN

Jesus Christ made an arresting declaration in His statement about this event:

> When the Son of Man comes in His glory, and all the holy angels with Him,
> then He will sit on the throne of His glory. All the nations will be gathered
> before Him, and He will separate them one from another, as a shepherd

divides his sheep from the goats. Then the King will say to those on His right hand, "Come, you blessed of My Father, inherit the kingdom prepared for you from the foundation of the world: for I was hungry and you gave Me food; I was thirsty and you gave Me drink; I was a stranger and you took Me in; I was naked and you clothed Me; I was sick and you visited Me; I was in prison and you came to Me" (Mt. 25:31–32, 34–36).

Jesus said the righteous will ask, "Lord, when did we see You hungry and feed You, or thirsty...a stranger...sick, or in prison?" (vv. 37–39). The King will reply, "Assuredly, I say to you, inasmuch as you did it to one of the least of these My brethren, you did it to Me" (v. 40).

Who are the "least of these My brethren"? There is no doubt, they are the chosen seed of Abraham—Israel.

Jesus echoed Joel's words that the basis for judging the Gentile nations before the Kingdom begins will be "on account of My people, My heritage Israel, whom they have scattered among the nations; they have also divided up My land" (Joel 3:2).

Jehovah's words to Abraham, therefore, ring clearer still: "I will bless those who bless you, and I will curse him who curses you" (Gen. 12:3). The Scriptures, Old Testament and New, tell us that whoever raises a hand against the Jewish people, even through the long night of their Dispersion, raises a hand against God and can expect to be fully requited for their arrogance. So the anguished Jewish cry of the centuries is answered. Justice will be served. Our God has assured us of it.

After God judges the nations in the Valley of Jehoshaphat (Joel 3:2, 12), "the LORD shall be King over all the earth. In that day it shall be—'The LORD is one, and His name one" (Zech. 14:9).

Thus will be ushered in the age when all of the biblical promises of Israel's full restoration and reestablishment will be fully realized. It will be the day of the final Aliyah: The Ascenders will have reached the summit.

RECONCILIATION

Jeremiah anticipated this day when he said,

But this is the covenant that I will make with the house of Israel after those days, says the LORD: I will put My law in their minds, and write it on their hearts; and I will be their God, and they shall be My people. No more shall every man teach his neighbor, and every man his brother, saying, "Know theLORD" for they all shall know Me, from the least of them to the greatest of them, says the LORD. For I will forgive their iniquity, and their sin I will remember no more (Jer. 31:33–34).

This is what Paul had in mind when he wrote, "all Israel will be saved" (Rom. 11:26). All of the Jewish people at that time will know the Lord. The nation will become a theocracy in the truest sense of the term. Redeemed Jews and Gentiles will unite under the banner of the reigning Messiah-Savior. Ancient animosities will be put away forever, and a glorious spiritual union will finally exist.

REGATHERING

Moses, Isaiah, Ezekiel, and Jeremiah joined the chorus of prophetic heralds who spoke confidently of the regathering and full restoration of the scattered nation of Israel. This illustrious quartet offered superb harmony concerning the certainty of the final return.

Moses: "The LORD your God will bring you back from captivity, and have compassion on you, and gather you again from all the nations where the LORD your God has scattered you" (Dt. 30:3).

Isaiah: "Fear not, for I am with you; I will bring your descendants from the east, and gather you from the west; I will say to the north, 'Give them up!' and to the south, 'Do not keep them back!' Bring My sons from afar, and My daughters from the ends of the earth" (Isa. 43:5–6).

Jeremiah: "'Behold, I will send for many fishermen,' says the LORD, 'and they shall fish them; and afterward I will send for many hunters, and they shall hunt them from every mountain and every hill, and out of the holes of the rocks'" (Jer. 16:16).

Ezekiel: "Therefore thus says the Lord GOD: 'Now I will bring back the captives of Jacob, and have mercy on the whole house of Israel; and I will be jealous for My holy name'" (Ezek. 39:25).

Today Zionists, Jews, and many Christians recognize the validity of the Jewish people's right to a national homeland in the Middle East. In this yet future day, the full scope of that right will be fully realized.

REESTABLISHMENT

The Messiah's throne will be established in an Israel that will occupy the expansive geographical area that God promised to the patriarch Abraham. All current territorial arguments will be irrelevant when the King announces Israel's boundaries.

Jerusalem will be the capital of the world, the center of all religious and political activity. One of the most expressive statements regarding this time comes from the prophet Zechariah:

"Yes, many peoples and strong nations shall come to seek the LORD of hosts in Jerusalem, and to pray before the LORD." Thus says the LORD of hosts: "In those days ten men from every language of the nations shall grasp the sleeve of a Jewish man, saying, 'Let us go with you, for we have heard that God is with you'" (Zech. 8:22–23).

Everyone will join in homage to God at the magnificent Temple described in Ezekiel 40—44, where memorial worship to the Messiah's sacrificial ministry will be observed. The sheer splendor of this age, as described by the prophets, is thoroughly captivating. It will be marked by peace, equity, productivity, and righteousness. Isaiah summed it all up in this classic and beautiful description of the quality and extent of the Messianic Kingdom: "They shall not hurt nor destroy in all My holy mountain, for the earth shall be full of the knowledge of the LORD as the waters cover the sea" (Isa. 11:9).

Of course, central to everything will be the King Himself. All processes will flow around His supreme presence. God, in the person of the Messiah, will dwell in the midst of His people. Little can be said to add anything to the weight of this momentous revelation. Let Zechariah say it for us:

And the LORD shall be King over all the earth. In that day it shall be—"The LORD is one," and His name one. And it shall come to pass that everyone who is left of all the nations which came against Jerusalem shall go up from year to year to worship the King, the LORD of hosts, and to keep the Feast of Tabernacles (Zech. 14:9, 16).

And all these wonderful things are just the beginning. Everything we have considered that will take place during the Millennial Age of the Messiah's reign is but a transcending prelude to the eternal glories God has prepared for His people.

EPILOGUE

THE POEMS

Of all the instruments of communication available to us, poetry occupies a unique position. It emanates from a heart sparked by passion, rather than from information gathered by accumulating facts, figures, and commentary.

The huge amassing of poetry and songs that stream through the pages of Scripture overflow with deep, personal emotion. It is of no little consequence that Israel's greatest king, David—a warrior, sovereign, and deliverer of the nation—is remembered as "the sweet psalmist of Israel" (2 Sam. 23:1).

When great historical events, such as the birth of the modern State of Israel in 1948, captivate a people and alter the course of world history, an irrepressible, spontaneous outpouring of emotion takes place.

In the poems included in this book, I've attempted to capture the sense of overwhelming awe and depth of heart that a long-displaced people felt when they witnessed the preservation and restoration of their universal dream.

The Jerusalem poems—*Jerusalem, The Holy City,* and *The Wailing Wall*—were written in the 1970s, when I was doing research in Israel for the first edition of *It Is No Dream.* I interviewed many Israeli military officials, political leaders, soldiers, archaeologists, historians, early pioneer settlers, and people who had made it safely to the Jewish homeland after enduring the horrifying Holocaust.

From those conversations, I discovered a universal cord. It was one that could not be captured by communicating details of great battles won against insurmountable odds or by enumerating the international political transactions confirming the Jewish people's right to the land of their fathers.

This cord was better felt than articulated. An indefinable something came over these people as they spoke of the moments when something eternal seemed to reach out to embrace them.

Well-known Israeli photographer David Rubinger captured that indefinable something in his famous portrait of the three young paratroopers gazing up at the great stones of the Western Wall for the first time when Israel took the Old City in 1967. Seasoned military men and weathered Israeli officials found themselves speechless. When Israel's Chief Rabbi Shlomo Goren sounded the shofar at the Wall, it not only declared the unification of Jerusalem but also beckoned the Jews of the Diaspora to come home.

Hopefully, some semblance of that unique sentiment made its way into the

Jerusalem poems, which were so well received in Israel and abroad. I received many encouraging letters about them. Among them were those from Jerusalem's mayor at the time, Teddy Kollek: "I found each one sensitive and moving." Then-Prime Minister Golda Meir referred to them as "the lovely poems" and expressed gratitude that they were so widely published. The minister of information at the Israeli embassy in Washington wrote that, on receiving "the beautiful poems . . . I am forwarding them to our Foreign Office in Israel, so they too may enjoy them." Another official said he had placed the poem *The Jew* under glass on his desk as a constant reminder of the past and present wonder of the Jewish return to Israel.

I've included these poems in the hope that, in the same intangible way, you might share in the experience felt by these Israelis, other Jewish people around the world, and Christian lovers of the Jewish people.

For Christians who treasure Israel and its people, there exists a bond of sorts—an empathy with Jewish emotions. I saw it many times when followers of Jesus wept freely upon seeing the open door at the Garden Tomb for the first time. I also witnessed it while in the Church of the Nativity and in the small caves in the shepherds' fields near Bethlehem.

Lovers of Jesus and Israel burst into spontaneous waves of songs and hymns—unannounced, unequalled in enthusiasm, and with no need of a director to lead them. The inspiration flowed from what happened outside the city's walls more than 2,000 years ago, when the greatest of spiritual battles was fought and won on a nearby hill called Calvary.

For Israel, returning to the land in 1948 was a beginning that gave hope for the full acquisition of the dream of one day living in peace on the hills of Zion and Jerusalem. Thus, when the words *Next year in Jerusalem* are intoned at the close of Passover seders the world over, they represent so much more than a recitation born in antiquity. They express a vibrant aspiration that never has left the hearts of the Jewish exiles.

THE LAND

It has been said of King David that he possessed three loves: his God, his people, and his land.

Every time I peered through the window of one of those huge jetliners as it dipped a wing and swung over the Israeli coastline toward Ben Gurion Airport, I caught a sense of what the sweet psalmist of Israel felt about his land. I made the trip across the Atlantic at least 50 times. Yet the wonder of it never escaped me. Nor would I wish for it to.

To compare Israel in size to the state of New Jersey is statistically accurate but woefully inadequate in every other way. Israel is the land where God has chosen to place His name and where He will someday dwell again with His people. It is breathtakingly beautiful and must be seen to be truly appreciated.

Ideally, it's best to make the trip in person. Since that is not a fully achievable objective through the pages of a book, I have asked the publishers to include a brief photographic tour of the land, from towering Mount Hermon in the north to the Port of Eilat, the southernmost city beautifully situated on the shores of the Red Sea. Figuratively, it can be said we will see a bit of the favored land from "Dan to Beersheba."

A PARTING WORD

I've been asked countless times why, as a Gentile Christian, I've spent so much of my life in Israel, writing and speaking on Jewish themes. My answer appears in many places, some within the pages we have just shared. But beyond that, I want to take a moment to tell you why I have loved these people and their land and endorse their biblical destiny.

As a child, I heard people mock, scorn, and ridicule Jewish people. I remember conversations about the nefarious Illuminati and snatches of thoughts echoing the fiercely anti-Semitic *Protocols of the Elders of Zion*. At the time, it all meant nothing to me. I was far too busy growing up, and I knew no Jewish people.

However, I learned later that in our small town, at least three of the merchants operating businesses were Jewish. In fact, I later learned that the owners and operators of the local theater that screened newsreels of World War II, the Nazi blitzkrieg, and Adolf Hitler's war against Europe and its Jews were themselves Jewish.

Being unchurched, my conversion to faith in Christ totally transformed my life. Not in the sense of morality because our community, for the most part, already walked pretty closely to the line drawn by the Ten Commandments.

However, knowing Christ gripped me profoundly in another way. What I found in Jesus contradicted everything I had heard in the anti-Semitic overtones of my youth. When I did begin to meet Jewish people, they were Hebrew-Christians who, for the most part, served in Jewish mission agencies. Although rejected by their families and the Jewish community for their faith in Christ, they retained a deep love for their people.

I came to understand why the breach occurred. Crusaders, pogromists, anti-Semites, and genocidal maniacs wearing the mantle of Christianity had all left their scars. All such persecution in the name of Christ fed the Jewish rejection of Jesus as the Messiah. In fact, it became a driving force to incite more hatred of the Jewish people, whom many Christians falsely branded as "Christ killers."

As I matured as a Christian, I was increasingly drawn to understand that our Jewish neighbors, with whom we have so much in common, are "beloved for the sake of the fathers" (Rom. 11:28). God loves them, and He expects us to love them too.

I will never forget the day I stood with hundreds of others in a great hall in Jerusalem and witnessed an incident that gave witness to that biblical sentiment.

As we stood there, a 90-year-old concert pianist visiting Israel for the first time walked over to the piano. When he began to play "Hatikvah," the Israeli national anthem, a perceptible change came over the audience. He was using the instrument to pour out the passion of his heart for this land and his people in a way that touched every person, Jew and Gentile, in the room. And though he was a Jewish believer in Jesus, he encountered no adversaries in the hall that afternoon.

Later I heard him speak of his brethren with the same profound, fervent outpouring of heart he brought to the keyboard. His words were about his people and what they had brought to all of us through Christ.

To them "pertain the adoption, the glory, the covenants, the giving of the law, the service of God, and the promises; of whom are the fathers and from whom, according to the flesh, Christ came, who is over all, the eternally blessed God" (9:4–5).

After all the afflictions that have beset this tiny nation that God designated as a "peculiar people unto himself" (Dt. 14:2, KJV), God's Chosen People persist in blessing us in countless ways: breakthrough discoveries for healing our bodies and quelling diseases, new-wave technology for our prosperity, groundbreaking advances for our food production, and the arts for our enlightenment. They do not seek revenge for the persecution they've suffered at the hands of Gentiles.

Through the prophet Isaiah, God admonishes us, "Speak comfort to Jerusalem" (Isa. 40:1). To fully accomplish that task, we must first possess a love for His people; a love for His land; and above all, a love for the God who calls us to serve Him.

Now to Him who is able to keep you from stumbling, and to present you faultless before the presence of His glory with exceeding joy, to God our Savior, who alone is wise, be glory and majesty, dominion and power, both now and forever. Amen (Jude 24–28).

Mount Hermon

Aerial view of Galilee and Jordan Valley

A view of the Sea of Galilee from Mount Arbel

Coastline of Caesarea

Jezreel Valley

Tel Aviv skyline off the shore of the Mediterranean Sea

Jerusalem Old City - Haas Promenade

Tower of David in Jerusalem

The Knesset (Parliament) Building of Israel

Famous Golden Gate in the walls of the Old City

Sunset at sea in Ashkelon

Panorama of the Dead Sea.

Ein Gedi

Ein Gedi kibbutz

Solomon's Pillars, Timna Valley

Sandy beach of Eilat - famous resort and recreation city in Israel

THE DREAM

Think of it.
A people cruelly severed from their Land
to endure millennia in daunting exile.
Yet never relinquishing hope of a return
one day to the sacred inheritance.
Strange indeed to fathom how it could endure,
this sure-hope of what others could not see.
"Next year in Jerusalem" said in every language
known to man.
From places where seemed dim to speak the words,
that never weakened in intensity.
Their City of Gold awaiting 'promise-delivered'
as a final word.
And now we witness glimpses of the dream
beginning to come true.
A chosen people never more deemed wandering castaways,
assuring God-borne word of wonders yet to come.

JERUSALEM

Of all the regal cities fair
This planet can display,
None will ever yet compare
With that one far away.
A solitary maiden there
Upon the sun-drenched hills
Glistening domes and treasures rare
The voyager's vision fills.
From all the centuries of old
Dust -laden men have trod,
To wrest her from another's hold
And make them serve their god.
But one by one they're turned aside
That all men might confess:
What Gentile Lords have been denied,
Jehovah will possess.

THE HOLY CITY

Seat of David's hallowed throne,
Salem, City of Peace.
Plagued of death by sword and stone
Until all wars shall cease.
Long thy sons have wandered far
The captives chain to bear.
Now, back home, the royal star
They look with pride to wear.
The prophets warn of coming strife
To smite the remnant there,
But over this shine words of life
That vanquish brooding care.
For David's Greater Son, you see,
Will save and rule the nation,
The Holy City then shall be
The center of Creation.

THE WAILING WALL

See the Hebrew standing there
Before the ancient stones.
He lifts his voice o'er downcast eyes
In soft but plaintive tones.
He comes here to remember;
He comes here to forget.
To morn departed glories,
And dream what might be yet.
From memory, sunken faces
File by in gaunt parade.
Now comes the haughty Sabra
Resolute and unafraid.
Symbol to the scattered tribes,
Great sentinel of the years,
Emblem of all Jewry,
Receptacle of tears.
Mute witness to her sufferings
And yearnings for release,
Give substance to the promise
Of Israel's coming peace.

THE JEW

We well recall the wandering Jew
Bowed low and slow of gait,
Who crept the ghettoes, wore the patch,
Absorbed the scorn and hate.
He sold us matches, bought our rags,
Sewed clothes and fixed the shoes.
But seldom would we fraternize,
Strange ones, we thought, those Jews.
It seemed he never quite belonged;
His gaze was fixed afar.
It was as though he searched the skies
To find some rising star.
One day he left, quite suddenly,
That earnest son of Shem.
"I'm going home; I've found my star:
Beloved Jerusalem!"
He's down on Ben Yehuda Street,
Erect and bronzed and trim.
Now we stand by in wonderment
To see what's next for him.

INVADERS

Long they looked with hungry eyes
At Canaan's storied land.
Stealthily conspired to come
And take the deed in hand.
Columned armies, turbaned hosts,
Dark Bedouin marauder,
Swept with fury o'er the hills
To seize Jehovah's daughter.
With dented shield and blunted sword
They all would trudge away,
And learn that only Jacob's sons
Could enter there to stay.

THE SIX-DAY WAR

June, 1967
Little David stood one day
Before a glowering foe.
Trembling brothers watched from far
In fear he'd come to woe.
Sang his sling with high-pitched note
As stone launched from its seat.
Soon a quivering despot's form
Lay at the stripling's feet.

Little Israel stood one day
Before an enemy,
Who boasted loud and promised all
He'd drive them to the sea.
Midst turbine's whine and surging tanks,
With charging infantry,
David's sons brought down their foes
And rewrote history.

JEHOVAH ANSWERS

Ezekiel 38, 39

"I will call for a sword,"
Jehovah has said,
And leave the Red hordes
to number their dead.
To strike with great shaking,
the flood and great hail,
My spear flashing lightening
to pierce through their mail.
Dread silence will reign
on the face of the land,
All ears fallen deaf
to the sound of command.
Now frozen in death
hands that wielded the sword,
Brought low in the end.
by the voice of the Lord.
So birds wing their way
where once raged the strife,
To light midst the shambles,
bereft of all life.
Behold it is done,
and let it be known,
The arm of Jehovah
was bared for His own.

SURVIVORS

They streamed ashore from vessels hardly worthy of plying the seas,
these tired, tattered remnants with drawn faces and darkest memories.
Witnesses of horrors unknown to generations gone before, barely able
to contemplate the loss—shattered families, home and comforts gone.
Their past erased when blue numbers etched by genocidal monsters
plotted their future; the ovens or penned to starve behind the wire.
But as feet touched the sands of Haifa's harbor they looked into a new reality—
fraught with questions, yet within the bounds of certainty.
They had survived, and whatever lay ahead in refashioning what each had
left of life,
there was a common thread found in a word—Free!
A word once thought would never be within their reach again,
that all would end in torments like six million gone before.
A miracle to be numbered among the host that made it through?
Perhaps, but the greater miracle reposed before their eyes.
The Promised Land, and Holy Jerusalem had been reclaimed in time to stand
before and welcome them home!

NOTABLE QUOTES

"Now, when I hear that Christians are getting together in order to defend the people of Israel, of course it brings joy to my heart. And it simply says, look, people have learned from history." —Elie Wiesel

"We can forgive the Arabs for killing our children. We cannot forgive them for forcing us to kill their children....We will only have peace with the Arabs when they love their children more that they hate us." —Golda Meir

"I said, 'Mr. Balfour, if you were offered Paris instead of London, would you take it?'...He looked surprised. He said: 'But London is our own!' I said, 'Jerusalem was our own when London was a marsh.'" —Chaim Weizmann

"All things are mortal but the Jew; all other forces pass, but he remains. What is the secret of his immortality?" —Mark Twain

"Were I to sum up the Basle Congress in a word—which I shall guard against pronouncing publicly—it would be this: 'At Basle, I founded the Jewish State.' If I said this out loud today, I would be answered by universal laughter. If not in 5 years, certainly in 50, everyone will know it." —Theodor Herzl

The Jew is the symbol of eternity....He is the one who for so long had guarded the prophetic message and transmitted it to all mankind. A people such as this can never disappear." —Leo Tolstoy

TIMELINE

FROM THE PROMISE TO THE CAPTIVITY

2126 BC	God calls Abraham to the land of Canaan (Gen. 12:1–3).
1913 BC	God cuts an unconditional covenant with Abraham and tells him the boundaries of the land He has given to him and his seed forever (Gen. 15).
1800 BC	God confirms the Abrahamic Covenant with Isaac (Gen. 26:1–5).
1760 BC	God confirms the covenant with Jacob (Gen. 28:13–15).
1728 BC	Joseph is sold into slavery in Egypt (Gen. 37:36).
1706 BC	Jacob (now called Israel, Gen. 32:28) and family move to Egypt (Gen. 46:1–26).
1446 BC	The Exodus from Egypt (Ex. 14).
1406 BC	The Israelite conquest of Canaan begins.
1375 BC	Period of the judges.
1050–930 BC	The united kingdom (Saul, David, Solomon). In 1000 BC David conquers Jerusalem and makes it Israel's capital.
930–722 BC	The divided kingdom (called Israel in the north, Judah in the south). Jerusalem is the capital of Judah.
722 BC	Assyria conquers the northern kingdom.
605–586 BC	Babylon conquers the southern kingdom and destroys Solomon's Temple. The Babylonian Captivity begins.

FROM THE RETURN TO HEROD THE GREAT

539 BC	Babylon falls to Media-Persia (Dan. 5).
538 BC	Persian King Cyrus allows the Jewish people to return home (Ezra 1).
537 BC	Jewish people return to Jerusalem under Zerubbabel.
516 BC	Second Temple is completed.
458 BC	More Jewish people return under Ezra.
445 BC	Artaxerxes II sends Nehemiah to Jerusalem to rebuild its walls (Neh. 2).
430 BC	Malachi becomes the last prophetic voice, after which begin the 400 "silent" years.
333 BC	Alexander the Great conquers Persia, beginning the Greek, or Hellenistic, period.
323 BC	Alexander the Great dies and his kingdom is divided between his four generals.

167 BC	Antiochus IV (Epiphanes) defiles the Temple.
165 BC	Judas, or Judah, Maccabee leads a revolt against Antiochus, cleanses the Temple, and reestablishes Jewish independence under a Hasmonean dynasty.
63 BC	Roman General Pompey enters Jerusalem, ending Jewish independence; Julius Caesar assassinated.
37 BC	The Romans appoint Herod the Great "king of the Jews" and give him authority over Judea, Samaria, and Galilee.

FROM HEROD TO MUHAMMAD

20 BC	Herod begins remodeling the Temple.
6–5 BC	Jesus is born in Bethlehem.
4 BC	Herod dies; Caesar Augustus divides the territory: Archelaus gets Judea, Antipas gets the Galilee, and Philip gets northeast of Galilee.
26–36	Roman Procurator Pontius Pilate rules Judea.
30	Messiah Jesus dies, arises, and ascends to heaven. Church Age begins on Day of Pentecost (Shavuot).
66–73	First Jewish uprising. Romans destroy Jerusalem and the Temple (AD 70) and attack Masada, where 960 Jews commit suicide rather than surrender (AD 73).
132–135	Second Jewish uprising. Emperor Hadrian attempts to rebuild Jerusalem as a pagan city called Aeolia Capitolina. Rabbi Akiva leads a rebellion and proclaims military leader Simon Bar Kochba messiah. Jewish people lose access to Jerusalem only and disperse throughout the land. Rome renames Judah, Samaria, and Galilee Palestina, later known as Palestine.
200	Many dispersed Jews return.
312–313	Emperor Constantine embraces Christianity.
330	Constantine moves to Byzantium, renames it Constantinople (Istanbul, Turkey), and keeps control over Palestine.
570	Muhammad is born in Mecca (Saudi Arabia).

FROM MUHAMMAD TO THE OTTOMAN TURKS

| 622 | Muhammad moves to Medina (Saudi Arabia). His move is called the hijrah, Arabic for "emigrate." The Muslim calendar begins with this date, which is 1 AH. |
| 610 | Muhammad claims the angel Gabriel showed him a tablet stating he was to become God's messenger. From then until his death, Muhammad has "visions." Thus begins the Muslim religion of Islam, meaning "submission to Allah." |

630	Arab Omayyads become the first Muslim presence in Jerusalem.
632	Muhammad dies.
639–661	Arab Muslims rule. This 22-year-period is the only time Arabs ever rule the land. Even then it was part of a greater empire.
661–1099	Muslims rule Palestine; however, they are not Arabs. The Abbassids came from Baghdad; the Fatimids, from Cairo; the Seljuks from Turkey.
1099–1187	Catholic Crusaders under Pope Urban II conquer Jerusalem and massacre Jews and Muslims.
1187	Saladin, a Muslim Kurd from Damascus, recaptures Jerusalem and a large part of Palestine.
1244–1303	Asian Mongols depose Saladin's dynasty. Muslim Mameluks and Mongols struggle for power. The Crusader presence ends in 1291.
1513–17	Muslim Ottoman Turks conquer Palestine.

FROM THE OTTOMAN TURKS TO THE BRITISH

1517	Muslim Ottoman Turks rule Palestine as part of their empire.
1840	Turkish rule fully restored. English leaders begin to discuss the possibility of restoring the Jewish people to their homeland.
1882	Jewish people make aliyah from Romania to Palestine.
1890–91	Large wave of Jewish people arrive from Russia.
1894–95	French Capt. Alfred Dreyfus is convicted of espionage on falsified evidence amid rampant anti-Semitism.
1896	Theodor Herzl writes *Der Judenstaat,* "The Jewish State."
1897	First Zionist Congress meets in Basle, Switzerland, convened by Herzl. More than 200 participate from 17 countries, establishing the World Zionist Organization "to create for the Jewish people a home in Eretz-Israel secured by law." The Congress met every year from 1897 to 1901, then every second year, and still meets today.
1901	Zionist Congress establishes the Jewish National Fund (JNF) to raise funds to purchase land in EretzYisrael. The JNF is the largest landowner in Israel (12.5 percent of all land) and purchased more than half of that amount before the reestablishment of the nation.
1904	Second wave of immigration, mainly from Russia and Poland.
1906	First Hebrew high school is founded in Jaffa and art school founded in Jerusalem.
1908–14	Second Yemenite aliyah.
1909	Tel Aviv, the first all-Jewish city, is founded in Palestine.
1910	Kibbutz Degania is founded.
1914–18	World War I.

1917	British General Edmund Allenby conquers Palestine, east and west of the Jordan, ending the Ottoman reign. In November the British issue the Balfour Declaration, supporting a "Jewish Homeland."
1920	League of Nations gives Britain a mandate over Palestine, with orders to implement the Balfour Declaration.

FROM SAN REMO TO NAZI GERMANY

1918	British General Edmund Allenby defeats the Ottoman Turks and occupies all of Palestine.
1919–23	Third wave of Jewish immigration arrives, mostly from Russia.
1920	Britain receives League of Nations mandate over Palestine at San Remo Conference and is told to facilitate creation of a national Jewish homeland there; Arabs riot.
1921	First Jewish moshav, Nahalal, is founded. Arabs riot in Jaffa.
1922	Churchill White Paper reduces British commitment to the Jewish people and gives 77 percent of area designated for them to Abdullah and the Arabs (Transjordan).
1924–32	Fourth wave of immigration arrives, mostly from Poland.
1925	Hebrew University founded in Jerusalem.
1926	Arabs riot in Hebron, killing Jews.
1929	Arabs riot in Jerusalem and massacre Jews in Hebron and Safed. Second White Paper further reneges on Britain's Jewish commitment and limits Jewish immigration.
1933	Hitler comes to power.
1933–36	Fifth wave of immigration, mostly from Poland and Germany.
1934	Trying to flee Hitler, Jews begin "illegal" immigration because Britain refuses them entry while allowing massive, illegal Arab immigration— 36,000 Arabs from Syria alone in just a few months.
1935–36	Record 65,000 Jewish people immigrate.
1936	Arabs revolt and go on strike, demanding Jewish immigration stop; 500 Jews killed; British Capt. Orde Wingate establishes "night squads" to defend Jewish settlers. Massive illegal Arab immigration continues.
1937	Peel Commission recommends partitioning remaining 23 percent of the land designated for the Jews into two countries: one Jewish, one Arab.
1939	Hitler invades Poland. White Paper limits Jewish immigration to a mere 60,000 for five years. Ben-Gurion states, "We shall fight the war as if there is no White Paper and we shall fight the White Paper as if there is no war."

FROM NAZI GERMANY TO INDEPENDENCE

1939	Third British White Paper rejects partition concept, further restricts immigration, and severely limits land sales to Jews. Massive illegal Arab immigration continues, and Arabs appropriate the land Jews are clearing for Holocaust refugees.
1940	While Britain fights Hitler, Haj Amin al-Husseini, grand mufti of Jerusalem, moves to Berlin to help Hitler.
1941	Britain refuses entry to the ship *Struma,* carrying 767 Romanian-Jewish refugees. It sinks. All aboard die.
1943	Warsaw Ghetto uprising. Meanwhile, Britain deports "illegal" Jewish refugees to Cyprus while allowing illegal Arab immigrants.
1945	World War II ends. Jews smuggle Holocaust survivors into Palestine. Jewish underground works against the British.
1946	The Jewish Irgun blows up the west wing of the King David Hotel. Transjordan becomes the independent, Hashemite kingdom of Jordan.
1947	The British repel the ship *Exodus.* Its 4,500 Jewish refugees are returned to displaced-persons camps in war-torn Europe.
November 29, 1947	UN partitions Palestine into two states: one Arab, one Jewish. The Arabs reject the plan; the Jews accept it.
November 29, 1947–May 14, 1948	Jews defend themselves against Arab gangs. Guerrilla warfare rages. Arabs blockade road to Jerusalem. More than 1,200 Jewish people are killed, more than half of them civilians.
May 14, 1948	Ben-Gurion declares independence. Within minutes, U.S. President Harry Truman recognizes the new State of Israel.

FROM INDEPENDENCE TO THE YOM KIPPUR WAR

May 15, 1948–January 1949	Five Arab nations attack. The yearlong War of Independence ensues.
1948-50	Over 725,000 Palestinian Arabs leave their homes despite Israel's pleas for unity.
1956	Suez Canal crisis.
1964	Fatah forms, with Yasser Arafat as its leader.
1967	George Habash forms the Popular Front for the Liberation of Palestine (PFLP).

1967	Six-Day War (June 5–10). Israel defends itself against five Arab nations; captures the Sinai and Gaza Strip from Egypt, the Golan Heights from Syria, and the West Bank and East Jerusalem from Jordan. Israel reunites Jerusalem and assumes control of the Temple Mount. UN adopts Resolution 242.
1969	The PLO claims to speak for "all Palestinians." Arafat is its head. Golda Meir becomes Israel's prime minister.
September 1970	Syria and militant Palestinians threaten King Hussein's rule. Hussein strikes back in event called Black September. Jordanian forces kill well over 3,000 Palestinians.
1971	Palestinian terrorists move their bases to Lebanon.
October 6– November 11, 1973	On Yom Kippur Soviet-backed Egypt and Syria attack Israel and almost destroy her. The United States airlifts supplies to Israel, and by October 18 Israeli soldiers are outside Cairo. UN passes Resolution 338.

FROM THE YOM KIPPUR WAR TO NETANYAHU

1974	Arafat addresses the UN and calls for a united "Palestine" with a democratic, secular government "where Christian, Jew, and Muslim can live in justice, equality and fraternity."
1977	Menachem Begin becomes Israel's prime minister and supports keeping all disputed territories.
1979	Israel and Egypt sign Camp David Accords.
1982	Israel moves into Lebanon to protect Israel's northern border and stabilize a weak and struggling Lebanese people.
1987	Palestinian Intifada (uprising) against Israeli control explodes in the disputed territories.
1988	The PLO supposedly recognizes Israel and renounces terrorism, calling for negotiations. Yitzhak Shamir is elected Israel's prime minister.
1991	Gulf War. Iraqi Scud missiles attack Israel. United States deploys Patriot missiles to help Israel.
1992	Yitzhak Rabin becomes Israel's prime minister.
September 1993	U.S. President Bill Clinton, Rabin, and Arafat sign the Declaration of Principles (Oslo I) at the White House.
July 1994	Between 7,000–15,000 Palestinians organized by Hamas, Islamic Jihad, and PFLP protest Israeli-Palestinian negotiations. Israeli-Jordanian-Palestinian negotiators sign an agreement on water rights at Oslo.
July–August 1994	Palestinians and Israelis discuss transferring authority to the Palestinian Authority (PA) in the West Bank.

December 1994	Arafat, Israeli Foreign Minister Shimon Peres, and Israeli Prime Minister Rabin receive the Nobel Prize.
January 1995	Israel recognizes Palestinian passports, permits Palestinian vehicles on Israeli roads, and lets Palestinian men over 50 and students cross between Gaza and Jericho.
September 1995	Arafat and Rabin sign Oslo II, allowing expansion of Palestinian self-rule in the West Bank.
November 1995	Rabin assassinated. Peres becomes acting prime minister.
January 1996	Palestinians elect Arafat president.
March 1996	Hamas detonates bus bomb that kills 19 people. Peres declares war on Hamas, increases security, and begins destroying homes of suicide bombers and their families.
May 1996	Benjamin Netanyahu elected Israel's prime minister.

FROM NETANYAHU TO THE ROAD MAP

September 1996	"Al-Aqsa tunnel riots." Arabs spread lie that an exit door Israel installed to an underground tunnel to help tourists endangers the al-Aqsa mosque. (The tunnel existed 800 years before the mosque.)
January 1997	Israel and Palestinians reach agreement on Israeli redeployment in Hebron.
March 21, 1997	Hamas suicide bomber detonates bomb at Cafe Apropos in central Tel Aviv.
July 30, 1997	Two suicide bombers hit Mahane Yehuda open-air market in Jerusalem, killing 12 and wounding at least 150.
October 1998	Wye River Plantation talks. Israel agrees to redeploy and release political prisoners in exchange for Palestinian promises to stop violating Oslo accords, including excess police force.
May 1999	Israel elects former General Ehud Barak as prime minister.
May 2000	Israel withdraws from Lebanon. UN declares Israel in compliance with Resolution 242, but Hezbollah continues terrorism.
July 2000	Barak, Clinton, and Arafat meet.
September 28, 2000	Palestinians initiate riots after Ariel Sharon legally visits the Temple Mount. Violence and terrorism mount and continue today, termed the Oslo War.
February 6, 2001	Sharon elected prime minister.
June 1, 2001	Suicide bombers hit Dolphinarium Discotheque in Tel Aviv; 20 killed, including many Israeli teenagers.
August 9, 2001	Islamic Jihad suicide bomber hits Sbarro pizzeria in Jerusalem; kills 15, wounds 130.

October 17, 2001	PFLP assassinates Israeli Tourism Minister Rehavam Ze'evi in an Israeli hotel.
January 3, 2002	Israel captures *Karine*—A ship carrying 50 tons of illegal, advanced weaponry to the Palestinian Authority.
March 27, 2002	Hamas suicide bombing kills 27 and maims scores at Passover seder in Netanya's Park Hotel.
March-April 2002	In retaliation for an unprecedented number of suicide bombings, Israel mounts Operation Defensive Wall.
May 30, 2002	Arafat signs PA transitional constitution to guarantee Palestinian rights. However, it is based on Islamic Sharia law; declares Islam the official religion of "Palestine"; and contradicts Arafat's "democratic, secular state" UN speech.
April 2003	Mahmoud Abbas (Abu Mazen) elected Palestinian prime minister; Arafat maneuvers to retain control. Violence continues unabated. U.S. releases Road Map peace plan.
July 2003	To protect itself from terrorism, Israel begins building a 500-mile security fence.
August 2005	Israel demolishes 21 Israeli communities in the Gaza Strip and expels 8,000 Israeli residents in hopes of securing peace with the Palestinians.
July 12, 2006	Hezbollah fires rockets from Lebanon into Israel. The Second Lebanon War begins.
August 14, 2006	The UN brokers a ceasefire between Israel and Hezbollah and blames Israel for the conflict.
2007	Hamas seizes control of the Gaza Strip and begins building massive tunnels to use for terrorism.
2009	Israel completes 300 miles of its security fence.
September 2011	The UN hosts its World Conference Against Racism in Durban, South Africa, which turns into an anti-Israel tirade to delegitimize Israel and promote Zionism as racism.
October 31, 2011	The United Nations Educational, Scientific and Cultural Organization (UNESCO) grants "Palestine" membership, giving the Palestinians full admittance into a UN organization for the first time.
September 28, 2016	Former Israeli Prime Minister Shimon Peres, one of the last of the generation that helped establish the State of Israel, dies.
December 2016	Between 2005 and 2016, terrorists use the Gaza Strip to fire more than 15,000 rockets and mortars into Israel.
December 23, 2016	The U.S. abstains from voting on the UN's anti-Israel Resolution 2334. Consequently, the UN condemns Israel and officially declares all the land that Israel won in the 1967 war "occupied" Palestinian territory, including eastern Jerusalem—which includes the Temple Mount, Mount of Olives, Garden Tomb, and Western Wall.

| May 2018 | Terrorists send incendiary kites and balloons into Israel, igniting more than 450 fires and destroying more than 1,800 acres of Israeli land. |
| May–August 2018 | More than 695 rockets and mortar rounds are fired into Israel from the Gaza Strip, destroying more than 7,400 acres. |

ENDNOTES

CHAPTER 1: THE PROPHETIC NATION

[1] Alfred Edersheim, *Bible History, Old Testament*, bk. 2, The Exodus and the Wanderings in the Wilderness (1890, reprint, 7 vols. in 1, Peabody, MA: Hendrickson, 1995), 147.

[2] Ibid., 153.

CHAPTER 3: THE LONG, LONELY ROAD

[1] *Israel Pocket Library*, "Anti-Semitism" (Jerusalem: Keter Publishing, 1974), 105–106.

[2] Ibid., 124.

[3] TOI Staff, "Hamas Revives Passover Blood Libel," *The Times of Israel*, November 30, 2015 <timesofisrael.com/hamas-revives-passover-blood-libel>.

[4] Ibid.

[5] *Israel Pocket Library*, 111.

[6] Philip Schaff, *History of the Christian Church*, Vol. 5 (Grand Rapids, MI: Eerdmans, 1970), 240–241.

CHAPTER 4: THEN THERE ARE CHRISTIANS

[1] *Israel Pocket Library*, "Anti-Semitism" (Jerusalem: Keter Publishing, 1974), 11.

[2] Ibid.

[3] Pinchas Lapide, *Three Popes and the Jews* (New York, NY: Hawthorn Books, 1967), 269.

[4] *Israel Pocket Library*, 23.

[5] Meir Kahane, "Christians for Zion," *The Jewish Press*, January 24, 1975, 34.

[6] Raphael Patai, ed., *Encyclopedia of Zionism and Israel* (New York, NY: Herzl Press/McGraw Hill, 1971).

[7] Michael Comay, *Zionism and Israel—Questions and Answers* (Jerusalem: Keter Publishing, 1976), 17.

[8] Elliot Jager, *The Balfour Declaration* (Gefen Publishing, Jerusalem: 2018), 58.

CHAPTER 5: BACK FROM THE DEAD

1 *Facts About Israel 1972* (Jerusalem: Keter Publishing, 1974), 26.
2 Raphael Posner, gen. ed., *Popular Judaica Library. The Return to Zion* (Jerusalem: Keter Publishing, 1974), 26.
3 Ibid.
4 Ibid., 24.
5 *Israel Pocket Library,* "History From 1880" (Jerusalem: Keter Publishing, 1973), 43.
6 *Facts About Israel 1973* (Jerusalem: Division of Information, Ministry of Foreign Affairs, 1973), 34.
7 "The Palestine Mandate," The Avalon Project, Yale Law School <avalon.law.yale.edu/20th_century/palmanda.asp>.
8 Ben Moshe, ed., *David Ben Gurion* (Jerusalem: Youval Tal Ltd.), 44.
9 Posner, 114.
10 Clark Clifford with Ambassador Richard Holbrooke, Counsel to the President, a Memoire, "Showdown in the Oval Office" (New York, NY: Random House, 1991), cited in "President Truman's Decision to Recognize Israel," Jerusalem Center for Public Affairs, May 1, 2008 <jcpa.org/article/president-truman's-decision-to-recognize-israel>.
11 Recognition of the State of Israel, trumanlibrary.org <tinyurl.com/y82gvt9k>.
12 *Israel Pocket Library,* "History From 1880," 141.

CHAPTER 6: ON EAGLES' WINGS

1 Dani Dayan, "Anti-Zionism Is Just Anti-Semitism by Another Name," Newsweek.com, January 27, 2018, <tinyurl.com/yb359uav>.
2 Mark Twain, *The Innocents Abroad* (1869: reprint, New York, NY: Signet Classics, 1966), 473–74.
3 "Buffett: Israel a top place for ideas, investments," israelnationalnews.com, February 5, 2013 <tinyurl.com/brvf7lf>.
4 Michelle Z. Donahue, "Found: Fresh Clues to Mystery of King Solomon's Mines," National Geographic.com, April 12, 2017 <tinyurl.com/ybrhkbpk>.
5 "The Mediterranean–Dead Sea Cooperative Initiative (MDCI)," <tinyurl.com/ybjzrmzg>.
6 Julian Cribb, "The Coming Famine: Risks and solutions for global food security," sciencealert.com, April 20, 2010 <tinyurl.com/y93bpmhc)
7 *Facts About Israel 1972,* 116.
8 *Israel Pocket Library,* "Economy" (Jerusalem: Keter Publishing, 1973), 228.

CHAPTER 7: WE ARE AT THE WALL

1 Larry Collins and Dominique Lapierre, *O Jerusalem* (New York, NY: Simon and Shuster, 1973), 191.

2 Randolph S. and Winston S. Churchill, *The Six-Day War* (London: Heinemann, 1967), 191..

3 Teddy Kollek and Moshe Pearlman, *Jerusalem: Sacred City of Mankind* (Jerusalem, Tel Aviv: Steinmatzky's Agency Ltd., 1975), 268.

CHAPTER 8: A QUIET DAY IN OCTOBER

1 Yeshayahu Ben-Porat, Hezi Carmel, Uri Dan, Yehonatan Gefen, Eitan Haber, Eli Landau, Eli Tabor, *Kippur* (Tel Aviv: Special Edition Publishers, 1973), 27.

2 Ibid., 267.

3 Major-General Chaim Herzog, *The War of Atonement* (Boston,MA: Little Brown, 1975), 278.

4 *Kippur*, 113.

5 Ibid., 115.

6 Herzog, 159.

7 *Kippur*, 8.

8 *The Yom Kippur War* (New York, NY: Doubleday), 134.

9 Herzog, 64.

10 *Kippur*, 181.

11 Herzog, 113.

12 Gideon Pick, "Becoming a Golani Soldier," onjewishmatters.com, July 22, 2014 <onjewishmatters.com/becoming-a-golani-soldier>.

13 Herzog, 284.

CHAPTER 9: THE STALKING BEAR

1 Yeshayahu Ben-Porat, Hezi Carmel, Uri Dan, Yehonatan Gefen, Eitan Haber, Eli Landau, Eli Tabor, *Kippur* (Tel Aviv: Special Edition Publishers, 1973), 122.

2 *The Yom Kippur War* (New York, NY: Doubleday), 407.

3 Dr. Mark Hitchcock, "The Battle of Gog and Magog," pre-trib.org <tinyurl.com/yara4phm>.

CHAPTER 10: TRAUMA AND TRIUMPH

1 "The Arab Spring, five years on: A season that began in hope, but ended in desolation," Patrick Cockburn, January 8, 2016, Independent.co.uk <tinyurl.com/

ycd6co2e>.

2 Ariel Ben Solomon, "ISIS Threatens Global War With Israel," May 19, 2016, jpost.com <tinyurl.com/ycx9e4pj>.

3 Andre Walker, "Terrorism in Europe Is Here to Stay Because We're Soft on Immigration," April 11, 2017, observer.com <tinyurl.com/y9uszv5q>.

4 Janine Di Giovanni and Conor Gaffey, "The New Exodus: Christians Flee ISIS in the Middle East," March 26, 2015, newsweek.com <tinyurl.com/q429w2b>.

BIBLIOGRAPHY

Churchill, Randolph S. and Winston S. *The Six-Day War.* London: Heinemann, 1967.

Collins, Larry and Lapierre, Dominique. *O Jerusalem.* New York, NY: Simon and Schuster, 1973.

Edersheim, Alfred. *History of the Jewish Nation.* Grand Rapids, MI. Baker Book House.

Herzog, Chaim. *The War of Atonement.* Boston MA, Toronto, ON: Little Brown and Co., 1975.

Insight Team of the London Times. *The Yom Kippur War.* New York, NY: Doubleday and Co.

Jager, Elliot. *The Balfour Declaration: Sixty-Seven Words, 100 Years of Conflict.* Jerusalem. Gefen Publishing, 2018.

Israel Pocket Library. *Anti-Semitism.* Jerusalem: Keter Publising House Jerusalem Ltd., 1974.

_____. *History From 1880.* Jerusalem: Keter Publishing House Jerusalem Ltd., 1974.

_____. *History Until 1880.* Jerusalem: Keter Publishing House Jerusalem Ltd., 1974.

_____. *Holocaust.* Jerusalem: Keter Publishing House Jerusalem Ltd., 1974.

Katz, Samuel. *Battleground: Fact and Fantasy in Palestine.* New York, NY: Bantam Books, 1973.

Kollek, Teddy and Pearlman, Moshe. *Jerusalem: Sacred City of Mankind.* Jerusalem: Steimatzky's Agency Ltd., 1975.

Lorch, Netanel. *The Edge of the Sword: Israel's War of Independence.* Jerusalem: Masada Press Ltd., 1961.

_____. *One Long War: Arab Versus Jew Since 1920.* New York, NY: Herzl Press, 1976.

Rubinstein, Aryeh, Editor. *The Return to Zion.* Jerusalem: Keter Books, 1974.

Schaff, Philip. *History of the Christian Church,* vol. V. Grand Rapids, MI: William B. Eerdmans Co., 1970.

ACKNOWLEDGMENTS

The author acknowledges, with sincere gratitude, the assistance of those whose contributions aided immeasurably in the preparation of this book.

The author acknowledges, with sincere gratitude, the assistance of those whose contributions aided immeasurably in the preparation of this book. These include the advisor on Church Relations, Consulate of Israel, New York; the Embassy of Israel, Washington, DC; Israel Defense Forces, Tel Aviv, Israel; and various departments within The Jewish Agency in Jerusalem that provided books and materials and arranged many interviews.

Scores of individuals in Israel and the United States who provided information, encouragement, and advice, particularly Editor-in-Chief Lorna Simcox and the editorial staff of The Friends of Israel Gospel Ministry.

Thank you to Tom Simcox and Steve Herzig for producing the timelines.

Above all, gratefully remembering the patience, love, advice, and innumerable sacrifices of my beloved wife, Maxine, now in glory, and our children, who cheerfully bore the separations and lonely hours while this book was in the making.

PHOTO CREDITS

p. 10 Shershel Frank/Government Press Office; **p. 16** nickolae/Adobe Stock; **p. 21** Stan Stein; **pp. 26–27** David Roberts/Public Domain; **p. 37** ZU_09/iStock; **p. 40** C.H. Jones; T.H. Hamilton; J. David Williams/Public Domain; **pp. 44–45** unknown/Yad Vashem; **p. 50** Erica Guilane-Nachez/Adobe Stock; **p. 59** Claudiad/iStock; **p. 71** unknown/The Friends of Israel; **p. 72** ZU_09/iStock; **p. 79l** unknown/Public Domain; **p. 79r** unknown/Government Press Office; **pp. 82–83** unknown/Government Press Office; **p. 89** Ullstein Bilderdienst/Public Domain; **p. 90** unknown/Government Press Office; **p. 92** unknown/Government Press Office; **p. 93l** George Grantham Bain/Public Domain; **p. 93r** unknown/Public Domain; **p. 95** Underwood & Underwood/Public Domain; **p. 96l** Koret Communications Ltd.; **p. 96r** Koret Communications Ltd.; **p. 98** Shershel Frank/Government Press Office; **p. 99** Koret Communications Ltd.; **p. 100** unknown/Yad Vashem; **p. 102** Pinn Hans/Government Press Office; **p. 105** Bettmann/Getty Images; **p. 106** Kluger Zoltan/Government Press Office; **p. 112** Pridan Moshe/Government Press Office; **p. 114** Eldan David/Government Press Office; **p. 118** Kluger Zoltan/Government Press Office; **p. 120** Kluger Zoltan/Government Press Office; **p. 122** Kluger Zoltan/Government Press Office; **p. 135l** Cohen Fritz/Government Press Office; **p. 135c** unknown/Government Press Office; **p. 135r** Milner Moshe/Government Press Office; **p. 136** David Rubinger/Government Press Office; **p. 139** Ilan Bruner/Government Press Office; **p. 140** Koret Communications Ltd.; **pp. 144–145** Kushnirov Avraham/Adobe Stock; **p. 150** AnastasiaUsoltceva/Adobe Stock; **p. 153** Milner Moshe/Government Press Office; **p. 157** Kogel Abraham/Government Press Office; **p. 158** Greenberg Yossi/Government Press Office; **p. 161** Frenkel Ron/Government Press Office; **p. 162** Sa'ar Ya'acov/Government Press Office; **p. 164** Koret Communications Ltd.; **p. 176** Milner Moshe/Government Press Office; **p. 182** Milner Moshe/Government Press Office; **p. 184** Milner Moshe/Government Press Office; **p. 197** unknown/Government Press Office; **p. 201** Claudiad/iStock; **p. 211** david/Adobe Stock; **p. 219t** boryak/iStock; **p. 219b** Phish Photography/Adobe Stock; **p. 220t** Michael Egenburg/Adobe Stock; **p. 220b** Emelianov Evgenii/Adobe Stock; **p. 221t** ilandavid/Adobe Stock; **p. 221b** STOCKSTUDIO/Adobe Stock; **p. 222t** alon/Adobe Stock; **p. 222b** SeanPavonePhoto/Adobe Stock; **p. 223t** SeanPavonePhoto/Adobe Stock; **p. 223b** proxima13/Adobe Stock; **p. 224t** Sergey Savich/iStock; **p. 224b** mstudio/Adobe Stock; **p. 225t** Catie Almacellas/The Friends of Israel; **p. 225b** amite/iStock; **p. 226t** Oleg Znamenskiy/Adobe Stock; **p. 226b** sergei_fish13/Adobe Stock